EXPLAINING
POST-CONFLICT
RECONSTRUCTION

EXPLAINING POST-CONFLICT RECONSTRUCTION

DESHA M. GIROD

OXFORD
UNIVERSITY PRESS

OXFORD
UNIVERSITY PRESS

Oxford University Press is a department of the University
of Oxford. It furthers the University's objective of excellence in research,
scholarship, and education by publishing worldwide.

Oxford   New York
Auckland   Cape Town   Dar es Salaam   Hong Kong   Karachi
Kuala Lumpur   Madrid   Melbourne   Mexico City   Nairobi
New Delhi   Shanghai   Taipei   Toronto

With offices in
Argentina   Austria   Brazil   Chile   Czech Republic   France   Greece
Guatemala   Hungary   Italy   Japan   Poland   Portugal   Singapore
South Korea   Switzerland   Thailand   Turkey   Ukraine   Vietnam

Oxford is a registered trademark of Oxford University Press
in the UK and certain other countries.

Published in the United States of America by
Oxford University Press
198 Madison Avenue, New York, NY 10016

© Oxford University Press 2015

All rights reserved. No part of this publication may be reproduced, stored in
a retrieval system, or transmitted, in any form or by any means, without the prior
permission in writing of Oxford University Press, or as expressly permitted by law,
by license, or under terms agreed with the appropriate reproduction rights organization.
Inquiries concerning reproduction outside the scope of the above should be sent to the
Rights Department, Oxford University Press, at the address above.

You must not circulate this work in any other form
and you must impose this same condition on any acquirer.

Library of Congress Cataloging-in-Publication Data
Girod, Desha M., author.
Explaining Post-Conflict Reconstruction / Desha M. Girod.
pages cm
Includes bibliographical references.
ISBN 978-0-19-938786-1 (hardback : alk. paper)—ISBN 978-0-19-938787-8 (pbk. : alk.
paper) 1. Postwar reconstruction. 2. Postwar reconstruction—Africa, Southern.
3. Economic assistance—International cooperation. 4. Economic assistance—Africa,
Southern—International cooperation. 5. Economic assistance—Political aspects.
6. Economic assistance—Political aspects—Africa, Southern. I. Title.
HV639.G57 2015
338.911724—dc23
2014020730

1 3 5 7 9 8 6 4 2
Printed in the United States of America
on acid-free paper

To Nick and Gretchen Maria

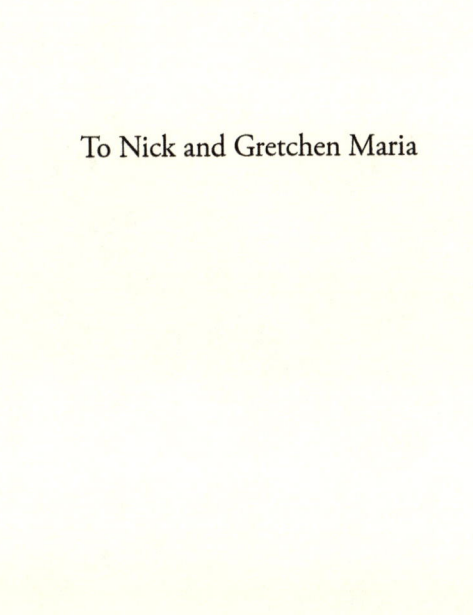

CONTENTS

List of Illustrations xi
Acknowledgments xiii
Abbreviations xvii
Prologue: A Phoenix State xix

1. Phoenix States after Civil War: The Problem and the Argument 1
   Post-Conflict Reconstruction is Crucial 2
   Can Foreign Aid Help? 3
   Phoenix States Challenge the Aid Curse 4
   The Need for a Testable Argument 4
   The Argument: Reconstruction Requires Incentives 5
   Scope of the Book 6
   Organization of the Book 7

2. Reconstruction Against All Odds 11
   Power Consolidation Following Civil War 13
   The Crucial Role of Income 15
   Testable Implications 24
   Alternative Explanations 26
   Summary 28

3. Statistical Analysis of Post-Conflict Reconstruction 30
   Testing the Nonstrategic-Desperation Hypothesis 32
      Preliminary Analysis 37
      Baseline Model 38
      Main Results 40
      Robustness 41
      Summary 45

4. Statistical Analysis of Post-Conflict Coup Risk 47
   Testing the Low-Windfall Coup-Proofing Hypothesis 48
      Main Results 51
      Robustness 55
      Summary 56

5. Similar Background, Different Windfall: Mozambique and Angola 58
   Civil War in Angola and Mozambique 61
   Windfall Income in Angola versus Mozambique 63
   Stonewalling versus Embracing Gatekeepers of Aid 65
      Nonstrategic Donor Response 71
   Differences in Who Pays for Post-Conflict Reconstruction 72
   Post-Conflict Reconstruction in Angola versus Mozambique 74
   Summary of Aid Effectiveness in Angola versus Mozambique 77
      Power Consolidation in Angola 78
      Power Consolidation in Mozambique 79
      Alternative Explanations 84
      Summary 97

6. Same Country, Change in Windfall: Uganda 99
   Brief Background: Civil War in Uganda 101
      Low Windfall 103
   Satisfying Gatekeepers of Nonstrategic Aid 105
      Nonstrategic Aid Increased 107
      Post-Conflict Reconstruction 108
      Power Consolidation 112
   Striking it Rich: Newfound Natural Resources and Strategic Importance 117
      Was it Good Leadership? 119
      Summary 121

7. Improving Aid Effectiveness after Civil War   122
    Supportive Cases   124
    Exceptional Cases with Low Windfall   128
    Exceptional Cases with High Windfall   130
    Policies to Counteract the Windfall Curse   134
    Future Research   144
    Conclusion   147

Notes   149
Bibliography   163
Subject Index   191

LIST OF ILLUSTRATIONS

Figures

3.1 Scatterplots of Nonstrategic Aid and Post-Conflict Reconstruction   37
3.2 Effect of Nonstrategic Aid on Reconstruction as Windfall Changes   43
4.1 Effect of Reconstruction on Coup Risk as Windfall and Nonstrategic Aid Change   53

Tables

2.1 Does Increasing Nonstrategic Aid Predict Post-Conflict Reconstruction?   24
3.1 Regression Analysis of Post-Conflict Reconstruction   42
4.1 Logit Analysis of Coup Risk   52
4.2 Logit Analysis of Coup Risk: Including Control Variables   54
4.3 Logit Analysis of Coup Risk: Excluding Outliers and Including Fixed Effects   56

ACKNOWLEDGMENTS

I BEGAN GRADUATE school at Stanford just as international efforts at reconstruction got under way in Afghanistan, and I became interested in a central question facing the leaders who were creating foreign policy at the time—could the United States and other international actors help weak or failed states like Afghanistan build governments that are responsive to the needs of their citizens? There was little academic literature on post-conflict reconstruction, and I wondered more generally whether any developing countries that had been broken by civil war in the last few decades managed to rebuild their states and significantly reconstruct their economies and societies. Did the international community help or hinder these efforts? What can success stories teach theory and policy on foreign aid, conflict dynamics, and state building?

These questions motivated me to write a dissertation on post-conflict reconstruction, a first step toward this book. As I developed my ideas in graduate school, I benefited greatly from many conversations with the four members of my dissertation committee: Jim Fearon (chair), Steve Krasner, David Laitin, and Jeremy Weinstein. My advisors fundamentally influenced how I think about civil war, international intervention, state-building, and social science. While at Stanford, I also received helpful comments on early drafts of this project from other faculty, including Lisa Blaydes, Josh Cohen, Larry Diamond, Alberto

Díaz-Cayeros, Avner Greif, Karen Jusko, Terry Karl, Phillip Lipscy, Beatriz Magaloni, Mike McFaul, Ken Schultz, Mike Tomz, and Barry Weingast.

I am especially grateful for the feedback from my graduate-student colleagues. I first shared my ideas about this project by outlining them on a napkin while working at a coffee shop with a colleague and friend, Claire Adida. For the conversation that ensued about my project on that day and for many other discussions about this project since then, I thank her. I also thank my other graduate-student colleagues, especially Sarah Anderson, Luz Marina Arias, Leo Arriola, Matt Carnes, Dara Cohen, Jesse Driscoll, Catherine Duggan, Joe Felter, Scott Handler, Ron Hassner, Kimuli Kasara, Alex Kuo, Bethany Lacina, David Patel, Christina Maimone, Yotam Margalit, Nikolay Marinov, Aila Matanock, Jake Shapiro, Jeremy Wallace, and Jessica Weeks. They all read early drafts and offered very helpful feedback. Pre- and post-doctoral funding from the Stanford Political Science program and the Stanford Center on Democracy, Development, and the Rule of Law also supported my research and writing.

I broadened and deepened the manuscript after becoming an assistant professor at Georgetown, where I regularly received constructive insights from Mike Bailey, Harley Balzer, Tom Banchoff, Andrew Bennett, Marc Busch, Dan Byman, Raj Desai, David Edelstein, Dan Hopkins, Lise Morjé Howard, Marc Morjé Howard, Charles King, Kate McNamara, Carol Lancaster, Eusebio Mujal-Leon, Abe Newman, Dan Nexon, George Shambaugh, Scott Taylor, Jenn Tobin, Erik Voeten, and Jim Vreeland. I am also grateful for the input from Georgetown students, including Alex Berg, Anjali Dayal, Jennifer Raymond Dresden, Liz Goldberg, Micah Jensen, Megan Stewart, Meir Walters, and Michel Weintraub.

Georgetown also offered financial support. The Government Department provided me with a grant for a daylong conference dedicated to discussion of my manuscript. In addition to the many Georgetown colleagues who participated, Joel Barkan, Thad Dunning, Caroline Harzell, Macartan Humphreys, and Nic van de Walle attended and provided extensive useful feedback. Georgetown's Graduate School of Arts and Sciences also supported my research and writing with a Summer Academic Grant. In addition, Georgetown provided institutional support.

I also received helpful comments from Faisal Ahmed, David Bearce, Jen Brass, Terry Chapman, Jeffrey Chwieroth, Jeff Colgan, Page Fortna, Bonnie Granat, Julia Gray, Zaryab Iqbal, Jordan Kyle, Amanda Licht, Camelia Minoiu, Gabriella Montinola, Kevin Morrison, Christopher O'Keefe, Glenn Palmer, Dane Rowlands, Burcu Savun, Laura Seay, Jessica Stanton, Tim Sisk, Elizabeth Sperber, Daniel Tirone, Joseph Wright, Vineeta Yadav, Greg Zarow, Christoph Zürcher, and the editors and anonymous reviewers at the *American Journal of Political Science* and *Conflict Management and Peace Science*. Seminar participants at Columbia, Cornell, Emory, Georgetown, Penn State, Stanford, the University of Denver, the U.S. Naval Academy, the University of Ottawa, the University of South Carolina, and Yale, and participants at the meetings of the African Studies Association, the American Political Science Association, the International Studies Association, the Midwest Political Science Association, and the Political Economy of International Organizations also offered insightful comments. I am also grateful for copyediting by Kathleen Kearns and feedback on writing for a broad audience from Liz Goldberg and Ruth Homrighaus. I also thank friends and family for many conversations about the book's argument and for feedback on the book cover.

I appreciate the input from Dave McBride at Oxford University Press and two anonymous reviewers who offered very valuable comments. I also thank the staff at Oxford for their guidance in publishing this manuscript.

John Wiley and Sons and Sage Publications graciously offered their permission to republish in this book research that I already published as academic journal articles in the *American Journal of Political Science* and *Conflict Management and Peace Science*, respectively.[1]

Finally, and most importantly, I thank my parents and sisters because they have taught me to tackle big projects one step at a time, an invaluable lesson for writing this book. I also thank Nick Guydosh for his daily inspiration in all things science and for believing in me. I wrote parts of the book while pregnant with our daughter, Gretchen Maria, and thank her too for the daily joy she provides. I dedicate this book to Nick and Gretchen.

ABBREVIATIONS

EITI	Extractive Industries Transparency Initiative
FLEC	Front for the Liberation of the Enclave of Cabinda
Frelimo	Liberation Front of Mozambique
GDP	Gross Domestic Product
IFI	International Financial Institution
IMF	International Monetary Fund
LRA	Lord's Resistance Army
MPLA	People's Movement for the Liberation of Angola
OECD	Organization for Economic Co-operation and Development
Renamo	Mozambican National Resistance
UK	United Kingdom
UN	United Nations
U.S.	United States
UNGA	United Nations General Assembly
UNITA	National Union for the Total Independence of Angola

PROLOGUE: A PHOENIX STATE

MOZAMBIQUE'S CIVIL WAR was one of Africa's worst in the 1980s, with 171,990 deaths from battle alone (Lacina and Gleditsch 2005), an estimated four to five million internally displaced individuals, and at least 1.5 million refugees (United Nations 1994a). The conflict destroyed much of the national infrastructure. Three weeks before a treaty was signed to end the civil war in 1992, the co-director of United Nations Humanitarian Affairs declared that Mozambique could become "the next Somalia" (quoted in Agence France Presse 1992). But Mozambique would not become the next Somalia.

Instead, Mozambique rose from the ashes of civil war. In the years following the war, Mozambican government officials managed to rebuild the country and oversee economic expansion that raised the national standard of living. The economy grew by 105% between 1992 and 2009, prompting a senior economist at the World Bank to say it was "like a dream" (quoted in Pickard-Cambridge 1998; Heston et al. 2011). More importantly, Mozambique's socioeconomic reconstruction benefited the general population (World Bank 2012a).

How and why did such reconstruction occur in a country that was devastated by sixteen years of civil war? The Mozambican town of Chibabava may offer some insight. With ten to fifteen people dying there daily as the civil war concluded in 1992, the town symbolized the hunger, insecurity, and destruction that had become the norm throughout Mozambique (Shaw 1992). Surrounded during the war by rebel-controlled areas, the overcrowded town, capital of the central Mozambican district of Sofala, had received minimal humanitarian relief during the war. According to a Red Cross worker in Chibabava at the end of the war, "you have no latrines, you have no water and no medics" (quoted in Manthorpe 1992).

After the peace treaty was signed, aid workers intervened aggressively throughout Mozambique. In Chibabava, workers from the Red Cross and other aid agencies vaccinated children against measles and built latrines. They also gave seeds to the displaced in Chibabava, and in so doing, helped reduce the population of the town from 20,000 to 2,000 in one month. "Everyone went home to plant corn," a reporter said (Keller 1993).

As emergency relief took hold, donors turned their attention to infrastructure for basic services. Chibabava received new schools, roads, and health centers. For example, with funds from the World Bank, donors completed a new hospital by the mid-2000s that expanded access to healthcare for the 285,000 living in the area (World Bank 2004). According to a foreign doctor working in the region, it was well-equipped: "X-ray (brand new and working), a very good lab, an operation theater, where they performed smaller surgery and cesarean. There was also a gym for physiotherapy... They also had a small blood bank."[1] The reconstruction in Chibabava persisted despite a massive flood in 2000, when "walls of water" displaced hundreds of thousands in the area and killed 700 (Carroll 2002). Mozambicans in Chibabava were no longer merely surviving and achieved these successes with approximately US$20 billion in aid (OECD 2012).[2]

A Puzzle

The experience of Chibabava, and of Mozambique more generally, raises important empirical questions about socioeconomic reconstruction. Is it possible (or desirable) to use foreign aid for reconstruction in post-conflict states? This question has important policy implications, given that post-conflict countries constituted fifteen of the top twenty recipients of development assistance between the end of the Cold War and 2010 (OECD 2012). In spite of these efforts, success has been uneven and elusive in many high-profile cases, such as Afghanistan and Iraq.

So how did socioeconomic reconstruction succeed in Mozambique, a country that faced significant destruction when its war ended? And did foreign aid help?

Much of the academic literature on foreign aid would predict that Mozambique would have experienced an "aid curse," where increases in aid represent windfall income for the government, income that inhibits development and fosters corruption because a leader rich in windfall need not turn to the population for tax revenues (Ahmed 2012; Bräutigam and Knack 2004; Bueno de Mesquita and Smith 2010; Easterly 2001; Morrison 2009; Moyo 2009; Smith 2008; van de Walle 2001). According to the literature, aid is only likely to help when a country has well-functioning governmental institutions that can absorb the aid and hold leaders accountable.[3]

The Mozambican government, like most post-conflict governments, lacked capacity to absorb the aid or mechanisms to hold leaders accountable when the civil war ended. But in the town of Chibabava and many others like it, donors distributed seeds, built infrastructure, staffed health clinics, and partnered with the government to strengthen its capacity so that it could offer continued support to the population. These contributions appear to have helped.

The government of Mozambique remains dependent on donors at this writing. As a result, the country's post-conflict reconstruction is not perfect. Mozambicans may have been better off had their leaders been forced to depend on taxes from the population instead of aid from donors. Mozambique's reconstruction is nevertheless puzzling. Explaining it will inform both donor policies following civil war and academic studies of post-conflict reconstruction, state building, and foreign aid.

Civil war continues to be common. Of 36 armed conflicts raging in 2009, fighting stopped in 19% (7 out of 36) by 2010, even as new armed conflict started in Mauritania and Tajikistan and was about to start in Libya and Syria (Gleditsch et al. 2002; Themnér and Wallensteen 2011). Determining when and why post-conflict socioeconomic reconstruction occurs can foster the effective use of aid following civil war and ameliorate an incalculable amount of human suffering. This book demonstrates how simple incentives can influence whether foreign aid helps a country achieve socioeconomic reconstruction following civil war. In doing so, I provide an argument that accounts for the paradoxical reconstruction rise of Phoenix States.

I

Phoenix States after Civil War: The Problem and the Argument

WHY DO SOME governments manage to successfully reconstruct their societies and economies following civil war? Why do some countries become Phoenix States,[1] when others do not?

"Post-conflict reconstruction"[2] became a popular term in the 1990s. Donors of foreign assistance used it to describe their state-building and development efforts in the aftermath of civil conflict. While the history of the concept long predates the phrase, the international state-building efforts in Afghanistan and Iraq in the 2000s in particular brought both the idea and the terminology to the fore. Transforming post-conflict countries into functioning states with governments that can offer their citizens basic public services has become a major foreign policy initiative of the United States and many European donors, in addition to major multilateral actors such as the United Nations, the World Bank, and the European Union. To Afghanistan alone, donor governments disbursed US$45.6 billion between 2001 and 2012, and US$64.6 billion to Iraq between 2003 and 2012 (Belasco 2009; European Union 2009; OECD 2012). Despite the investment in resources and in the lives of soldiers and aid workers lost doing the reconstruction, in both countries progress

1

has been slow to develop. The governments of Afghanistan and Iraq remain too weak to counteract ongoing violence and corruption or to offer reliable public services to their citizens.

Because these reconstruction efforts have failed to make much headway, they prompt the question of whether it is possible or even desirable for third parties to attempt post-conflict reconstruction (Brownlee 2007; Englebert and Tull 2008; Herbst 2004; Weinstein 2005). Before we can answer that question, we must understand the conditions and underlying incentives that promote reconstruction following civil war.

Post-Conflict Reconstruction is Crucial

Countries emerging from civil war face unique and daunting reconstruction challenges, including insecurity and corruption, weak infrastructure for transportation and communications, little formal economic activity, an unstable macroeconomic environment, and a lack of basic services, including health, water, and sanitation.[3] And without reconstruction, the citizens of post-conflict countries continue to suffer (Ghobarah, Huth and Russett 2003; Iqbal 2010). Disease (from internally displaced camps, for example) spreads rapidly due to a lack of health infrastructure and a dearth of medical professionals to contain the spread. Crime increases because the legal system and police remain weak, which makes it difficult for the government to enforce (and for citizens to respect) laws. Unemployment stays high because domestic and foreign investors fear unstable political, social, and economic conditions, not to mention the outbreak of new war. In fact, the probability that war resumes ten years after a ceasefire is 40% (Collier, Hoeffler and Söderbom 2008).

To turn the tide, a post-conflict country needs socioeconomic reconstruction; that is, it needs social and economic development that benefits a majority of citizens. When and why post-conflict governments manage to turn the tide matters greatly: 1.9 million people were killed fighting in post-conflict countries that fell back into civil war between 1970 and 2010, and foreign donors provided nearly US$1 trillion in reconstruction aid to prevent such horror.

Can Foreign Aid Help?

The academic literature suggests not. Instead, it predicts that the influx of aid to post-conflict countries may create an "aid curse." This theory holds that when aid comes from other countries or international organizations, governments no longer need to tax their citizens for income.[4] Instead of using aid for reconstruction, elites redirect that money to serve their own needs. The literature on foreign aid to all developing countries suggests that aid generally does not work because of the "curse," but if it helps at all, it does so when recipients have strong institutions.[5] Aid can help, for example, when leaders govern within a framework of broad-based institutions. When they depend on popular support, the leaders have to spend the money on development that benefits the population, just as the donors intend. Aid can also help when the recipient government has high-quality infrastructure and human capacity to spend the aid on development. However, in the immediate aftermath of civil war, weakness plagues institutions, so many scholars don't expect aid to promote socioeconomic reconstruction.[6]

Some evidence supports the existence of an aid curse following civil war. After the chaos of civil war in countries such as the Democratic Republic of the Congo and the Central African Republic, foreign actors have struggled to promote reconstruction. Combatants in these countries destroyed infrastructure, including communication and water systems and road networks, disrupted food markets, burned down or stole from homes, schools, and health clinics. In the wake of such destruction, these countries' civilian populations suffered from continuing high levels of crime and disease. Donors offered these two governments foreign aid specifically for basic services. The Democratic Republic of the Congo received US$35.3 billion in aid between 2002 and 2012, and the much smaller Central African Republic received US$1.6 billion in aid over the ten years following its 1997 ceasefire (OECD 2012). But within five years of the Democratic Republic of the Congo's 2002 ceasefire, at least 2.1 million people died of more violence, starvation, and disease, even in areas where fighting did not restart (Coghlan et al. 2007). As of 2014 in the Central African Republic, one third of the population lacks any clean water and thousands suffer from insecurity, poverty, crime, malnutrition, and epidemics (Médecins Sans Frontières 2011; UNICEF 2014; Wakabi

2006). These outcomes support the notion of an aid curse and cast doubt on the efficacy of foreign aid as a means of preventing human suffering in the wake of civil war. When countries with weak institutions receive aid, the problem may not be lack of money but paradoxically that plenty of money is coming in but not being used to improve living conditions.

Phoenix States Challenge the Aid Curse

However, some weak governments manage to improve living conditions in their countries—even after experiencing violence as devastating as that which beset the Central African Republic and the Democratic Republic of the Congo. Like Mozambique, El Salvador is also a Phoenix State. El Salvador experienced an "impressive economic recovery," according to the World Bank, after receiving US$5 billion in the ten years following its twelve-year civil war that had destroyed much of its infrastructure and human capital (Eriksson, Kreimer, and Arnold 2000, 13). Similarly, countries as diverse as Bosnia, Guatemala, and Rwanda also became Phoenix States, experiencing steady economic growth and improvements in living conditions after receiving US$11.2 billion, US$4.3 billion, and US$6.3 billion in aid, respectively, in the decade that followed their destructive civil wars (Heston, Summers, and Aten 2011; World Bank 2012a). In each of these countries, donors carried out extensive socioeconomic reconstruction projects, from the implementation of vaccination programs to the building of roads, schools, and health clinics.

Phoenix States raise questions about why some post-conflict governments are better at reconstruction than others. If post-conflict countries are less likely to have the strong institutions that foster the effective use of aid, how do Phoenix States manage to use aid to rebuild following civil war? This book argues that, in the absence of strong institutions, other factors influence countries that receive aid and affect the relationship between aid and reconstruction.

The Need for a Testable Argument

The academic and policy literature has yet to dedicate much attention to socioeconomic reconstruction, especially in a systematically comparative context.[7] Few scholars have analyzed why some countries manage to rebuild their societies and economies after a conflict while others don't.[8] In this book, I examine what conditions need to be present before aid will foster rebuilding following civil war. I offer an argument and test it using statistics, and I then use case studies to re-evaluate and fine-tune the argument. Then I look at the issues that surround this argument and raise several questions for policy: Can foreign aid be used effectively to reconstruct societies following a civil war? Might that aid actually make the problems worse? This book shows the specific circumstances under which foreign aid can help—and when it may have no effect or even hurt.

The Argument: Reconstruction Requires Incentives

I argue that foreign aid is more likely to promote social and economic reconstruction after civil war under two conditions: (1) when the government receiving the aid—that is, the aid recipient—lacks access to income from natural resources,[9] and (2) when donors do not provide the aid to support their own political, military, or other purposes. The income a government receives from natural resources, less production costs, is known as resource rent. Aid to countries with either high resource rents or high strategic importance after civil war may not promote social and economic reconstruction for the same reason: both the aid and the resource rents represent windfall (unearned) income (Ahmed 2012; Bueno de Mesquita and Smith 2010; Morrison 2009). Natural resources make no demands, so when countries that receive aid also receive large resource rents, they lack the financial incentives to meet donor expectations. Similarly, when donors disburse aid for strategic purposes, the recipient lacks incentives to use the aid for reconstruction because donors have not made the aid contingent upon meeting reconstruction goals (Bearce and Tirone 2010; Stone 2010).[10] When either resource rents or strategic importance is high, incentives to reach donor reconstruction goals are low.

However, when a recipient lacks resource rents and holds no strategic importance to the donor, that recipient faces strong incentives to pursue the reconstruction goals the donor articulates. By promoting social and economic reconstruction, these otherwise politically unimportant recipients maintain strong relationships with donors and secure continued flows of aid that allow the leader to hang on to power.

This line of thinking implies that positive aid outcomes following civil war are conditional, based on a combination of donor disinterest and recipient desperation. It suggests that development aid only "works" following civil war if the donors give the aid for nonstrategic reasons and if the recipient lacks alternative sources of income and is therefore desperate for aid.

Since the late 1990s, donors have been concerned with how a developing country can "get to Denmark"—in other words, how it can create a legitimate government that delivers high-quality public services to the vast majority of its population (Pritchett and Woolcock 2004). While some post-conflict countries can successfully reconstruct and become Phoenix States, they are unlikely to get all the way to Denmark, at least in the decades that immediately follow the war.

Post-conflict countries that use nonstrategic aid for reconstruction may remain dependent on that aid and therefore experience only a muted reconstruction success (Murshed 2010). If donors offer aid in exchange for meeting reconstruction goals, a developing country becomes dependent on a source of income that requires it to change. But this incentive to change is far from ideal. Legislators or citizens, who can be closer to, more knowledgeable about, and more demanding of their governments than donors, can create a far more powerful incentive. In fact, I find that nonstrategic donors will tolerate some corruption as long as leaders generally meet donor reconstruction goals. Nevertheless, my investigation also reveals that after civil war, when leaders with low windfall income receive nonstrategic aid, new political bodies emerge that are more sensitive to citizen needs than would be the case if their leaders had alternative sources of income. In short, post-conflict reconstruction in low-windfall countries that depend on nonstrategic aid may be muted, but it is more likely than post-conflict reconstruction in high windfall countries.

Scope of the Book

In this book, I focus my attention on post-conflict countries. I examine why aid helps only some of them, improving living conditions in certain countries and failing to do so in others. I focus on post-conflict countries because governmental institutions in such countries tend to be fragile or have failed. Given the scholarly consensus that foreign aid is most likely to be effective when institutions are strong, understanding the conditions under which aid is effective in post-conflict countries is important for advancing research on foreign aid. In addition, I focus on post-conflict countries because such countries are crucial for policy. The process that unfolds after civil war in countries like Libya and Syria may affect the national interests of many Western donors.[11] For these reasons, the book concentrates on countries that have recently experienced civil war.

The focus on foreign aid and natural resources limits the scope of the book to the last four decades. This is in part due to data availability. Data on aid begin in 1960 and data on resource rents begin in 1970. But data availability is not the only constraint on the time period under study. I do not expect the argument in this book to explain post-conflict reconstruction before foreign aid was commonplace (i.e., before the end of the Second World War). Even more constraining, the results may in fact only hold after 1970 because the resource curse, which is analogous to the aid curse, only began to afflict countries in the 1970s, when oil-producing countries took over the assets of foreign oil companies to a significant degree (Andersen and Ross 2014). Doing so gave these countries more direct access to resource rents and enabled them to create and maintain patronage networks (Ross 2012). The scope of the data range is therefore appropriate for testing the argument.

In determining the book's scope, I also took into account the literature on foreign aid. I analyzed aid flows from the 23 members of the Organization for Economic Development and Cooperation (OECD) Development Assistance Committee, which more or less means Western donors.[12] Cultural, policy, and institutional differences distinguish these 23 donors (van der Veen 2011), but extant cross-national studies generally focus on aggregated aid flows and overlook differences in types of donors. These differences may in fact partially explain why aid is more effective in some countries than in others following civil war. I focus on a specific characteristic of aid flows that has the potential to influence recipient incentives to implement aid agreements: whether a donor had a strategic interest in the recipient when it disbursed the aid.[13]

Organization of the Book

Chapter 2 offers a simple incentive based argument to explain when post-conflict leaders choose to promote reconstruction with aid and why only some of them do. I argue that recipients who mainly depend on nonstrategic aid generally use the aid for reconstruction as intended by donors in order to maintain a flow of income. The theoretical framework that I present simplifies complex concepts and interactions between and within donor and recipient countries so that I can derive meaningful hypotheses to test using quantitative and qualitative methods.

Chapters 3, 4, 5, and 6 test the argument in three different contexts: (1) across all countries that ended civil war during the last four decades; (2) by comparing two countries, Mozambique and Angola, that are very similar in important respects but differ in windfall income; and (3) within one country, Uganda, before and after it experiences windfall income. This three-pronged approach allows me to investigate the argument from different angles, adding confidence in the findings.

Chapters 3 and 4 look at what the numbers can tell us. They offer quantitative evidence about the impact of aid after all civil wars across the globe during the last four decades. Specifically, Chapter 3 demonstrates that increasing nonstrategic aid to low-windfall countries from US$10 to US$25 per capita improves socioeconomic reconstruction by 0.48%, while the same increase in nonstrategic aid to high windfall countries worsens the rate by 0.23%. In Chapter 4, I demonstrate that the combination of low windfall, nonstrategic aid, and socioeconomic reconstruction reduces the risk that a coup will occur following civil war. Global data thus support the argument, even if we re-examine the results using different models.

While the quantitative work demonstrates patterns that are consistent with the argument, detailed case studies allow me to examine how leaders and donors behave in practice. In Chapter 5, I link reconstruction spending and the strategies leaders use to ensure their political survival in two case studies: Mozambique after 1992 and Angola after 2002. The two countries share similar histories and had similar socioeconomic conditions at the end of their wars, but they differ in how much windfall income they had. Angola was rich in oil and diamond rents and strategic financial support from China while Mozambique had low windfall when its civil war ended. Only

Mozambique managed to experience broad-based development following the war.

The two case studies reveal the mechanisms underlying the argument, but comparing two countries is less than ideal. The optimal case study would allow me to observe the same government with and without windfall income. To approximate this, one can study a country that initially has no windfall, and then, after a sufficient period of observation, its government discovers a significant windfall. Such a comparison would hold many confounding factors constant. Therefore, in Chapter 6, I investigate post-conflict dynamics in Uganda, where the government's experience with windfall changed. Initially, at its 1986 ceasefire, Uganda had no significant windfall. But the country discovered natural resources in the mid-1990s, fundamentally changing its trajectory. Thus, I test the argument empirically, using a nested approach that combines quantitative empirics and qualitative analyses of case studies (Lieberman 2005).

Chapter 7 extends the findings through five additional cases that support the argument. These additional cases offer real-world support that the argument applies in countries other than Mozambique and Uganda. But, like any argument in the social sciences, my argument only explains some of the data. I therefore examine five cases that the argument doesn't explain in order to reveal additional variables that may be relevant to future research on post-conflict reconstruction. This concluding chapter also considers how donors can improve their ability to direct strategic aid toward socioeconomic reconstruction and persuade resource-rich governments to implement reforms that would improve living conditions in their states. It outlines the circumstances under which donors can improve aid effectiveness following civil war and help countries avoid the curse of windfall income.

I wrote this book with both specialists and nonspecialists in mind. Relying on social science methodology throughout the book allows me to examine the argument rigorously, but some chapters are more technical than others. Specialists and anyone interested in all the details of the argument may therefore wish to read the entire book. Nonspecialists, however, may want to read all of Chapters 1, 2, 5, 6, and 7 and only parts of Chapters 3 and 4, the quantitative chapters. I summarize the content of the quantitative chapters in their introductions, transitions, and conclusions, so the nonspecialist reader can understand what the statistics tell us without digging into the technical details.

The slow, uncertain progress of social and economic rebuilding in Afghanistan and Iraq has shaped recent scholarly and policy thinking on reconstruction in conflict-ridden states. After enormous investment of resources by external actors in these countries, scholars and policy analysts are now trying to evaluate whether post-conflict reconstruction is impossible or simply requires more resources. My findings suggest that such strategically important or mineral-rich governments as those in Iraq and Afghanistan will continue to encounter reasons not to invest in reconstruction. Aid appears to be a suitable tool to promote reconstruction after civil war only in countries where, paradoxically, donors have the least at stake.

2

Reconstruction Against All Odds

WHY DO SOME post-conflict countries become Phoenix States and achieve successful social and economic reconstruction? Can aid play a positive role in this process?

Foreign aid is controversial. The history of aid is replete with examples of good intentions gone awry because aid recipients stole the money or donors misspent it (Easterly 2003; Maren 1997). After the 2002 ceasefire in the Democratic Republic of the Congo, the World Bank offered the country US$493 million in an ambitious state-building operation that involved an array of other multilateral agencies, including UN peacekeepers and bilateral donors. At the time, the World Bank's country director argued that "success depends on the rapid availability of external support" (quoted in World Bank 2002). But the aid failed to reconstruct the country, and at least 2.1 million people died between 2002 and 2007 from ongoing violence as well as from starvation and disease (Coghlan et al. 2007). Perhaps disease and hunger would have spread more rapidly and reached more people without the aid, but at the very least, the failure of aid to raise the standard of living of the population contrasts sharply with donors' initial hopes.[1]

Six years after the U.S.-led state-building effort started in Afghanistan, the UN special envoy reported that the operation was in peril because external support was "under-resourced" and disorganized (quoted in DeYoung 2008). Then-U.S. senator Joe Biden also argued that "Afghanistan is slipping toward failure" (Biden 2008). To rectify the situation, he said, the United States needed to bolster its military effort and "to make good on President Bush's pledge for a Marshall Plan for Afghanistan" (Biden 2008).

Post-conflict reconstruction is expensive for donors and payoffs are rare. As a result, understanding why only some countries manage to bring about reconstruction can lead to better policy. Did the Democratic Republic of the Congo fail to meet donors' expectations because donor programs did not work, or did the government choose not to implement the aid agreements in the first place?

In this chapter, I explain why some leaders have more incentive than others to use aid for reconstruction. In addition to benefiting policy, understanding post-conflict reconstruction helps explain theoretical paradoxes in academic studies of foreign aid, political violence and development. One paradox is that in some post-conflict countries, socioeconomic reconstruction appears to occur as a result of aid, despite the existing theory that introducing aid into weak institutional environments can only worsen development prospects. Another paradox is that post-conflict countries that don't have windfall income achieve better social and economic reconstruction than countries that do.

I build an argument to answer *when* post-conflict reconstruction happens and to explain the decision-making process that accounts for *why* this reconstruction occurs. To determine *when*, I consider the conditions under which aid creates socioeconomic reconstruction. The *why* refers to the mechanism: can incentives explain why only a specific subset of post-conflict leaders chooses to invest in socioeconomic reconstruction? In this chapter, I develop hypotheses to address each of these components.[2]

My argument rests on the assumption that a country's leader wants to preserve his or her political survival. If we assume that post-conflict leaders act rationally, we can also assume that they will seek the easiest sources of income to secure their own survival. In turn, understanding how income sources determine leaders' strategies for protecting themselves from coups ("coup-proofing") can explain the stark variation in post-conflict socioeconomic reconstruction.[3]

I will begin by discussing the incentives that motivate post-conflict leaders and how they go about consolidating their political power in the face of rivals and weak institutions. Next I explore the crucial role different kinds of income—namely windfall income and nonstrategic aid—have in determining reconstruction outcomes. I then state my argument, detail how I will analyze my hypotheses, and consider alternative explanations.

Power Consolidation Following Civil War

Leaders emerging from civil war are likely concerned with coup-proofing both because they rule with fragile institutions and because post-conflict countries are prone to coups.[4] Generally, their countries are unstable and have a history of coups (Belkin and Schofer 2003; Londregan and Poole 1990; Powell 2012). In Uganda, for example, coups brought about four out of the six regime changes that preceded Yoweri Museveni's rule. In the Central African Republic, coups caused two of the four regime changes before the 1997 ceasefire. In Afghanistan, seven out of nine regimes since 1973 have been overthrown.

My analysis assumes that post-conflict leaders and their potential rivals seek to protect and expand their political positions. By "leaders," I refer to the executives in charge of the post-conflict government, and by "potential rivals," I refer to opposition leaders and other individuals in the state apparatus with the capacity to coordinate against the regime leader, including those inside the government's own political party as well as military officers.

Clearly, leaders and rivals are more than rational actors motivated simply by zero-sum calculations and their own political self-interest. Some may be motivated by sincere ideological or political beliefs or personal enrichment, and are therefore less concerned with maximizing income for political survival. Even if multiple factors motivate leaders and potential rivals, the supposition that they are rational actors is nevertheless useful because it allows for meaningful exploration of two questions: First, how do leaders secure resources to protect themselves from emerging threats after a civil war ends? And second, how do rivals view the expected costs and benefits of overthrowing the regime leader?

I define a "coup" as the capture of the executive by elites within the government using force, and "coup-proofing" refers to the steps a leader takes to consolidate power within the government.[5] This definition of a coup includes more than threats from military and security elites, but it does not include threats from rebellion. This "middle ground" definition[6] is consistent with the latest work on coups, and it allows the concept of coup-proofing to encompass strategies of power consolidation against any elite part of the state apparatus, not just the military. My definition of coup is thus broader than the definition used in much extant research on coup-proofing that is focused on threats from security forces.[7] But my definition is not so broad as to include seizures of power by actors outside the state structure.[8] By defining a coup as a threat from within the government and not including rebellions from outside the government, coups are not conflated with the resumption of civil war, which has different causes.[9]

Strategies of Potential Rivals

Potential rivals and their followers likely weigh the expected benefits of overthrowing the leader against the costs. Clearly, rivals can increase their income if they overthrow the leader and obtain access to government revenues. But attempting to overthrow the leader is risky because leaders are likely to incarcerate or execute any coup plotters they discover. Potential rivals are aware of this risk, as are their followers (Arriola 2009). On the other hand, followers stand to gain from supporting a rival who succeeds. For example, followers who directly help a rival coordinate a coup can become cabinet members in the new government. Thus, assuming potential rivals and their followers seek to maximize their own income, they must weigh the uncertainty of successfully executing a coup against the certain gains that the established government can provide. In general, potential rivals are less likely to coordinate a coup as the costs of executing the coup increase or as the anticipated benefits of coup success decline.

Increasing the Costs of a Coup: Strengthening Defense

A leader can increase the costs facing rivals who seek to coordinate a coup by bolstering the security infrastructure (Collier 1999; Ghobarah et al. 2003; Luttwak 1968). Coup-proofing to consolidate post-conflict power may include improving leader security by creating paramilitary infrastructures and duplicating intelligence structures, by giving officer positions that favor important ethnoreligious loyalties, and by professionalizing the military (Quinlivan 1999). Strengthened security forces can detect a potential coup more rapidly and respond more quickly and effectively, reducing the chances a coup attempt will succeed. By increasing uncertainty about the expected success of a coup, leaders can discourage coup attempts.

Decreasing the Benefits of a Coup: Paying Off Potential Rivals

From a potential rival's perspective, overthrowing the government might appear increasingly unattractive if the gap between potential and present benefits narrows. Cash handouts are therefore important for power consolidation. A leader hoping to co-opt potential opponents can induce cooperation by paying supporters and rewarding rivals for switching sides (Bueno de Mesquita et al. 2003). Importantly, the net reward for a successful coup is smaller for a rival who is actively receiving payoffs from the leader.[10] Handouts can alleviate the grievances of potential rivals and allow them to benefit from the status quo, thereby reducing their incentive to initiate a coup.

The Crucial Role of Income

Because coup-proofing involves elite payoffs and strengthening defense, power consolidation is expensive, immediate, and ongoing, and requires steady revenue (Quinlivan 1999). Income is therefore crucial following civil war. So how do post-conflict leaders secure income to protect themselves from a coup? Because coup risk is high, post-conflict leaders are likely to pursue the easiest and most profitable income options. Appreciating how income sources drive leaders' incentives towards reconstruction as they try to reduce coup risk following civil war is fundamental to my argument here, as is the distinction between windfall and nonwindfall income.

Windfall Income: Natural Resources and Strategic Aid

The easiest and most attractive sources of significant income for post-conflict leaders are natural resource rents and strategic aid.[11] Both represent windfall income with no reconstruction strings attached. To the extent that windfall income from resource rents or strategic aid allows recipients to make payoffs and strengthen the security infrastructure, these sources of income increase the odds that potential rivals will incur serious losses during a coup attempt.

Natural resource rents represent a potential source of immediate windfall income for post-conflict leaders, especially if the windfall requires little labor (oil) or little technology (gold and diamonds) to extract. Natural resources that require little labor or capital to extract are often relatively easy to protect during the war. Unlike plantations, for example, which are widespread in a region and can be easily targeted by combatants, windfall-generating natural resources are often "point" facilities confined to specific enclosed mining areas or, as in the case of oil, offshore (Le Billon 2001a). Also, even if damaged by the war, protected natural resource areas are readily rebuilt by signing deals with foreign extraction companies. Thus, while civil war may destroy significant amounts of infrastructure, protected natural resource holdings generate continued rents after a ceasefire. Between 1970 and 2008, 37% of post-conflict governments received at least US$100 per capita annually in windfall income from natural resources, demonstrating that post-conflict countries indeed receive resource rents following civil war (Hamilton and Clemens 1999).

From the leaders' perspective, the next-best option to exploiting resources like oil and diamonds is receiving aid that is contingent on donor geostrategic interests. Donors are likely to disburse strategic aid to former colonies because donors often maintain political interests in their former colonies (Alesina and Dollar 2000) and because donors often have military strategic interests in the recipient country.[12] To obtain strategic aid, a recipient can, for example, sell rights to its air space; rights to land at military bases; the right to conduct military operations; votes on the United Nations Security Council; or other explicit support for donor foreign policy priorities in the region (Dreher, Sturm, and Vreeland 2009a; Dreher, Sturm, and Vreeland 2009b; Kuziemko and Werker 2006). A recipient can also "sell" the donor state's ideology—something valued especially highly during the Cold War.

Strategic aid is less attractive than resource rents because the aid is contingent on meeting donor security goals, and leaders likely prefer to have free reign over the money they receive. Nevertheless, donor security goals in post-conflict countries generally involve helping the leader stay in power (Carter 2009). Thus, strategic aid represents income that is, in part, directly intended to help leaders protect their regimes from coups.

In addition, strategic aid that is specifically earmarked for reconstruction is often used for coup-proofing. The incentive to comply with donor expectations to spend a portion of strategic aid on reconstruction is weak because the aid contingency is based more on donor strategic interests than on reconstruction goals (Martens et al. 2002).[13] Because the recipient is important to advancing the donor's strategic interests, the recipient can "do no wrong" when it comes to implementing other donor demands. As a former senior U.S. official said, in the 1980s, in strategically important countries, "we had multiple tracks. . . . What was important to the economic folks, and what was important to the diplomatic folks were two different things sometimes. And this got triaged."[14] As a result, post-conflict aid based on strategic importance comes with unenforceable demands for reconstruction.[15] Post-conflict aid based on strategic importance can therefore operate almost entirely like natural resources, generating an immediate windfall for the recipient government.

Indeed, leaders view strategic aid as an offering that is similar to windfall income from natural resources. For example, an analyst of foreign assistance to the mineral-rich Democratic Republic of the Congo when it was known as Zaire, wrote that the elite "sees development assistance"—most of which appeared to be strategic—"as yet another means to accumulate personal wealth" (Leslie 1987, 6).[16] Kiren Aziz Chaudhry observed that aid to the Yemeni government from strategically-motivated Gulf states created the same institutions as oil rents in oil-rich states: "Until 1981, the Gulf states paid the total current cost budget of the state, enabling the government to maintain itself without enforcing the collection of direct taxes. By providing a foreign source of state revenue, aid diminished the importance of the Ministry of Finance and supported the rise of highly centralized planning institutions, similar to those found in oil exporters" (Chaudhry 1989, 130). Strategic aid can thus operate like natural resource rents in providing windfall income for post-conflict leaders.

Nonstrategic Aid

After windfall, nonstrategic aid is the next easiest-to-acquire source of income following civil war.[17] While nonstrategic donors are less interested in protecting specific leaders than in reconstruction, nonstrategic donors are keenly interested in maintaining sufficient stability to promote reconstruction.[18]

HOW NONSTRATEGIC AID PAYS FOR SECURITY AND HANDOUTS

From a nonstrategic donor's perspective, a secure government makes socioeconomic reconstruction more likely. The World Bank's operations manual, for example, states that "economic and social stability and human security are pre-conditions for sustainable development" (World Bank 2001, 1). Similarly, the OECD's 2001 guidelines for official bilateral development assistance indicate that "Helping developing countries build legitimate and accountable systems of security—in defence, police, judicial and penal systems—has become a high priority. . ." (OECD 2001, 19). These guidelines set out what actions donors who want to promote development can take to achieve that goal. The United States, for example, directly funded the training, equipment, and deployment of El Salvador's national police after that country's post–Cold War ceasefire, when it no longer held significant strategic importance to the United States (U.S. General Accounting Office 1994). Thus, nonstrategic aid—even if its goal is reconstruction—can provide some security and thereby reduce the chance of a coup.[19]

Nonstrategic aid can also help post-conflict leaders offer payoffs to elites. For example, in the lead-up to the Solomon Islands elections in 2001, the country's leaders (with support from Australia) paid $5.95 million to the politicians, rebels, and police who had organized a coup attempt the previous year (O'Callaghan 2001). Nonstrategic donors may also invest large sums in war-torn countries to incorporate opposition parties into a democratic political system that can potentially mediate future conflict among elites peacefully (Doyle and Sambanis 2006; Fortna 2008). In other words, donors sometimes offer aid to buy support for the political system because they seek to obtain sufficient stability for socioeconomic reconstruction. Specific reconstruction initiatives might also benefit some sectors privately. For example, police and lawyers privately benefit from policies that invest in the rule of law (Bueno de Mesquita et al. 2003, 31). Nonstrategic aid can thus be used to coup-proof, but nonstrategic aid is not windfall.

Unlike strategic aid, nonstrategic aid can come with enforceable reconstruction strings attached. Leaders must meet donor objectives, which means they must implement donor guidelines on development aid, or risk donor withdrawal.[20] Nonstrategic donors generally call for reform of public finances and wider allocation of wealth to the poor (Devarajan et al. 2001).

NONSTRATEGIC DONOR DEMANDS

Nonstrategic donors make two general demands of post-conflict countries: first, maintain good standing with the international financial institutions (in other words, work toward macroeconomic stability), and second, meet specific political and development goals.

Before a nonstrategic donor disburses aid to a post-conflict country, the International Monetary Fund (IMF) takes the lead in negotiating the recipient country's budget. As a Fund economist said,

> Bilateral donors want to see in place a functioning IMF program for them to engage... in the country. But they [bilateral donors] do not affect directly the way in which we negotiate the budget with the authorities.... [B]ilateral donors do not directly impose standard conditionality regarding the budget. Even the World Bank doesn't. The only organization that does that is the IMF since we are the only ones negotiating the budget with the authorities.[21]

When the IMF negotiates the budget with the recipient government, it attempts to stabilize the country's fiscal position and its macroeconomic environment. To do this, it looks for ways to increase government revenues and cut spending.

In addition to demands regarding the budget, the IMF and other donors include structural demands, requirements that the recipient country change the structure of its economy by, for instance, increasing market competition or reducing government control. The IMF and the World Bank specifically ask recipients of their assistance to implement policies on macroeconomics, tax administration, public expenditures, and overall transparency and accountability. Because the IMF and the World Bank play a crucial role in encouraging or discouraging bilateral nonstrategic donors to disburse aid, bilateral donors "indirectly... endorse the conditionality... imposed by these two institutions."[22] But bilateral donors also add on their own specific demands regarding everything from strengthening legislatures and protecting human rights to building schools, rehabilitating roads, or improving access to health services. Thus, recipient countries have to meet the demands of nonstrategic donors, including the goals set by the international financial institutions and goals set by bilateral donors.

HOW NONSTRATEGIC AID CREATES PHOENIX STATES

Importantly, aid can facilitate socioeconomic reconstruction.[23] By successful reconstruction I mean that living conditions improve for the majority of its citizens. The United Nations Development Program has defined such development this way: "Human development is a process of enlarging people's choices. The most critical ones are to lead a long and healthy life, to be educated and to enjoy a decent standard of living" (United Nations 2010, 12).

To prevent further human tragedy and to reduce poverty after civil war, nonstrategic donors typically fund humanitarian relief (food, shelter, medical attention), in addition to vaccination programs, health clinics, water and sanitation systems, road rehabilitation, and other programs that address basic needs. Studies indicate that such initiatives do in fact reduce poverty, and donors expect that, if implemented, agreements to provide aid for basic needs will promote socioeconomic reconstruction.[24]

One might ask how poverty declines in a country that implements IMF and World Bank policies, given that some have argued that compliance with these policies exacerbates poverty (van de Walle 2001; Vreeland 2003). By the late 1980s, aid workers (especially those from nongovernmental organizations), policy makers, and academics charged that the Fund and the Bank required governments that received aid to cut expenditures on social sectors such as health, education, or food.

Others dispute the degree to which the Fund and the Bank actually called for these measures, with some arguing that cuts were only meant to eliminate "ghost workers" (nonexistent people who appear on a payroll) and other corruption.[25] Nevertheless, the critics' views prompted campaigns for donors to stop requiring that governments make structural changes in their economies, to offer debt relief, or at least to modify structural adjustment into "adjustment with a human face," which would put more emphasis on social sectors (Cornia, Jolly, and Stewart 1987). By the early 1990s, the IMF and the World Bank began explicitly protecting social sectors when they negotiated with governments in crisis, and by the early 2000s the two institutions were actively protecting what they call "priority spending" or "pro-poor spending" (i.e., funding for health, education, and infrastructure).

If IMF and World Bank staff did indeed call for cuts to spending on social sectors prior to the 1990s, is it still plausible to see socioeconomic reconstruction based on nonstrategic aid during the last four decades? There are two reasons to believe so. First, when the Fund credibly threatened to punish noncompliance during this period, recipients complied with the conditions on the loans and their economies benefited (Stone 2002). Similarly, when Western donors credibly threatened to withdraw aid during this period, recipients implemented the largely neoliberal policies the donors sought and experienced economic development (Bearce and Tirone 2010).

Second, the austerity measures the IMF and the World Bank required may not have inhibited socioeconomic reconstruction because compliance with these measures seems to have attracted aid from other donors that targeted poverty directly. Even if the IMF and World Bank policies directly reduced social spending, the indirect and larger effect of these "gatekeepers" was to attract additional aid that could offset negative consequences. According to a former senior World Bank official involved with Bank efforts in Sub-Saharan African countries in the 1980s, "Civil society and others were pushing like nobody's business. . . putting a lot of resources to address this imbalance that had occurred."[26] Thus, socioeconomic reconstruction is possible in spite of structural adjustment. Aside from championing big policy ideas like structural adjustment, donors have funded projects that are far less controversial (health clinics, schools, roads, and so on) and that appear—*when implemented*—more likely to bring about socioeconomic reconstruction.

How would a country leader's choices with regard to strategic or nonstrategic aid affect a nongovernmental organization administering a health clinic in the hinterlands of a post-conflict country? The leader can determine whether aid workers get access to certain populations, whether medicines and equipment get stuck in transport due to fees, whether officials at checkpoints are supportive, and so on. Leaders can do more (or less) to facilitate socioeconomic reconstruction when they have a greater (or lesser) interest in it—when they have (or lack) "political will." This book suggests that this political will depends in part on whether recipient leaders depend on nonstrategic aid and consider as credible donors' threats to withdraw that aid.

ARE THREATS TO WITHDRAW NONSTRATEGIC AID CREDIBLE?

Donors regularly express frustration at being unable to compel recipients to implement their aid agreements, yet donors continue to give aid. Studies show that donors continue to disburse funds to try to ameliorate crises, reward development successes, or compel recipients to buy products from the donor country via "tied aid" (Easterly 2003). However, a credible threat exists that donors can withdraw aid if the recipient fails to meet basic reconstruction objectives.

In an important 1975 essay, James Buchanan cautioned of a "Samaritan's Dilemma" wherein donors gain simply by giving, so they continue to disburse aid even if the recipients fail to meet donor objectives (Buchanan 1975). Donors make their donations, according to Buchanan, in order to feel good about themselves—regardless of the aid's effectiveness. Overcoming this dilemma is possible if the Samaritan comprehends the "prospects open to him and begins to behave accordingly. . . . Vague threats or promises to cut off his charity in the absence of work on the part of the recipient. . . will remain empty unless there's demonstrated willingness to carry out such threats" (Buchanan 1975, 76).[27]

More recent evidence suggests that donors can credibly threaten to withdraw aid from leaders who lack strategic importance and fail to implement aid agreements.[28] The IMF automatically stops funding to countries that go "off-track" (Stone 2004). Many donors who lacked strategic interests in Uganda reduced aid to the government in 2005 and again in 2010 when the government failed to comply with donor expectations (Girod, Krasner, and Stoner-Weiss 2009; Milner, Nielson, and Findley 2013). In general, the threat to withdraw is implicit. According to a former senior official at the World Bank:

> In some critical issues, one would go behind closed doors, tell the president or tell the finance minister, if you guys cross this red line, you're going to make it very difficult for us to go to our Board and

get approval for this. You're going to make it very difficult for us to go to the donors and ask them to open their pockets to support your development program. You're going to undercut us as spokespeople or advocates. . . .[29]

But are these threats indeed credible given that aid agency workers are more likely to advance their own careers if they disburse the aid? Aid agency workers who are worried about meeting their disbursement targets may not stop providing funds even if the recipient is not meeting donor goals (Easterly 2003). The degree to which this perverse incentive structure exists within donors is under debate. A senior official at the World Bank called it "an exaggerated myth" and explained that, "there are people, probably, who think that 'the only way I'm going to be promoted is to show that I can really get these loans going.' But there are also are a lot of people who have guts and stand up for things they believe in who are also valued and promoted. So it's a far more colored picture."[30] Nevertheless, to the extent that this problem exists, it likely undermines the ability of donors to make threats credible. This internal incentive structure, however, does not stop the most senior aid managers and their boards from disrupting aid disbursement, especially budget support, as the case studies later in this book will show. Thus, donors may become more effective at credibly threatening to withdraw if they change their internal career incentive structures, but the evidence indicates that nonstrategic donors are already relatively effective at convincing recipients of their willingness to withdraw.

While socioeconomic reconstruction may occur in some post-conflict countries, Powell (2012) finds that economic development is not, in general, associated with reducing coup risk. Thus, post-conflict leaders are likely to promote socioeconomic reconstruction only to the extent that it helps them obtain aid funds, some of which can be used toward consolidating power within the state apparatus and thereby reducing the risk of coup. From leaders' perspective, nonstrategic aid is less optimal than windfall income because some nonstrategic aid must be used toward socioeconomic reconstruction. But for low-windfall leaders, socioeconomic reconstruction represents the best mechanism to ensure continued nonstrategic aid to fund coup-proofing.

Testable Implications

Given that aid for post-conflict reconstruction may be worthwhile only under certain circumstances, I constructed an incentive-based model to help explain why that aid results in socioeconomic reconstruction for some post-conflict countries and not others. The argument advanced here consists of two empirically testable hypotheses that predict the broad circumstances necessary for aid to be effective in promoting socioeconomic reconstruction.

When Does Post-Conflict Reconstruction Occur?

Only post-conflict leaders with low resource rents and low strategic importance are likely to bring about socioeconomic reconstruction with aid because they, unlike windfall-rich leaders, desperately need the money and will therefore meet donor goals to continue the flow of aid. The positive effect of aid on reconstruction is therefore conditionally dependent on the absence of windfall income. This idea, which I summarize as the nonstrategic-desperation hypothesis, predicts *when* aid is likely to work.

> *Nonstrategic-Desperation Hypothesis: Nonstrategic aid is more likely to promote socioeconomic reconstruction following civil war in recipient countries that have low windfall income.*

If this hypothesis is correct, increases in aid should promote socioeconomic reconstruction only when resource rents and strategic importance are both low (see Table 2.1). The hypothesis also suggests that socioeconomic reconstruction should not occur in relation to aid levels when either resource rents or strategic importance are high. Because leaders with windfall genuinely do not need nonstrategic aid money, they have no incentive to use nonstrategic aid for socioeconomic reconstruction.

Table 2.1 Does Increasing Nonstrategic Aid Predict Post-Conflict Reconstruction?

	High windfall	Low windfall
High nonstrategic aid	No	Yes
Low nonstrategic aid	No	No

If this hypothesis is invalid, we will find that nonstrategic aid fails to help low-windfall countries achieve social and economic reconstruction. For example, nonstrategic aid could hinder reconstruction if recipients generally fail to implement aid agreements, such that the post-conflict governments become wealthy from aid while their citizens suffer. Nonstrategic aid could also hinder reconstruction because nonstrategic donors fail to enforce conditions on aid (Easterly 2003). If the nonstrategic-desperation hypothesis is invalid for these or other reasons, reconstruction will not improve significantly with increasing levels of nonstrategic aid in post-conflict countries lacking windfall income.

Why Does Post-Conflict Reconstruction Occur?

My second empirically testable hypothesis attempts to explain *why* only some post-conflict leaders foster socioeconomic reconstruction. It addresses the paradox that low-windfall countries with nonstrategic aid outperform high-windfall countries in post-conflict reconstruction. Post-conflict leaders who lack windfall have little choice but to embark on reconstruction programs in exchange for nonstrategic aid. Leaders with low windfall need the continued flow of aid money to survive, so they have a strong incentive to meet donor demands regarding reconstruction. Nonstrategic donors help these leaders bolster security infrastructure and payoffs, both of which combine to reduce coup risk. Successful socioeconomic reconstruction should ensure continued nonstrategic aid, demonstrating the incentive-based mechanism that predicts that high nonstrategic aid and high reconstruction post-conflict should reduce the risk of coup only in low-windfall countries.

Low-Windfall Coup-Proofing Hypothesis: Following civil war, the interaction of low windfall, nonstrategic aid, and reconstruction should reduce coup risk.

By investigating how the three-way interaction of nonstrategic aid, reconstruction, and windfall affect coup risk, I can assess whether low-windfall leaders who spend aid on donor goals are more likely to reduce coup risk than low-windfall leaders who steal the aid. If the low-windfall coup-proofing hypothesis is valid, coup risk should decline with increases in the interaction of nonstrategic aid and reconstruction following civil war, but only for low-windfall countries.[31] However, it is plausible that this hypothesis is invalid and the interaction of nonstrategic aid and reconstruction fails to reduce coup risk for countries low in windfall income. For example, reconstruction could increase the vulnerability of low-windfall leaders by strengthening their opposition. Further, aid increases money in government coffers, enlarging the potential prize for any opposition group considering a coup attempt. Consequently, one might not see a negative and statistically significant interaction of low windfall, nonstrategic aid, and reconstruction. If the hypothesis is invalid for these or other reasons, coup risk should not decline with increases in the interaction of nonstrategic aid and reconstruction in countries that lack windfall income.

I can test both hypotheses using statistics on civil wars that ended during the last four decades. Equally importantly, I can examine case studies to discover how nonstrategic aid helps reconstruction and coup-proofing in practice following civil war. Case study methodology should reveal that donors, leaders, and rivals are aware of these variables and relationships, and that these variables and relationships directly affect their decisions. If the argument is valid, case studies should demonstrate that leaders who are rich in windfall income do not prioritize socioeconomic reconstruction. These leaders should also fail to implement nonstrategic aid agreements because such agreements place constraints on government spending. In contrast, leaders with low windfall income should give nonstrategic aid donors leverage over their post-conflict budgets and follow through with agreements because these leaders need the continued flow of money to protect against coups.

Alternative Explanations

A number of important alternative factors could also account for differences in post-conflict reconstruction. For example, existing institutions, the strength of opposition groups after the war ends, and the leader's interest in increasing popularity could account for why some leaders choose to reconstruct their states while others do not. I describe the potential impact of each of these factors here and demonstrate in subsequent chapters that they do not seem to invalidate my argument.

Institutions

Existing institutions—also known as background institutions—are the most important alternative factor (Collier and Hoeffler 2004a; Flores and Nooruddin 2009; Kang and Meernik 2005). Some post-conflict countries have more state capacity, more physical resources, and more human resources to offer basic services when the war ends. Governments with greater capacity are better able to dispatch health services to areas in need, to communicate health risks to the population at large, to build health clinics and schools as needed, to facilitate transportation throughout the country, to create and support new areas of economic activity, and to prevent crime. For these reasons, governments with more capacity should be more capable of promoting socioeconomic reconstruction. Levels of state capacity could therefore explain variation in reconstruction outcomes.

Strong political institutions that emphasize good governance, such as democracy, could also explain the variation in post-conflict socioeconomic reconstruction (Flores and Nooruddin 2009; Kang and Meernik 2005). More democracy means more pressure on the leader to spend on the population. In more democratic contexts, leaders depend on broader coalitions and must therefore serve those coalitions in order to stay in office (Bueno de Mesquita and Smith 2010; Lake and Baum 2001). More constraints on the leader limit predation (Bates 2008; Olson 1993). It is important to note, however, that autocracies appear to be as likely as democracies to reduce poverty, measured by infant and child mortality rates (Ross 2006b). Given the uncertainty surrounding the impact of some background institutions, I account for institutions using various measures when analyzing post-conflict reconstruction.

Persistent Opposition

Strong opposition factions can spoil reconstruction initiatives (Licklider 1995; Toft 2010; Walter 1997). Analysis of post-conflict reconstruction thus needs to account for whether the conflict ended with a negotiated settlement, rather than ending decisively or waning on its own. Further, reconstruction may be more likely when leaders govern countries that have been at peace longer. More time heading a post-conflict country gives leaders more post-conflict governing experience and may allow them to consolidate more power than leaders whose countries have just emerged from war. My analysis therefore also accounts for the amount of time since the conflict ended.

Leader Popularity

Popularity may reduce coup risk by making it more difficult for rivals to recruit supporters because when a leader is popular, fewer individuals should have grievances. In addition, popularity should increase the leader's legitimacy. If coup plotters succeed in overthrowing a popular government, they should find it difficult to win support from domestic and international groups. For leaders lacking windfall income to pay for security infrastructure and elite handouts, popularity may be an additional means to reduce coup risk. Although this alternative explanation cannot be examined with quantitative analysis, the case studies allow us to investigate leaders' interest in popularity.

Summary

The mystery is not why foreign aid so often fails to promote socioeconomic reconstruction after a civil war. The real mystery is why foreign aid ever succeeds in creating Phoenix States. Rebuilding infrastructure and social institutions requires long-term thinking. However, post-conflict leaders are likely preoccupied with their immediate need to defend and consolidate their hold on power. Forgoing spending on today's security to invest instead in the country's future may increase a leader's vulnerability and thereby reduce the odds of political survival. Assuming that the challenge of basic survival is more pressing than broad social and economic development, leaders are likely to spend on socioeconomic reconstruction only to the extent that such spending directly ensures their own short-term survival. If reconstruction spending helps secure their political position, leaders invest in reconstruction; if it hinders their ability to protect themselves, they don't.

I argue that the key to understanding post-conflict leader decisions about reconstruction is appreciating the incentive structure that government income imposes. Where a post-conflict leader has access to windfall income, little incentive exists to promote socioeconomic reconstruction. Where a leader depends on nonstrategic donors, the government promotes reconstruction because that is the easiest way to keep income flowing to the leader.

Therefore, the nonstrategic-desperation hypothesis suggests that post-conflict reconstruction is most likely in countries where (1) aid is mainly from nonstrategic donors and (2) the post-conflict government lacks access to natural resource income and is therefore desperate for income. Further, according to the low-windfall coup-proofing hypothesis, nonstrategic aid should only reduce coup risk for leaders who lack access to windfall income and carry out reconstruction projects. The next chapters test these hypotheses with data and examine how they hold up in case studies.

3

Statistical Analysis of Post-Conflict Reconstruction

TO CONFIRM THAT differences in types of government income explain the variation in post-conflict reconstruction outcomes, I turn first to data. Successful reconstruction should be more likely if the post-conflict government lacks access to natural resources and strategic aid. Because the leader of such a government is desperate for income to coup-proof the regime, the incentives for reconstruction are present: the leader may choose to comply with reconstruction agreements because he or she desperately needs nonstrategic aid income, some of which can be used to consolidate power.

In this chapter, I test the first of the two hypotheses that follow from my argument. I proposed that increasing nonstrategic aid is likely to foster socioeconomic reconstruction only when the recipient government lacks windfall income. This nonstrategic-desperation hypothesis explains when reconstruction occurs, but not why. To explain why reconstruction occurs, I offered the low-windfall coup-proofing hypothesis, which predicts that only leaders with low windfall income are likely to invest in reconstruction in order to reduce coup risk following civil war. I test this second hypothesis in Chapter 4.

I test both hypotheses using annual data following 89 civil wars that ended between January 1, 1970 and January 1, 2009,[1] totaling 1,260 post-conflict years.[2] Descriptive statistics appear in Online Appendix Table 1.[3] The regression models that follow allow me to study differences across post-conflict governments over time with data that directly measure factors I hypothesize matter to the actors involved: resource rents, foreign aid, and reconstruction.

The data on civil war come from the Armed Conflicts Database (Gleditsch et al. 2002; Themnér and Wallensteen 2011). I define a civil war as an armed conflict where combatants fought against the government and at least 500 died annually on average. Following Fearon (2010) and Walter (2011), I consider a war to end when violence declines to twenty-five battle deaths or fewer per year for at least two consecutive years. The results are consistent if this threshold is changed to three consecutive years (Online Appendix Table 2). A post-conflict period ends on the final year of the sample, or sooner if civil war resumes in the country.

The macro-level cross-national approach used here faces a limitation that is common to this type of methodology: I cannot make causal claims strongly because nonstrategic aid and windfall income are not distributed randomly in the world. For example, country attributes such as their reconstruction prospects may play some role in determining why some countries receive more nonstrategic aid than others. If I could disburse nonstrategic aid or windfall income (my treatment variables) randomly to countries, I could infer that differences between the treated group and the control group actually depend on differences in their (randomly distributed) government finances.

Increasingly, scholars research aid at the micro-level instead of the macro, cross-national level after convincing a nongovernmental organization to randomize its intervention.[4] By randomly assigning treatment variables, micro-level experiments minimize problems of causal inference that plague the macro-level, cross-national studies, where treatments can rarely be assigned randomly (Humphreys and Weinstein 2009).

This book asks *when* and *why* post-conflict governments are likely to foster reconstruction, and micro-level interventions focused on the effects of specific projects on reconstruction would not help answer these questions. Nevertheless, the fact that foreign aid and other treatment variables in this study cannot be randomly assigned presents threats to the validity of results.

To mitigate these threats, I use a wide variety of robustness checks. These checks include the analysis of potentially confounding control variables, different measures of reconstruction and windfall income, fixed effects by region and decade, the endogeneity of aid (i.e., reverse causality), outliers, and a joint-modeling strategy that ties the error structure of the reconstruction and coup risk models together. I also analyze multiple rival explanations for the relationship between aid and reconstruction and for the relationship between reconstruction and leader survival in office. I conclude that the theoretical framework offered here represents a valid explanation for reconstruction outcomes.

The findings support the nonstrategic-desperation hypothesis and the low-windfall coup-proofing hypothesis. In Chapter 3, I explain the research design and findings for the nonstrategic-desperation hypothesis, and in Chapter 4 I do the same for the low-windfall coup-proofing hypothesis.

The purpose of this quantitative chapter is to statistically test the nonstrategic-desperation hypothesis developed in Chapter 2 in order to answer my argument's "when" question: under what circumstance do leaders bring about successful post-conflict reconstruction? In Chapter 2, I argued that leaders who depend on nonstrategic aid reconstruct their states in order to satisfy nonstrategic donors. This argument highlights leader incentives. Post-conflict leaders need income to strengthen security and buy out elites. When post-conflict leaders depend on windfall, donors have no leverage. But when leaders depend on nonstrategic aid, they face incentives to implement donor goals with the hope of securing aid flows. My argument thus helps explain why only a narrow subset of post-conflict leaders appears to have the political will to reconstruct their states.

Testing the Nonstrategic-Desperation Hypothesis

> *Nonstrategic aid is more likely to promote socioeconomic reconstruction following civil war in recipient countries that have low windfall income.*

I test the nonstrategic-desperation hypothesis across three multiple regression models in this chapter and 23 additional multiple regression models in the Online Appendix. The dependent variable of interest is socioeconomic reconstruction, measured as the inverse of the percent change in infant mortality, and the independent variables of interest are nonstrategic aid and windfall income.

Dependent Variable: Post-Conflict Socioeconomic Reconstruction

I posit that governments foster reconstruction to meet donor development goals. I follow the existing literature on development and measure socioeconomic reconstruction (broad-based development) using infant mortality rates (Boone 1996; Burnside and Dollar 1998; Gerring, Thacker, and Alfaro 2012; Ross 2006b). Infant mortality is the probability that a live-born infant dies before reaching one year of age. It is measured per 1,000 live births, and the data come from the World Bank (2012a). Results are also consistent when the dependent variable is measured as other attributes of broad-based socioeconomic reconstruction: per capita income growth; life expectancy; or percentage of children vaccinated for diptheria, tetanus and pertussis (Online Appendix, Tables 3 and 4).[5] While the data on these factors are often missing and may also not be as reliable or as comparable across countries as the infant mortality data (Gerring et al. 2012; Ross 2006b), the analysis nevertheless shows that the results remain robust across a broad set of reconstruction measures.

Since reductions in infant mortality rates indicate improvement, the change in infant mortality is multiplied by "-1" so that positive values indicate successful reconstruction. Thus, the dependent variable, *Socioeconomic Reconstruction*, is measured as the percent change in the inverse of infant mortality from the previous year.

Independent Variables: Nonstrategic Aid × Windfall Income

The independent variables of interest are *Nonstrategic Aid* and *Windfall Income*. Aid refers to gross official development assistance per capita from OECD donors in constant 2005 U.S. dollars. The data on aid agreements come from OECD and include agreements for concessional financial assistance with at least 25% being in the form of grants (OECD 2012). These aid agreements are supposed to benefit development. In spite of differences among donor countries, OECD members state that the sole substantive requirement of development assistance is that it "is administered with the promotion of the economic development and welfare of developing countries as its main objective" (OECD 2008, 1). The aid covers any project that aims to foster social or economic development, refugee support, police training for establishing the rule of law, or United Nations peacekeeping support, particularly for monitoring elections, demobilizing and reintegrating soldiers, training police, establishing governance mechanisms, and implementing economic reform. The aid data does not separate out disaster rehabilitation from development aid, but before the mid-1990s, donors themselves rarely distinguished between the two (Kreimer et al. 1998). The aid data exclude military or counter-terrorism assistance unless external troops are offering humanitarian assistance or implementing development projects; such as building schools or health clinics.

Aid can come from donors with a strategic interest or from donors who lack a strategic interest in the recipient. Although data on military or counter-terrorism assistance are unavailable for almost all donors, the literature on foreign aid has identified three variables that are important determinants of strategic aid disbursement: (1) colonial history; (2) a military alliance between donor and aid recipient; or (3) aid agreements with a non-neutral donor during the Cold War.[6] Donors who disburse aid based on colonial relationships, a military alliance, or Cold War relationships are not expected to credibly threaten to withdraw their support if the recipient fails to implement the donor's development agenda.

Shared colonial history represents strategic importance because donors generally maintain political-economic links with their former colonies (Alesina and Dollar 2000). The data come from Rose (2005) with each observation coded as "1" when donor and recipient share colonial history and "0" otherwise.

A *military alliance* represents a formal agreement between donor and aid recipient for defensive action, offensive action, neutrality, nonaggression, or consultation when military conflict, or its prospect, emerges (Bobba and Powell 2007; Leeds et al. 2002). The data come from Brett Ashley Leeds (Leeds 2005). Because the donor prioritizes the military relationship over the recipient's commitment to donor development goals, a nondevelopmental outcome is associated with a military alliance. Each observation is coded as "1" when donor and recipient share a military alliance and "0" otherwise.

Recipients of aid that entered aid agreements with non-neutral donors during the Cold War were likely receiving strategic aid because foreign aid disbursement was a tool used by the governments of the United States, the Soviet Union, and their allies to win support and buy loyalty (Bearce and Tirone 2010; Dunning 2004).[7] A donor-recipient pair is coded as "1" if the donor was not neutral during the Cold War and "0" otherwise.[8]

A recipient is coded as having low strategic importance (coded as "0") if and only if (1) it and the donor share no colonial history, (2) the two share no military alliance, and (3) aid disbursement during the Cold War came from a neutral donor. I weigh the three factors equally because each appears to represent similarly low levels of strategic value to the donor. For example, following its 1972 ceasefire, Sudan's strategic importance to the United Kingdom can be measured by the fact that it had once been a British colony. Pakistan's military alliance with the U.S. government after its 1999 ceasefire gave it strategic value. The strategic importance of the Democratic Republic of the Congo (then Zaire) to the United States after its 1978 ceasefire can be measured by its Cold War relationship to the U.S. government, which sought influence in central Africa. If the recipient has at least one of these three factors, the donor-recipient dyad is defined as having high strategic importance (coded as "1"). Results are consistent when I measure strategic importance using only Cold War aid agreements, as in the literature on the effectiveness of strategic aid (Online Appendix Table 5, model 2) (Bearce and Tirone 2010; Dunning 2004).

Having established a measure of strategic importance, I can calculate strategic and nonstrategic aid. *Nonstrategic aid* is the sum of aid from donors that lack a strategic interest in the recipient. *Strategic aid* is the sum of aid from donors with a strategic interest in the recipient. On average, 51% of aid to post-conflict countries is strategic. Sixty-one percent of strategic aid in the sample comes from donors who share colonial history with the recipient, 33% comes from non-neutral donors during the Cold War, and 21% comes from donors with a military alliance with the recipient.

Earlier, *resource rents* were defined as income a government receives after accounting for the costs of producing natural resources. I chose to study commodities that take little labor or technology to extract and therefore represent the most profitable natural resources (Dunning 2008; Humphreys 2005; Ross 2006a), such as gold, silver, bauxite, lead, timber, oil, and gas. Profiting from oil, for example, requires little labor, while profiting from hard minerals, such as gold, usually requires little technology. By measuring rents directly, this study analyzes the attribute of natural resources that arguably influences the political economy of development after civil war. The resource rents variable refers to rents per capita in constant 2005 U.S. dollars. Data on rents come from the World Bank's Genuine Savings Project (Hamilton and Clemens 1999). The data exclude rents from illicit markets. Because illicit markets are expected to amplify the negative effects of the resource curse on reconstruction (Le Billon 2001a), excluding illicit rents means that some countries may be inaccurately coded as having low windfall when they actually have rents from natural resources like certain narcotics. However, this data problem causes little concern because it makes it harder for the existing data to support the hypothesis. The missing data bias the results against finding an effect of nonstrategic aid on reconstruction in low-windfall countries.

I define *windfall income* operationally as the sum of income from natural resource rents and aid income from strategic donors. As I have said, these sources provide income with no strings attached. Increases represent increases in windfall income. To facilitate interpretation of results involving windfall's interaction with other variables, I multiply windfall by "-1" and refer to the inverted windfall variable as *Inverted Windfall*, where increases represent reductions in windfall. I have only included the inverted windfall variable in models where windfall interacts with other variables.

On average, the median amount of windfall income post-conflict countries received is US$60 per capita. Examples of countries with high windfall include Laos in 1973, which received US$105 per capita when it was strategically important to Western donors, and the Democratic Republic of the Congo (then Zaire), which received US$103 per capita in 1980 when it was becoming both the world's leading cobalt producer and strategically important to Western donors. Post-conflict countries with low windfall income include Lebanon, which received US$5 in per capita in 1991, and Cambodia, which received US$3 per capita in 2001.

Preliminary Analysis

Raw data are consistent with the nonstrategic-desperation hypothesis. Figure 3.1 (panels A and B) displays scatter plots of nonstrategic aid and reconstruction for subsamples with low versus high windfall.[9] To ensure the measure of low windfall income captures governments that are likely desperate for income, I consider recipients below the 33th percentile in windfall income to have low windfall, and all others to have high windfall. I use this threshold throughout the chapter.[10] In Figure 3.1A, the significant positive slope as nonstrategic aid increases indicates that reconstruction increases only when recipients have low

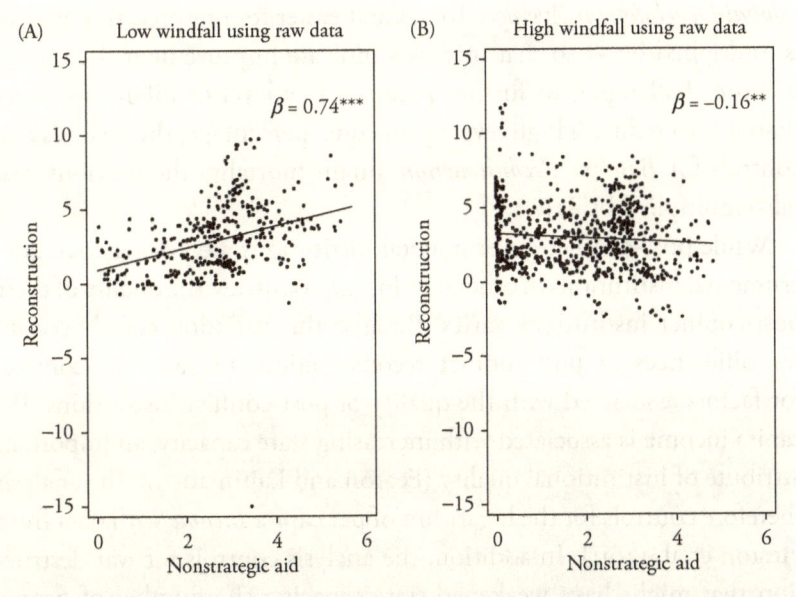

Figure 3.1 Scatterplots of Nonstrategic Aid and Post-Conflict Reconstruction. Panels A and B are based on the raw data. Reconstruction is the inverted annual percent change in infant mortality. Nonstrategic aid (log) is lagged by one year. Windfall income (not inverted here) is lagged by 3 years. β indicates the slope. *sig at 10%; **sig at 5%; *** sig at 1%. Positive coefficients indicate increases in reconstruction. Panel A (low windfall) has a significant upward slope while Panel B does not, consistent with the nonstrategic-desperation hypothesis.

windfall income. In Figure 3.1B, the slope is negative, reflecting the negative effect that nonstrategic aid to governments with high windfall has on reconstruction.

Baseline Model

It is important to hold constant any factor that may confound the influence of nonstrategic aid on social and economic reconstruction, expressed here as the inverse of the percent change in infant mortality. While there is no consensus on a model of infant mortality, this analysis controls for variables typically included in studies of infant mortality as well as variables associated with post-conflict dynamics. Unless otherwise noted, all control variables are lagged by one year. Because global infant mortality improves over time as a result of better technologies and advances in our understanding of human health, the analysis controls for the average global change in infant mortality, the *Global Development Average*. To make it easier to interpret, this average is multiplied by −1 so that increases indicate improvement. Because it is more challenging to further reduce a low level of infant mortality than it is to reduce a high level by an equal percentage, the analysis also controls for *Baseline Reconstruction*, infant mortality the previous year (also multiplied by −1).

While post-conflict governmental institutions are weaker than governmental institutions in other developing countries, the quality of these post-conflict institutions varies. Because this variation could account for differences in post-conflict reconstruction, the analysis controls for factors associated with the quality of post-conflict institutions. Per capita income is associated with increasing state capacity, an important attribute of institutional quality (Fearon and Laitin 2003). The analysis therefore controls for the logarithm of per capita *Income* with data from Heston et al. (2011). In addition, the analysis controls for war destruction that might have weakened state capacity: the number of people killed during the civil war (logarithm of *War Deaths*) and the duration of the civil war (the logarithm of *War Duration*—in months). The data on war deaths come from Lacina and Gleditsch (2005), and the data on war duration come from the Armed Conflicts Database (Gleditsch et al. 2002; Themnér and Wallensteen 2011).

To account for the quality of democratic governance, another institutional factor related to post-conflict reconstruction, the analysis controls for *Democracy* (Flores and Nooruddin 2009; Kang and Meernik 2005). The democracy variable is scaled from –6 to 7 using the X-POLITY variable coded by James Vreeland (Vreeland 2008), who eliminated political violence from the POLITY measure of democracy developed by Monty Marshall, Keith Jaggers, and Ted Robert Gurr (2009). Higher values reflect increases in the democracy scale.

Variation in challenges to power consolidation could also account for differences in post-conflict reconstruction. Perhaps post-conflict leaders facing fewer challenges to power after the war feel less desperate for nonstrategic aid and are therefore less likely to invest in meeting donor development goals. To account for challenges to power consolidation following the war, I control for the number of *Years since War Ended* using data from the Armed Conflicts Database (Gleditsch et al. 2002; Themnér and Wallensteen 2011) and whether the war ended with a *Negotiated Settlement* using data from Kreutz (2010).[11] I code observations as "1" if combatants ended the war with a negotiated settlement such that both parties may be strong enough to restart conflict. Otherwise, I code it as "0" to mean that the war did not end decisively or wane on its own (Licklider 1995; Toft 2010; Walter 1997).

UN Security Guarantees may confound the effects of aid on reconstruction by creating peace or by attracting foreign direct investment (Kang and Meernik 2005). Where such guarantees are in force, peacekeepers from the United Nations threaten to punish any combatant who defects from the ceasefire (Fortna 2008; Harzell and Hoddie 2003; Walter 1997; Wantchekon 2004). I code observations as "1" if UN security guarantees are present and "0" otherwise, using data from the United Nations (2012). Note that the baseline model does not control for foreign direct investment or exports because so much of that data is missing. Results are nevertheless consistent when I include exports and foreign direct investment as a percent of gross domestic product[12] to check the model's robustness (Online Appendix Table 6, model 2).

Because in countries with high diversity, public services are low, I also control for *Ethnic Fractionalization* (Habyarimana et al. 2007).[13]

Equation (1) presents the model:

$$\begin{aligned}Reconstruction = \alpha_{i,t} &+ \beta_1 \, InvertedWindfall_{i,t-3} * NonstrategicAid_{i,t-1}\\&+ \beta_2 NonstrategicAid_{i,t-1} + \beta_3 InvertedWindfall_{i,t-3}\\&+ \beta * Controls_{i,t-1} + \varepsilon_{i,t}\end{aligned} \quad (1)$$

I analyze the influence of increasing nonstrategic aid per capita on post-conflict reconstruction by modeling reconstruction in each post-conflict country (i) year (t) using ordinary-least squares, with standard errors clustered by country to adjust for correlation of more than one civil war that ended within the same country over time. Reconstruction is measured from time $t-1$ to time t. This change depends on nonstrategic aid and windfall income. Thus, the model includes the two-way interaction of *inverted windfall* × *nonstrategic aid*. Nonstrategic aid is lagged by one year, $t-1$, to mitigate potential endogeneity of reconstruction and aid. I analyze this potential threat to the validity of results following discussion of the main results. Windfall is lagged by three years, $t-3$, to see if windfall interacted with subsequent nonstrategic aid influences reconstruction at time t. I stagger windfall and nonstrategic aid to show the influence of windfall income and subsequent nonstrategic aid on reconstruction. The model also includes a vector of control variables, lagged by one year, $t-1$, and an error term (ε). Results are consistent when all independent variables are lagged by one year (Online Appendix Table 5, model 4).

Main Results

I evaluate the nonstrategic-desperation hypothesis directly by assessing the two-way interaction of inverted windfall and nonstrategic aid in models predicting reconstruction. Using this multiplicative interaction approach, the hypothesis is valid only if the two-way interaction is positive and statistically significant. Model 1 in Table 3.1 introduces the inverted windfall × nonstrategic aid interaction. The positive two-way interaction in model 1 shows that the marginal effect of nonstrategic aid on reconstruction differentially increases as windfall income goes from high to low, consistent with the nonstrategic-desperation hypothesis. Figure 3.2 graphically displays this two-way interaction, revealing that only countries with low windfall income show a significant positive marginal effect of nonstrategic aid on reconstruction. The effect of nonstrategic aid on reconstruction is only statistically significant (the confidence intervals do not overlap with zero) on the right-hand side of the figure, where windfall is low.

The influence of increasing nonstrategic aid on reconstruction is further demonstrated in Table 3.1 across two subsamples: where recipients have low windfall income (Table 3.1, model 2) and high windfall income (Table 3.1, model 3). Consistent with the hypothesis, the influence of increasing nonstrategic aid on reconstruction is only positive and statistically significant when aid recipients have low windfall income (Table 3.1, model 2, not model 3). Based on models 2 and 3, increasing nonstrategic aid from US$10 per capita to US$25 per capita in countries with low windfall income improves the annual rate of reconstruction by 0.48% while a similar increase in nonstrategic aid worsens the reconstruction rate by 0.23% in high windfall countries.

Thus, the pattern for countries with low windfall income differs from other countries in two important regards. First, Table 3.1 confirms the upward slope of the data in Figure 3.1A. Increasing levels of nonstrategic aid promotes reconstruction for recipients with low windfall but not for recipients with high windfall. Second, and more important from a policy perspective, not much aid is needed to significantly rehabilitate low-windfall countries (see Figure 3.1A). For countries with low windfall, even relatively small increases in nonstrategic aid improve reconstruction after civil war, while for other countries, five times as much nonstrategic aid fails to help.

Robustness

To ensure that the results are valid and not an artifact of outliers, unique attributes of regions, time periods, recipient institutional background, or endogeneity of aid, I conducted robustness checks.

Results are robust to the exclusion of outliers. In Figure 3.1, outliers of the regression are visually obvious. Because outliers can disproportionately influence the slope of a regression line, it is important to determine whether results are robust to the exclusion of outliers in the dataset. The nonstrategic-desperation hypothesis is supported

Table 3.1 Regression Analysis of Post-Conflict Reconstruction

	(1) Full sample	(2) Low windfall	(3) High windfall
Inverted windfall × Nonstrategic aid	0.270***		
	(0.064)		
Nonstrategic aid	1.082***	0.519***	−0.254**
	(0.287)	(0.162)	(0.113)
Inverted windfall	−0.339**		
	(0.168)		
Global development average	0.262	−0.027	0.451
	(0.275)	(0.396)	(0.282)
Baseline reconstruction	0.975**	1.478*	1.078**
	(0.475)	(0.758)	(0.474)
Per capita income	0.636	−0.332	0.840**
	(0.434)	(0.628)	(0.415)
War deaths	−0.011	−0.286**	0.068
	(0.119)	(0.130)	(0.129)
War duration	0.031	0.532***	−0.069
	(0.172)	(0.154)	(0.182)
Democracy	−0.033	0.102**	−0.086
	(0.058)	(0.049)	(0.068)
Years since war ended	−0.016	0.017	−0.039
	(0.035)	(0.029)	(0.035)
Negotiated settlement	0.067	−2.462***	0.468
	(0.669)	(0.575)	(1.146)
UN security guarantees	0.505	−0.311	0.259
	(0.653)	(0.650)	(1.005)
Ethnic fractionalization	−2.471***	−3.368**	−2.535***
	(0.781)	(1.285)	(0.847)
Constant	1.227	12.537	1.188
	(4.953)	(7.874)	(4.755)
Observations	749	215	534
R^2	0.449	0.573	0.496

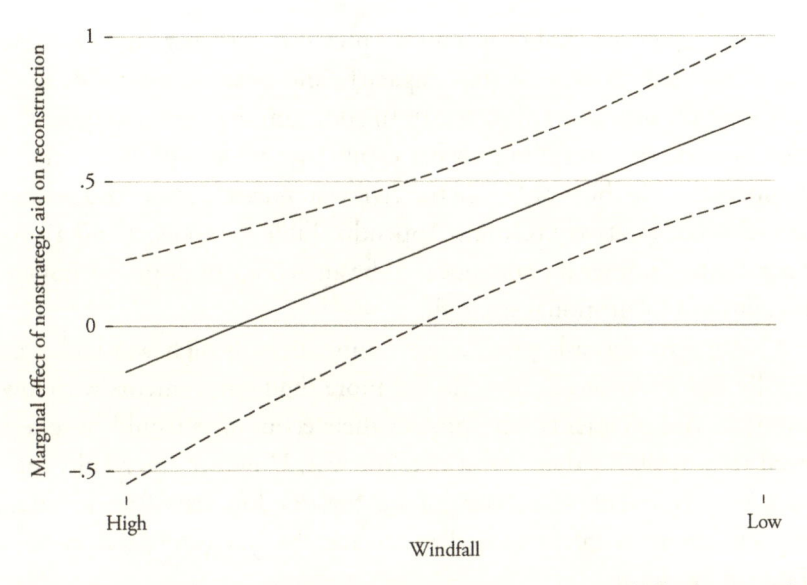

Figure 3.2 Effect of Nonstrategic Aid on Reconstruction as Windfall Changes. The code used to generate the figure was adapted from Brambor, Clark, and Golder (2006). The dashed lines represent the 95% confidence interval. Reconstruction is the inverted annual percent change in infant mortality. Increases indicate reconstruction. Nonstrategic aid (log) is lagged by one year. Windfall income (not inverted here) is lagged by three years. The marginal effect of nonstrategic aid on reconstruction is positive and significant only when windfall income is low, supporting the nonstrategic-desperation hypothesis.

when the findings are replicated with outliers removed (Online Appendix Table 7, model 1).

It is also possible that the findings are biased due to unobserved attributes of particular regions that are correlated with reconstruction or due to unobserved attributes of the decade of observation. For example, perhaps African governments face unique challenges in using nonstrategic aid to reconstruct their states after civil war. Or perhaps aid recipients were unusually likely to use aid to foster reconstruction during the 1990s, after the end of the Cold War. I assessed whether the hypothesis is supported when including region- and decade-fixed effects (Online Appendix Table 7, models 2 and 3). The results remain the same across each of these models.

Another possible threat to validity is that post-conflict institutions may be stronger when aid recipients have low windfall income than when aid recipients have high windfall. To account for this potential issue, the regressions hold constant the previous year's per capita income (an often-used measure of state capacity) and position on the democracy scale (Fearon and Laitin 2003). In addition, the results support the argument when controlling for per capita income and position on the democracy scale the year before the civil war, *prewar income* and *prewar democracy*, respectively (Online Appendix Table 8, models 1 and 2). As a result, the findings do not appear to be an artifact of disproportionate background institutional strength.

One might also ask whether governments with high windfall protect living conditions during the war more than governments with low windfall. Aid recipients who protect their economies would have less need to reconstruct their states after the war. However, the results support the argument when controlling for development (the inverted rate of change in infant mortality) during the war (Online Appendix Table 8, model 3).

If the causal arrows are reversed, the potential reductions or increases in reconstruction attract nonstrategic aid flows. To address the problem of this possible endogeneity, nonstrategic aid as described in these regressions temporally precedes reconstruction. This staggering allows us to analyze aid decisions made by nonstrategic donors prior to realized changes in reconstruction. However, because donors may be able to predict reconstruction outcomes as they make disbursement decisions (de Ree and Nillesen 2009; Savun and Tirone 2011), an additional robustness check is useful.

Therefore, I consider a two-stage least squares model. In the first stage, the instrumental variable produces an estimate of nonstrategic aid that should be independent of donor motivations to support certain aid recipients. I use the predicted values to estimate the effect of nonstrategic aid on reconstruction in the second stage.

The analysis uses *nonstrategic donor gross domestic product* (GDP) *per capita* as an instrument (Savun and Tirone 2011) because donor governments should be less willing to disburse aid while suffering economic loss (Dabla-Norris, Minoiu and Zanna 2010). To give donors time to respond to the shock of such loss, nonstrategic donor per capita GDP is lagged by two years ($t-2$). The instrument satisfies the exclusion restriction because it is not plausibly related to socioeconomic reconstruction in post-conflict countries except through its influence on aid. In the first-stage regression, nonstrategic donor GDP has a positive and statistically significant effect on nonstrategic aid flows.[14] Consistent with the nonstrategic-desperation hypothesis, increases in nonstrategic aid only foster reconstruction when windfall is low (Online Appendix Table 9). Thus, the results do not appear to be an artifact of endogeneity in this analysis. To complement empirical testing with and without instrumental variables, the case studies in Chapters 5 and 6 will further demonstrate that the results from empirical analyses do not appear to be an artifact of endogeneity.[15]

Combined, these findings support the hypothesis that nonstrategic aid fosters reconstruction following civil war only when recipients have low windfall income. These recipients face incentives to meet aid agreements. The raw data supports the hypothesis, and the hypothesis appears to be robust to potentially confounding factors, outlier exclusion, fixed effects by region or decade, alternative measures of reconstruction, nonstrategic aid and windfall income, and the potential endogeneity of aid.

The results also suggest that post-conflict leaders face unique challenges in comparison to leaders of developing countries that lack a history of war or that are experiencing war. The two-way interaction of nonstrategic aid and windfall income is not statistically significant in a sample of developing countries without a history of war during the time period under study (Online Appendix Table 10, model 1), or in a sample of developing countries experiencing war (Online Appendix Table 10, model 2). These results suggest that post-conflict leaders face different incentives than other leaders considering the use of aid.

Summary

Examples of aid fostering reconstruction after a civil war are puzzling. These unusual examples contrast with the broader literature on aid, which tends to find that aid works (if it works at all) when recipient institutions are strong—not when institutions are fragile, as in countries emerging from civil war. Strong institutions pressure aid recipients to foster reconstruction by creating incentives for investing in citizens. The analysis provided here reveals, however, that recipient income sources also provide incentives—and disincentives—for fostering reconstruction.

When the government is endowed with significant resource rents or possesses strategic importance to the donor, the recipient has little incentive to reach reconstruction goals. The recipient lacks incentives to reach reconstruction goals because it has high resource rents and therefore does not really need the money or because it is highly important strategically to the donor and therefore the aid is more contingent on donor strategic interests than on reconstruction goals. Increases in aid only predict successful reconstruction in cases where resource rents and strategic importance are both low, consistent with the nonstrategic-desperation hypothesis. An increase of nonstrategic aid per capita from US$10 to US$25 to such recipients improves the annual reconstruction rate by 0.48% while the same increase to other recipients worsens the reconstruction rate by 0.23%.

Having established when leaders are likely to bring about successful post-conflict reconstruction, we turn to the mechanisms that allow them to do so. Discerning those mechanisms requires an analysis of post-conflict coup risk, the subject of the following chapter.

4

Statistical Analysis of Post-Conflict Coup Risk

IN THIS CHAPTER, I test the low-windfall coup-proofing hypothesis statistically to determine why some leaders bring about successful post-conflict reconstruction. Despite heroic donor efforts, post-conflict development outcomes vary greatly, as I have noted, and only some countries become Phoenix States. Increases in aid may have positive effects on reconstruction after civil war, but the previous chapter showed that these effects appear to be conditional. Strong positive effects are only evident when recipients lack strategic importance to donors and lack access to rents from natural resources. This suggests the possibility that an exploration of incentives may reveal why and under what circumstances post-conflict leaders use aid toward development. Chapter 2 developed such a mechanism and derived the low-windfall coup-proofing hypothesis. The hypothesis predicts that low-windfall countries reduce the risk of coups as nonstrategic aid and reconstruction increases, but the same increase in nonstrategic aid or reconstruction is unlikely to help high-windfall countries prevent coups.

To reiterate, the argument developed in Chapter 2 begins with the premise that post-conflict leaders allocate spending to ensure their own survival. Accordingly, post-conflict leaders will spend on reconstruction only if such spending reduces their coup risk. When leaders lack windfall income, their easiest source of financing is aid from donors who are mainly interested in reconstruction (nonstrategic aid). To foster stability, nonstrategic donors pay for regime security and offer payoffs to encourage rivals to participate in the political system. Nonstrategic donors lack strategic interest in the recipient, so they may terminate aid flows if the recipient fails to comply with donor prescriptions. With the hope of continuing nonstrategic aid flows, low-windfall leaders reconstruct their states. In this way, nonstrategic aid and reconstruction combine to reduce coup risk for post-conflict leaders with low windfall.

For leaders rich in windfall income, the calculus is different. Donors may demand that these leaders spend existing wealth to reduce poverty. Post-conflict leaders with windfall income are not desperate for money, so they can forego nonstrategic-donor assistance and use their windfall income toward coup-proofing.

If this low-windfall coup-proofing hypothesis is valid, the combination of low windfall, nonstrategic aid, and reconstruction should reduce coup risk following civil war. The data support this hypothesis. As nonstrategic aid increases from US$10 per capita to US$25 per capita in low-windfall countries with high reconstruction, yearly coup risk declines by 75%. The same increase in nonstrategic aid to countries with high reconstruction but high windfall does not reduce coup risk.

Testing the Low-Windfall Coup-Proofing Hypothesis

> *Following civil war, the interaction of low windfall, nonstrategic aid, and reconstruction should reduce coup risk.*

Dependent Variable: Coup Risk

To test whether only low-windfall governments reduce coup risk with reconstruction and nonstrategic aid following civil war, the dependent variable is the probability of a coup after civil war.[1] I code each post-conflict year as "1" if the leader experiences a coup and "0" otherwise, using coup data from Powell and Thyne (2011). These data build upon other widely used sources, such as the Cross-National Time-Series Data Archive, the Center for Systemic Peace dataset on coups, and Archigos (Banks 2011; Goemans et al. 2009; Marshall and Marshall 2010). Examples of coups in the data include Chad in 1975, when the armed forces overthrew the president they once served, François

Tombalbaye; the 2003 coup in Guinea-Bissau where General Veríssimo Correia Seabra overthrew President Kumba Ialá; or the 1999 coup in which General Pervez Musharraf toppled Pakistani Prime Minister Nawaz Sharif.

I chose the risk of coup rather than other measures like coup attempts or resumption of war. Data are unreliable concerning coup attempts and fail to capture the actual risk associated with a coup. Resumption of war may not directly threaten the leader's survival and may therefore concern the reconstruction calculus of leaders less than coup risk (Roessler 2011). Indeed, the interaction of inverted windfall, nonstrategic aid, and reconstruction does not explain the resumption of war (Online Appendix Table 11).

Because coups are binary events, I modeled the probability of coup using logistic regression with standard errors clustered by country to adjust for more than one civil war within the same country.[2]

Independent Variable: Windfall Income × Nonstrategic Aid × Reconstruction

The argument that low windfall, high nonstrategic aid, and high reconstruction (each operationally defined in Chapter 3) combine to reduce coup risk implies a three-way interaction. After a civil war, leaders in countries with windfall already have the cash to coup-proof without reconstructing their states, but leaders in countries without windfall need to foster reconstruction to ensure the flow of nonstrategic aid, some of which they can use to coup-proof. The argument therefore implies that when both nonstrategic aid and reconstruction are high, low-windfall (and not high-windfall) countries should experience a reduction in coup risk, a three-way interaction. Thus, the probability of coup in each post-ceasefire (i) year (t) depends on *inverted windfall × nonstrategic aid × reconstruction*.[3]

Because I expect windfall to combine with nonstrategic aid and reconstruction to reduce coup risk, windfall is lagged by three years ($t-3$), nonstrategic aid is lagged by one year ($t-1$), and socioeconomic reconstruction measures the change in infant mortality (inverted) from $t-1$ to t. Results do not appear to depend on the specific lag structure. They are consistent, for example, if all independent variables are lagged by one year (Online Appendix Table 12, model 4). The baseline model controls for changes in global health, *Global Development Average*, and initial reconstruction levels, *Baseline Reconstruction*, either of which could confound the influence of reconstruction on coup risk. To account for temporal dependence, the model includes a cubic polynomial approximation of time, T (Carter and Signorino 2010). The model also includes an error term (ε). Equation 2 presents the model:

$$\begin{aligned}\Pr(Y=1) = \Phi[&\alpha_{i,t} + \beta_1 \textit{InvertedWindfall}_{i,t-3} * \textit{NonstrategicAid}_{i,t-1} * \textit{Reconstruction}_{i,t} \\ &+ \beta_2 \textit{InvertedWindfall}_{i,t-3} * \textit{NonstrategicAid}_{i,t-1} \\ &+ \beta_3 \textit{NonstrategicAid}_{i,t-1} * \textit{Reconstruction}_{i,t} \\ &+ \beta_4 \textit{InvertedWindfall}_{i,t-3} * \textit{Reconstruction}_{i,t} \\ &+ \beta_5 \textit{InvertedWindfall}_{i,t-3} + \beta_6 \textit{NonstrategicAid}_{i,t-1} \\ &+ \beta_7 \textit{Reconstruction}_{i,t} + \beta_8 \textit{GlobalDevAve}_{i,t} \\ &+ \beta_9 \textit{BaselineDev}_{i,t-1} + \beta_{10} T_{i,t} + \beta_{11} T^2_{i,t} \\ &+ \beta_{12} T^3_{i,t} + \beta * \textit{Controls}_{i,t-1} + \varepsilon_{i,t}] \end{aligned} \quad (2)$$

The baseline model includes twelve independent variables before accounting for additional control variables. By virtue of including the three-way interaction, the baseline model automatically includes an additional six independent variables, representing the two-way and single component terms of the interaction. None of these component terms provide useful insight on the hypothesis because simple coefficients that form interactions express effects when the other term(s) in the interaction are set at zero (Brambor, Clark, and Golder 2006). In addition to these seven variables, the model includes three time dummy variables, the global development average, and baseline reconstruction, totaling 12 independent variables.

Given the number of independent variables already included in the baseline model, adding a large set of controls could result in overfitting and missing data. Nevertheless, control variables could confound the effects of windfall, nonstrategic aid, or reconstruction on coup risk. I therefore add one or two control variables at a time to the baseline specification to ensure results are robust to the inclusion of these variables. I also test the hypothesis with a model that includes all control variables by imputing missing data.[4]

Coups should be less likely when leaders govern within a framework of strong institutions (Belkin and Schofer 2003), so I control for the institutional quality variables described in the previous section: *Income, Democracy*, and levels of destruction from the war, including *War Dead* and *War Duration*.

Leaders who enter office through irregular means (i.e., coups or revolutions) are more likely to be overthrown than leaders who enter office through regular means, but that effect decreases the longer a leader is in office (Goemans et al. 2009). Thus, I control for *Incumbent Tenure, Irregular Entry* (both of which were also defined earlier), and the interaction between them.[5]

The analysis also controls for demographic factors associated with coup risk. I control for *Population Density* since the cost of carrying out a coup increases with population density (Kimenyi and Mbaku 1993). Also, *Ethnic Fractionalization* is included because higher ethnic diversity may threaten leader survival in office (Morrison 2009).

Because the reconstruction and coup risk models are similar and theoretically linked, I ensured results are robust when linking their error structures. Results support the hypothesis when modeling coup risk and reconstruction jointly using a seemingly unrelated estimation regression (Online Appendix Table 13).

Main Results

According to the low-windfall coup-proofing hypothesis, windfall income should significantly moderate the relationship between nonstrategic aid, reconstruction, and coup risk. To test the hypothesis directly, model 1 in Table 4.1 introduces the three-way interaction of Inverted Windfall × Nonstrategic Aid × Reconstruction. If the probability of a coup declines as windfall declines with increases in nonstrategic aid and reconstruction, a negative, statistically significant three-way interaction would be expected. Consistent with the hypothesis, the three-way interaction is negative and statistically significant. This result demonstrates that increases in aid and reconstruction are likely to decrease coup risk when windfall is low.

Figure 4.1 demonstrates the three-way interaction using a binary measure of windfall, where low windfall is less than the 33rd percentile (see Table 4.1, model 2). Based on model 2 in Table 4.1, the left-hand panel of Figure 4.1 shows that the marginal effect of reconstruction

Table 4.1 Logit Analysis of Coup Risk

	(1) Windfall: continuous	(2) Windfall: binary
Inverted windfall × Nonstrategic aid × Reconstruction	−0.095***	−0.428**
	(0.033)	(0.209)
Inverted windfall × Nonstrategic aid	0.330**	1.041
	(0.151)	(0.666)
Nonstrategic aid × Reconstruction	−0.400**	0.157
	(0.160)	(0.162)
Inverted windfall × Reconstruction	0.194**	0.521
	(0.099)	(0.581)
Inverted windfall	−0.767**	−1.698
	(0.375)	(1.379)
Nonstrategic aid	1.299**	−0.470
	(0.604)	(0.583)
Reconstruction	0.794	−0.283
	(0.496)	(0.242)
Global development average	0.521	0.537
	(0.613)	(0.620)
Baseline reconstruction	−0.985**	−1.023***
	(0.458)	(0.352)
Constant	−13.039***	−9.356***
	(3.460)	(2.179)
Time dummies	Yes	Yes
Observations	1057	1057

on coup risk is negative and statistically significant as nonstrategic aid increases in countries with low windfall income (i.e., the confidence interval does not overlap with zero).[6] The right-hand panel shows a positive marginal effect, indicating increased coup risk. However, the effect is statistically insignificant (i.e., the confidence interval overlaps with zero throughout the range of nonstrategic aid). Thus, nonstrategic aid amplifies the negative marginal effect of reconstruction on coup risk only when windfall income is low, consistent with the hypothesis. For countries with low windfall and high reconstruction (above the

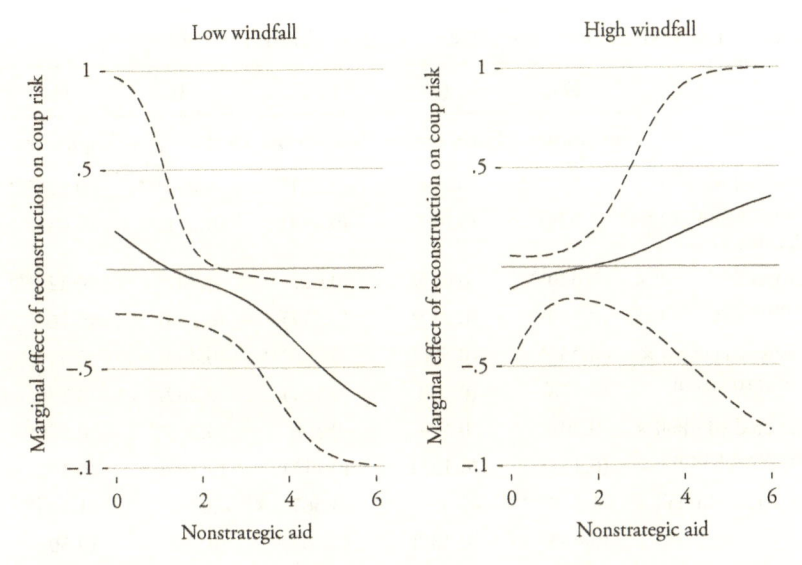

Figure 4.1 Effect of reconstruction on coup risk as windfall and nonstrategic aid change. The figure is based on Table 4.1, model 2. The code used to generate the figure was adapted from Brambor, Clark, and Golder (2006). The dashed lines represent the 95% confidence interval. Reconstruction measures the inverted percent annual change in infant mortality. Nonstrategic aid (log) is lagged by one year. Windfall income (not inverted here) is lagged by three years. The marginal effect of reconstruction on coup risk is negative and significant only when windfall income is low, supporting the low-windfall coup-proofing hypothesis.

90th percentile), increasing nonstrategic aid from US$10 per capita to US$25 per capita cuts coup risk by 75% from 0.4% to 0.1%. The same increase in nonstrategic aid in countries with the same level of reconstruction and high windfall more than triples coup risk from 1.3% to 5.0%, although the effect is statistically insignificant.[7]

The low-windfall coup-proofing hypothesis might only explain coup risk in post-conflict countries, as the hypothesis is not supported in data from countries that have no civil war during the time period under study (Online Appendix Table 15, model 1) or from countries that are at war (Online Appendix Table 15, model 2). These findings are consistent with the results in the previous section that test the nonstrategic-desperation hypothesis across developing countries. Combined, these findings suggest the intuitive conclusion that post-conflict leaders operate under different pressures than leaders of other countries.

Table 4.2 Logit Analysis of Coup Risk: Including Control Variables

	(1) Institutions	(2) Entry-tenure	(3) Interaction	(4) Demography	(5) Imputation
Inverted windfall × Nonstrategic aid × Reconstruction	-0.137*** (0.038)	-0.161*** (0.047)	-0.161*** (0.048)	-0.095*** (0.031)	-0.129*** (0.047)
Inverted windfall × Nonstrategic aid	0.630*** (0.169)	0.625*** (0.213)	0.627*** (0.217)	0.301** (0.150)	0.428*** (0.164)
Nonstrategic aid × Reconstruction	-0.533* (0.278)	-0.506*** (0.192)	-0.496*** (0.181)	-0.409** (0.169)	-0.540** (0.270)
Inverted windfall × Reconstruction	0.202 (0.133)	0.104 (0.121)	0.106 (0.116)	0.205** (0.105)	0.289* (0.162)
Inverted windfall	-1.188*** (0.455)	-0.659 (0.488)	-0.667 (0.467)	-0.767* (0.398)	-1.194** (0.502)
Nonstrategic aid	2.271** (0.924)	1.953** (0.797)	1.933** (0.788)	1.216* (0.639)	1.694** (0.800)
Reconstruction	0.715 (0.793)	0.329 (0.706)	0.316 (0.692)	0.877* (0.524)	1.285 (0.923)
Global development average	0.433 (0.644)	-0.587 (0.564)	-0.608 (0.606)	0.495 (0.603)	0.308 (0.581)
Baseline reconstruction	-1.283* (0.676)	-1.641*** (0.374)	-1.610*** (0.396)	-1.061* (0.558)	-1.071 (0.657)
Per capita income	-0.342 (0.465)				-0.374 (0.365)
Democracy	0.056 (0.096)				0.001 (0.078)
War deaths	-0.298* (0.172)				-0.259* (0.134)
War duration	0.410* (0.237)				0.303 (0.200)
Incumbent tenure		-0.026 (0.032)	-0.034 (0.032)		-0.020 (0.029)
Irregular entry		-0.821 (0.836)	-1.189 (1.616)		0.114 (0.888)
Irregular entry × Incumbent tenure			0.030 (0.100)		-0.033 (0.072)

Population density				–0.869	–0.276
				(3.610)	(2.911)
Ethnic fractionalization				–0.000	0.027
				(1.033)	(0.934)
Time dummies	Yes	Yes	Yes	Yes	Yes
Observations	779	752	752	1008	1260

Robustness

The hypothesis remains supported when including control variables (Table 4.2). Results also remain consistent when I replicate the findings removing observations greater than the 95th percentile in reconstruction, nonstrategic aid, or inverted windfall (Table 4.3, model 1). However, it is still possible that the results are an artifact of unique attributes of time periods, regions, or of endogeneity of aid to coups. I perform robustness checks to address these additional potential threats.

First, unobserved attributes of particular decades of observation may be correlated with coup risk. Perhaps coups were particularly more likely during the Cold War or in certain regions (Goemans and Marinov 2011). When including region- or decade-fixed effects, however, results remain consistent with the hypothesis (Table 4.3, models 2–3).

It is also possible that the results are an artifact of the endogeneity of aid, reversing the causal arrows. Strategic and nonstrategic donors may respond to coups or coup prospects with increases or decreases in aid (Girod and Walters 2012). To mitigate this potential threat to the validity of results, the regressions presented here measure strategic and nonstrategic aid lagged to be a year prior to assessment of whether a coup occurred. Because I measure both aid variables in the year prior to coup assessment, the coup (or its prospect) is less likely to have caused the aid disbursement. Finally, I include donor GDP per capita two years prior to aid disbursement as an instrument for nonstrategic aid in a two-stage least squares regression, and the effect of the three-way interaction on coup risk remains consistent (Online Appendix Table 16).[8] Thus, the findings supporting the hypothesis do not appear to result from the potential endogeneity of aid to coup risk.

In summary, as with the nonstrategic-desperation hypothesis, the data appear to support the low-windfall coup-proofing hypothesis after

Table 4.3 Logit Analysis of Coup Risk: Excluding Outliers and Including Fixed Effects

	(1) Excl. outliers	(2) Region FE	(3) Decade FE
Inverted windfall × Nonstrategic aid × Reconstruction	−0.121** (0.056)	−0.100*** (0.033)	−0.097*** (0.037)
Inverted windfall × Nonstrategic aid	0.474** (0.221)	0.375** (0.159)	0.344* (0.179)
Nonstrategic aid × Reconstruction	−0.603*** (0.220)	−0.418** (0.178)	−0.402*** (0.155)
Inverted windfall × Reconstruction	0.228** (0.116)	0.202** (0.098)	0.198* (0.102)
Inverted windfall	−0.965** (0.415)	−0.894** (0.383)	−0.803** (0.382)
Nonstrategic aid	2.139** (0.902)	1.437** (0.669)	1.330** (0.629)
Reconstruction	1.002* (0.583)	0.856 (0.526)	0.797 (0.494)
Global development average	0.729 (0.633)	0.488 (0.580)	0.496 (0.578)
Baseline reconstruction	−0.964* (0.550)	−0.023 (0.441)	−0.995** (0.453)
Time dummies	Yes	Yes	Yes
Observations	909	863	1057

accounting for potential threats to validity, including different measures of key variables, potentially confounding variables, removal of outliers, fixed effects by region and decade, and the endogeneity of aid.

Summary

Why do leaders reconstruct their states following civil war when institutions are weak and when the risk of coup is significant and immediate? The explanation that emerges here begins with the assumption—common to political economy studies—that leaders spend on reconstruction if reconstruction promotes their political survival. Because income structures constrain choices, the effects of reconstruction vary according to income source. Income source is therefore critical in explaining why only a subset of leaders fosters reconstruction following civil war. The low-windfall coup-proofing hypothesis suggests that reconstruction paid for with nonstrategic aid reduces coup risk following civil war only for post-conflict states with low windfall. And the data appear to support this hypothesis.

5

Similar Background, Different Windfall
Mozambique and Angola

WHILE THE REGRESSIONS in Chapters 3 and 4 provide empirical evidence of a link between income sources, reconstruction, and coup risk, cross-national statistics cannot reveal how leaders, in practice, implement aid programs and spend to reduce coup risk following civil war.

Case study methodology allows us to observe implementation of aid programs and to track government spending for reconstruction. Do leaders with high windfall behave differently than leaders with low windfall? I assess this question by examining in this chapter a pair of countries that are well-matched except for windfall income and also by assessing a country that had a change in windfall status following civil war in Chapter 6.

In this chapter, I compare post-conflict dynamics in Mozambique and Angola. These cases demonstrate the differences in how the leaders of one high-windfall country and one low-windfall country used their income sources toward socioeconomic reconstruction. Consistent with the argument in this book, leaders in windfall-rich Angola stonewalled donors, while leaders in Mozambique implemented aid agreements to foster socioeconomic reconstruction, and this reconstruction attracted additional nonstrategic aid, part of which appears to have been used for coup-proofing. The Uganda case study in Chapter 6 allows further analysis of the argument because the government there had low windfall income immediately following civil war and behaved as expected of a low-windfall government regarding aid and reconstruction. But when windfall was realized, the Ugandan government behaved as expected of a high windfall government.

This chapter begins the narrative approach to examining the puzzle of why only some post-conflict countries become Phoenix States by looking at the experiences of Mozambique and Angola. How did the government of Mozambique achieve a remarkable feat of reconstruction in the aftermath of violent conflict? How did it rebuild infrastructure, improve governance, stabilize the economy, expand access to basic services, improve the rule of law, and more generally bring about economic development that benefited living conditions for much of the population? Mozambique's success is puzzling given that the government possessed little human capital and grappled with vast destruction from the civil war. And if the government of Mozambique could accomplish such reconstruction, why was the Angolan government less successful after a similarly destructive conflict.

The argument developed in Chapter 2 indicated that nonstrategic aid promotes post-conflict reconstruction in states with low windfall but has no such effect in states with high windfall and, further, that the mechanism for the positive effects of nonstrategic aid is the willingness of donors to hold recipients accountable to the conditions under which the aid was granted. This chapter now offers an explanation to account for why low-windfall leaders in Mozambique implemented aid agreements and brought about successful reconstruction while their resource-rich counterparts in Angola stonewalled donors and kept their state in socioeconomic collapse.

I selected Mozambique and Angola with care. Because these two countries share important similarities in their institutional histories and in the nature of their civil wars, I could focus on income sources to explain their different post-conflict reconstruction outcomes (Tarrow 2010).[1] In other words, the similarities between the two countries cannot account for the differences in their post-conflict reconstruction.

To summarize the comparison, Mozambique and Angola share similar institutional histories. Both were Portuguese colonies in Africa, and in both, liberation movements fought a war against Portuguese rule. Both obtained independence in 1975, which led to new civil wars that involved rebels backed by South Africa. Both established socialist governments led by a Marxist-Leninist party.[2] Both received support from the Soviets and other communist countries to finance their governments and to fight their civil wars. As their civil wars ended, both lacked the strong state institutions that can bring about successful reconstruction, such as a strong justice system and a functioning physical infrastructure. These two cases therefore serve as a relatively compelling "most-similar" comparison that allows us to focus on an important difference between them: windfall income (George and Bennett 2005). The Angolan budget consisted mainly of rents from oil and diamonds along with strategic financial support from China. Excluding unavailable data on Chinese support,[3] two years after the end of civil war 0.01% of Angola's budget came from grants from foreign governments or international organizations while Mozambique's budget was entirely funded by these external sources, which generally lacked strategic interests in Mozambique (IMF 1998, 91–92; IMF 2007, 62).

Though the two cases are similar and well-matched, of course Mozambique and Angola have other differences besides windfall. During colonial rule, Angola was more industrialized than Mozambique. Angola's main civil war ended decisively in 2002 while Mozambique's ended in 1992 with a negotiated settlement administered by UN peacekeepers. Post-conflict, Angola democratized less than Mozambique. Angola's civil war was followed by a small-scale secessionist insurgency, while Mozambique has remained largely at peace. And Mozambique's leadership appears to have been intrinsically more interested in socioeconomic reconstruction than Angola's. These differences constitute plausible alternative explanations for why Mozambique outperformed Angola. I examine each of these differences at the end of the chapter.

Before investigating alternative explanations, however, I analyze the observable implications of my argument. As posited by that argument, the chapter shows that when Mozambique embraced nonstrategic donors, those donors responded by supporting reconstruction, while Angola's resistance led donors to eschew support for that country's reconstruction. Donors had leverage over Mozambique's leaders because they effectively paid the reconstruction bill and provided funds that could help leaders consolidate power. However, these same donors lacked leverage in Angola, where they were asking leaders to redirect the country's own wealth to benefit the poor. Consistent with the argument, Mozambique's leaders appear to consolidate power by securing nonstrategic aid while Angola's leaders appear to consolidate power by maintaining control over windfall income. The chapter begins with a brief background to contextualize the two cases and to demonstrate the relatively similar challenges to power consolidation the two countries faced when their respective civil wars ended.

Civil War in Angola and Mozambique

Civil war broke out in both Angola and Mozambique soon after independence. At Angola's independence, two armed liberation groups remained: the People's Movement for the Liberation of Angola (MPLA) and the National Union for the Total Independence of Angola (UNITA).[4] UNITA represented the most populous ethnic group (Ovimbundu), but the MPLA had more powerful armed forces and controlled the Angolan capital, Luanda. Because the MPLA controlled Luanda, the MPLA became the governing party in Angola following independence from Portugal. But the MPLA's hold on power was fragile. Soon after independence, the MPLA and UNITA continued to fight, but in a war against each other.[5]

While the Soviet Union and its satellites supported MPLA leaders, China and South Africa provided funding for UNITA leaders (the Chinese and Soviets competed in Angola).[6] UNITA leaders also relied on income from diamonds in territories they controlled. Early on, UNITA leaders began using military force to take over diamond mines both to grow the group's resource base and to reduce the MPLA government's access to diamond revenue (Le Billon 2001b, 67). By the 1990s, the value of diamonds in UNITA areas totaled between US$3 billion and US$4 billion (Le Billon 2001b, 69).

In addition to support from the Soviets and Cubans, the MPLA also funded its military operations with oil. Oil revenue first started pouring into Angola in 1968, when the colonial Portuguese in control of Angola signed a contract with Gulf Oil to drill in Cabinda, a strip of land between the Democratic Republic of the Congo and the Congo Republic that belongs to Angola. MPLA leaders took over the Gulf Oil contracts after they came to power in Luanda and used oil revenues to buy military equipment as well as to back commercial loans to purchase additional military supplies (Le Billon 2001b, 77).

Civil war officially ended when the government under President José Eduardo dos Santos defeated UNITA rebels by killing their longtime leader, Jonas Savimbi, in February 2002. A ceasefire signed on April 4, 2002, formalized the victory.

In Mozambique, open rebellion against the post-independence government also had origins in the colonial struggle and began shortly after independence.[7] Rhodesians and Portuguese intelligence officers originally created the rebel group Mozambican National Resistance (Renamo) to thwart the liberation struggle of the Liberation Front of Mozambique (Frelimo). After Frelimo leaders came to power, the Renamo group reconstituted itself with support from South Africa. Meanwhile, the Soviet Union and Scandinavian countries provided Frelimo leaders' primary backing (Hanlon 1991).

The leadership of both Frelimo and Renamo faced severe income shortages by 1990, as the end of the Cold War diminished global powers' interest in African proxy wars and the South African government moved toward ending apartheid. With both movements running on empty, the war began to wind down. Mozambique's civil war officially ended on October 4, 1992, when the warring factions signed a peace accord that called for demobilization, military unification, and national elections. The combatants also agreed to a two-year United Nations mandate that would allow that body to verify the ceasefire, provide humanitarian aid, and coordinate the national elections. Frelimo leaders were to stay in power during the transition period between the end of war and the national elections.

Though the civil wars in Angola and Mozambique ended differently, the two countries' controlling parties (the MPLA and Frelimo, respectively) encountered similar and substantial lingering challenges. Both parties faced powerful rivals. The MPLA's military operations had weakened UNITA organizationally, but UNITA had the potential of reorganizing under new leadership. UNITA represented the largest ethnic group in Angola and still had support throughout the country. MPLA leaders thus needed resources to continue to dominate militarily while coopting and subverting UNITA leaders.

UNITA leaders may have had a larger following than Renamo leaders because Renamo was a construct of Rhodesia and South Africa while UNITA was homegrown. Still, Renamo's top leader, Afonso Dhlakama, developed a strong following in north and central Mozambique during the war because he championed traditional forms of rule and freed citizens from the collective-labor schemes that Frelimo's leadership organized (Chabal and Vidal 2008; Weinstein 2002). Dhlakama's following remained strong and well organized after the war because Frelimo's military was unable to win the war decisively. Thus, after the peace agreement, Frelimo's leader, Mozambican president Joaquim Chissano, still had to contend with Dhlakama, who controlled approximately 19% of the country (Vines 1996, 3). Like dos Santos in Angola, Chissano faced challenges to power consolidation and needed resources to dominate militarily and to both coopt and subvert potential rivals.

Windfall Income in Angola versus Mozambique

The government of Angola had large amounts of resource wealth when the civil war there ended while the government of Mozambique was essentially desperate for income. The Angolan government had controlled oil wealth since independence, and took over diamond mines that had been historically under UNITA control. Officially, diamonds generated US$1 billion in revenues by 2005 (IMF 2007, 53). Oil alone, however, constituted approximately 92% of government revenues between 2002 and 2005 (IMF 2007, 56).

Angola's oil rents depended on the national oil company, Sonangol (Hodges 2004; Soares de Oliveira 2007; Roque 2011). Unlike most state institutions in Angola, Sonangol ran as a corporation, with elaborate and efficient techniques for handling its many assets, domestic and offshore accounts, and contracts with foreign oil companies and foreign governments. As Angolan analyst Ricardo Soares de Oliveira said, Sonangol was "an island of competence thriving in tandem with the implosion of most other Angolan state institutions" (Soares de

Oliveira 2007, 595). But rather than fostering good governance, this highly capable institution ultimately seems to have fostered corruption by generating a steady flow of rents to the executive (Soares de Oliveira 2007, 595). The World Bank referred to Sonangol-based government expenditures as the government's "non-conventional spending system" (World Bank 2005a, ii).

By 2004, the Angolan government also identified the Chinese government as a partner with a large source of potential income and a willingness not to influence Angola's public finances (World Bank 2007a, 16). The Chinese government offered a US$2 billion credit for reconstruction that year. Chinese loans totaled between US$12 and US$18 billion by 2009 (Soares de Oliveira 2011, 301).

In contrast to the government of Angola, the government of Mozambique possessed little windfall when the war ended and thus became dependent on nonstrategic donors. At the time, the Mozambican government lacked easy-to-access natural resources like oil or diamonds. Mozambique also lacked any non-reconstruction-related attractions for foreign donors (Howard 2008, 188). After independence, the Soviets sent the Mozambican government strategic aid, but they reduced aid to developing countries by 41% between 1979 and 1983 (Stockholm International Peace Research Institute 1984, 177). By the mid-1980s, Mozambique suffered declines in Soviet aid, and by 1989, the Mozabmican government confronted the full collapse of Soviet support. Thus, the government of Mozambique, which had received windfall income from the Soviet Union for much of its short history, became a low-windfall government by the late 1980s, when the Soviet Union withdrew support.

The Mozambican government also could not obtain strategic aid from the U.S. government at the time. A former senior official at the U.S. Agency for International Development indicated that the U.S. government's general view as the Cold War concluded was: "now that the Soviet Union had collapsed, we don't see any strategic threats in Africa that require security assistance."[8] Therefore, the only major source of government revenue in Mozambique at the ceasefire was nonstrategic donor aid; that is, aid from donors seeking only to promote social and economic development along with peace.

Stonewalling versus Embracing Gatekeepers of Aid

Because the governments of Angola and Mozambique depended on different sources of income, the governments of these two countries responded differently to demands made by the international financial institutions. While the Angolan government refused the international financial institutions and their calls to redirect oil revenues toward poverty reduction, the Mozambican government embraced these same institutions and allowed them to define spending priorities in Mozambique. As the next section demonstrates, the two governments' different attitudes influenced how much aid OECD bilateral and multilateral donors disbursed to the two countries, with consequences for post-conflict reconstruction.

Angola: Stonewalling Gatekeepers of Aid

As the argument in this book predicted, the Angolan government refused to implement the international financial institutions' reforms because it would have had to give up control over national revenues. The lead donor agency in the budgeting discussions in Angola following the war was the International Monetary Fund. Fund officials sought to implement a structural adjustment program calling for a national budget that aimed to dismantle Angola's nonconventional spending system. World Bank officials supported the Fund's demands by threatening not to organize a conference to coordinate aid from OECD bilateral and multilateral donors (such as the UN Development Program) unless the government implemented the Fund's program. These donors sought to avoid disbursing aid to a rich government that was unwilling to use its own money for reconstruction. According to a former senior official at the World Bank,

> If you have a country that has opportunities to generate revenues, and is not transparently using these revenues for development, you can't then organize a group of donors to come together and talk about assisting this country. The first question [from Western donors] is 'OK we want to know what the Angolans are doing with their oil money'... We were not convinced that this was a country that was using its own resources for the development of its people.[9]

Because the Angolan government could not account for billions of dollars in revenues lost in the five years preceding the end of the war, OECD donors—including senior U.S. officials—rallied behind the Fund (Human Rights Watch 2004; Soares de Oliveira 2011, 301).

Western donors were essentially asking the Angolan government to allocate oil money for socioeconomic reconstruction in exchange for aid. The donors wanted to combine their aid with Angola's windfall to fund reconstruction initiatives that would reduce poverty and ameliorate suffering from the war. An analysis funded by the United Kingdom's aid agency, the Department for International Development (DFID), offers evidence of this view, pointing out that because Angola had plenty of resources to spend on reconstruction, Western donors came to see themselves less as potential "donors" and more as potential "development partners": "Unlike in many other African countries, the role for partners like DFID is not so much as donors of money (which is usually rather small compared to Angola's budget) but as providers of technical assistance and cooperation in certain areas of Angola's development" (Shaxson et al. 2008, 11). Similarly, a former senior official at the U.S. Agency for International Development indicated in an interview: "our view was: they have oil, why don't they use their own wealth [for development]?"[10] The resident coordinator of the United Nations also argued that the Angolan government should contribute "a greater part of the burden" (quoted in Soares de Oliveira 2011, 300). However, the prospect of these partnerships was not enough to entice Angolan leaders to give up the nonconventional spending system.

Western donors believed that resistance to reform of public finances to benefit socioeconomic reconstruction came from the highest levels of the Angolan government. By 2005, after years of failed discussions, the World Bank stated that efforts to convince the Angolan government to reform the nonconventional spending system may not succeed because "implementation of the needed reforms may face still political resistance from influential quarters in Angola" (World Bank 2005a, 89). A United Nations official similarly indicated that "development strategy [in Angola] is beyond our remit as the government treats this as a sovereign issue" (quoted in Soares de Oliveira 2011, 305).[11] The government of Angola essentially turned away the Western aid community, including the international financial institutions and the Western donors that supported these agencies.[12]

In addition, Angolan government staff appears to have failed to facilitate some of the humanitarian aid that did arrive, suggesting further that the Angolan government did not prioritize socioeconomic reconstruction. For example, the government appears to have redirected food aid intended for specific nutritional centers, leading the UN to threaten that "food and other humanitarian supplies could be cut off if more transparency in management was not demonstrated" (UN Integrated Regional Information Networks 2004). Angolan officials also appear to have failed to expedite the influx of food aid. In early 2003, 4,210 metric tons of food aid sat in Angolan ports while Angolans starved (UN Integrated Regional Information Networks 2004). This government inaction suggests that the interests of the government and Western donors did not align.[13]

Thus, post-conflict, Angolan government officials gave the impression that they would follow their own reconstruction plans into the future and not give up control of their windfall income.

Mozambique: Embracing Gatekeepers of Aid

The Mozambican government embraced demands from the international financial institutions, as the argument in this book anticipated. Similar to Angola, staff from the International Monetary Fund and the World Bank led discussions about public finances and structural adjustment more generally with Mozambican government officials following the war. Also similar to Angola, Fund and Bank officials appeared to require compliance with their demands before Mozambique could obtain substantial support from other multilateral donors and OECD bilateral donors. Unlike the government of Angola, however, the government of Mozambique met Western donors' reconstruction goals.

The Mozambican government implemented the fiscal and government reform (structural adjustment) policies the Bank and the Fund sought at the time, from devaluing the currency to privatization (Landau 1998). The government also met public-finance goals even if the Bank and Fund staff designed Mozambique's budget and drafted most of the new post-conflict economic policies in Washington with minor input from Mozambican government staff (Arndt, Jensen, and Tarp 2000, 303; Hodges and Tibana 2005).[14] According to the World Bank itself, "partly by design, partly by default," by 1993 the Bank held "a near monopoly on development strategy dialogue with the [Mozambican] Government" (quoted in Hall and Young 1997, 226). Despite donor control over development policy, the government of Mozambique complied with reform efforts throughout the 1990s. The World Bank's independent internal auditing group indicates that Mozambique's government complied at least satisfactorily with 89% of the conditions the Bank attached to aid agreements between 1992 and 1999 (World Bank 2006b).

Consistent with my argument, the prospect of more aid appears to have motivated compliance with donor policies.[15] As a Bank official who worked in Mozambique said, "the Bank is de facto managing a donors' cartel. . . .[And] not following Bank advice tends to mean non-access to other (bilateral) sources of financial assistance" (quoted in Hanlon 1996, 48).[16] Mozambican government officials who described their own motivations for embracing Bank and Fund initiatives provide evidence that the prospect of more aid shaped their thinking. For example, a former senior official of the government of Mozambique remarked, "There was a decision. . . not to challenge IFIs [international financial institutions]. That we can prove with experience if they are wrong, but we won't challenge them from within. We assumed there would be some price to pay if we challenged them. There was no other way to go."[17] Similarly, a senior Mozambican legislator said,

> We agreed to [macroeconomic] conditionality because donors insisted. So who was going to stand against conditionality in that environment? Of course, there were disagreements over how reform happened, but there was agreement that it needed to happen. Back then, we had very little room to say anything. We needed the money. Now we have more room, but still, they have a lot of power. They have their matrices, and any time we don't meet one of their metrics, there are discussions as to why and whether the government itself is responsible, and funding can be withheld.[18]

Yet another senior official in the Mozambican government at the time explained, "We followed the market-economy model because it would get us help."[19] A civil servant remarked, "Everyone knows that. . .[compliance]. . .is important to the World Bank. . . . We understood that aid had to be used properly or it might be lost."[20] Mozambican President Chissano, who was broadly described in interviews as very pragramatic, also explained that aid dependence was an important driver of Mozambican reform efforts: "We are totally dependent on inputs from outside"[21] (Saul 1991, 106).

Some of the senior aid officials negotiating with the government believed the incentive structure for effective use of aid in Mozambique was sufficiently obvious that explicit threats to withdraw were not necessary. For example, a former senior World Bank official explained that Mozambican government leaders were "so aid dependent. . . they couldn't say 'well give us your money and put it in the budget and we'll then take it and use it on something else.' They had to listen to the donors and what the donors thought development programs should look like."[22] But other senior officials in donor agencies were quite explicit about their threat to withdraw, even detailing how and why withdrawal would occur if Mozambican government efforts failed to meet donor goals. For example, in 1989, in the lead-up to the ceasefire, a senior official at the U.S. Agency for International Development described to a senior Mozambican official the consequences of misusing food aid:

> [T]here's massive looting of food by your security forces and you have to stop it. . . . It's become scandalous, and the U.S. Congress is calling me in and we may have to stop all aid to you if you don't stop this. . . . Do you know what happens when the U.S. Congress gets involved?. . . . They have congressional hearings. It's on TV. It becomes part of people's political campaigns. They issue orders you have to follow, they put restrictions in your budgets. . . . You do not want to be the object of congressional hearings. . . . You would be very embarrassed, and it would be very bad for [US]AID and for you.[23]

The remarks seem to have carried weight. The Mozambican official approached the U.S. official twenty years later and said, "I remember everything you said in that meeting, and it influenced me a lot."[24]

According to the U.S. official, "[The Mozambican official meant] not just there, but every time they did other programs. . . . He repeated what I said in some detail, which sort of shocked me because it was so long ago. So it made an impression [on him]."[25]

Mozambican leaders' rhetoric highlights the priority they placed on keeping nonstrategic donors engaged. In contrast to their counterparts in Angola, Mozambique's senior officials responded to donor demands and were sensitive to the possibility of donor withdrawal (whether threats were implicit or explicit).

Two Caveats

First, Mozambican officials faced incentives to say the sorts of things they said in interviews with me, to newspaper reporters, and in their own reports. The leaders may say they "had no choice" as a way of appeasing domestic groups that preferred a socialist economy (Vreeland 2003). But even if they could have chosen not to do so, Mozambican government officials chose to implement aid agreements. Details from the case demonstrate that the Mozmabican government truly was dependent on nonstrategic aid and donors did threaten the government (even if implicitly) suggesting that the government would have foregone substantial amounts of aid money if it failed to meet donor expectations.

Second, whether compliance with structural adjustment policies championed by the international financial institutions actually led to socioeconomic reconstruction in Mozambique remains an open question, as I pointed out in Chapters 1 and 2. Some argue that implementing these reforms brings about macroeconomic stability, lower inflation, and economic growth, all of which can foster employment opportunities as well as improved market opportunities for local producers (Bearce and Tirone 2010; Stone 2002). On the other hand, ample evidence from Mozambique's experiences raises doubts about the wisdom behind these economic policies. As one prominent example, the structural reforms included liberalization of the cashew industry, which the government correctly viewed as harmful to the economy (de Renzio and Hanlon 2007). Even former senior officials at the World Bank now agree that asking Mozambique to liberalize this industry was a mistake.[26] In addition, structural adjustment may have had negative effects on reconstruction because Mozambican government officials seem to have manipulated some of the privatization reforms to support elite networks in ways that benefited elites at the expense of the population at large (Pitcher 2002).[27] As I will demonstrate, Mozambique likely achieved reconstruction in spite of these structural reforms because a large number of aid-funded projects directly benefited basic services and infrastructure. Funds for these projects, however, only flowed into the country once the gatekeepers of aid—the Fund and the Bank—gave the government a stamp of approval for complying with their structural demands.

Nonstrategic Donor Response

Nonstrategic donors responded to the Angolan government's failure to implement aid agreements by limiting support for Angola and responded to the Mozambican government's successful implementation of aid programs by offering continued aid to Mozambique.

By 2007, nonstrategic donors had essentially withdrawn from Angola. The international financial institutions and OECD donors did not want to disburse aid to a country that lacked commitment to reconstruction while earning billions from oil production (US$22.7 billion in 2005 alone) (IMF 2007, 56). In addition, nongovernmental organizations like Concern and United Nations agencies like the World Food Program lacked enough support from the leading Western donors to keep addressing reconstruction needs in Angola. For example, the World Food Program received less than the expected donor contributions in 2006 and therefore reduced its presence: "We plan to scale back to a small office in Luanda, which will provide only technical assistance to the Government, starting in 2007" (UN News Centre 2006). As of 2007, five years after Angola's civil war ended, foreign aid grants constituted 0.001% of Angola's revenues, down 90% from 0.01% two years after the war (IMF 2009, 24).

Evidence of donor withdrawal in Angola contrasts with the view (described in Chapters 1 and 2) that donors continue to disburse aid to recipients regardless of recipient performance. Local aid program managers were forced to withdraw when leaders of bilateral and multilateral aid agencies saw little inclination to redirect the country's own wealth toward reconstruction. Donors appear to have decided to stop disbursement mainly because the government rejected their guidelines on how to spend the government's windfall.

In contrast, World Bank officials were satisfied with the Mozambican government's compliance and organized donor conferences (Consultative Group meetings) among OECD bilateral donors and multilateral donors to coordinate aid disbursement to Mozambique. These donors disbursed aid to Mozambique specifically in response to government compliance. According to a report on a Consultative Group discussion in 1993, participants highlighted government reform efforts: "Donor governments and international institutions commended Mozambique for reducing price controls, reforming the banking sector and proceeding toward sale of 243 state-owned companies" (Borst 1993). In response to these reform efforts by the Mozambican government, donors at the conference committed US$1.4 billion, essentially matching Mozambique's requests for aid that year (Borst 1993). And support from the aid community persisted as Mozambican reforms continued. As a 1998 World Bank review said, "Donor satisfaction with Mozambique's progress [with 'nonsocialist economic management'] has been reflected in recurrent endorsement of the government's program at CG [Consultative Group] meetings [in the 1990s]. . . and the continuing high levels of aid. . ." (quoted in Landau 1998, 3). Foreign aid grants supplied 87% of Mozambique's government revenues on average during the 1990s (IMF 1998, 91–92; IMF 2001, 88–89). Thus, between 1992 and 1997, Mozambique received 169% more aid than Angola received during the five years that followed its civil war (OECD 2012).

Post-conflict, Angolan leaders appeared less interested in maximizing aid flows from nonstrategic donors than Mozambican leaders, arguably because only Mozambican leaders needed the money. Mozambique's government budget therefore became dependent on nonstrategic aid while the Angolan government budget remained rich in windfall income. This difference in income helps explain the variation in the reconstruction trajectories of the two countries.

Differences in Who Pays for Post-Conflict Reconstruction

Thus far, I have demonstrated that the governments of Angola and Mozambique depended on different income sources, that these income sources influenced how the two governments responded to demands made by Western donors, and that the response to donor demands in turn influenced donor interest in supplying further aid. As a result, OECD donors and multilateral agencies paid for post–civil war reconstruction in Mozambique, but not in Angola.

In general, China financed Angola's reconstruction projects, Chinese laborers completed them, and China did not demand that the government reform its public finances or social policies (Foster et al. 2008). Nonstrategic donors were essentially unwilling to fund these projects because the projects aimed to benefit resource extraction or the elite in Angola with few gains for the general population (Campos and Vines 2008; Lum et al. 2009).

In contrast, nonstrategic donors in Mozambique paid the reconstruction bill. Officials from the Fund, the Bank, and from OECD donors came together behind four reconstruction priorities in Mozambique beyond liberalizing the economy: disaster relief; poverty reduction through smallholder agriculture; a safety net via direct income transfers for impoverished households in the cities; and rehabilitation of basic services throughout the country (Government of Mozambique 1994, 5). Thousands of aid agencies (ranging from the United Nations to nongovernmental organizations like Concern and World Vision) descended upon Mozambique to implement aid projects around these four priorities.

The United Nations funded 486 "quick impact" disaster relief projects between 1992 and 1994 that reintegrated former combatants and provided basic services to the estimated 1.5 million refugees returning after the war (United Nations 1994a, 55). These projects targeted health, education, water, and infrastructure. Donors promoted agriculture and assisted district administrators in deciding what their communities should request of the government and donors (Landau 1998, 72). In addition, donors—and especially the World Bank—funded much of the road rehabilitation and maintenance between 1996 and 2002 (Arndt, Jones, and Tarp 2006). Aid also allowed the government to offer direct income transfers to 80,000 urban poor (Government of Mozambique 1994, 5; Landau 1998, 68). Finally, to improve basic services, aid allowed the government to expand water and sanitation systems as well as health and education programs (United Nations 2000, 118).

The National Health Service alone oversaw 405 donor health projects by 1996 (Pfeiffer 2003, 728). In collaboration with donors, the Ministry of Health designed the Health Sector Recovery Program to coordinate inflows of health aid with the specific goal to reduce infant mortality (Landau 1998, 27).[28] Also, using aid, each year from 1992 to 2004 the government built an average of 500 schools and added 3,500 teachers (Arndt et al. 2006, 40). Other reconstruction projects in the 1990s emphasized rural development as well as development of the social sectors.

Giving donors control may have increased the amount of aid allocated for reconstruction in Mozambique, but it also fostered dependence on aid. As a result, Mozambique's reconstruction success has been muted at best. The government has not become dependent on Mozambican citizens, who are the most sensitive to and knowledgeable about their own needs. While the next section demonstrates that the aid-dependent Mozambican government accomplished more socioeconomic reconstruction than the Angolan government following their respective wars, Mozambique's reconstruction is far from ideal.[29]

In summary, Western donors offered to pay for essentially all reconstruction activities in Mozambique because the government appears to have maintained its commitment to donor goals. In contrast, reconstruction spending in Angola depended mainly on Chinese investment and generally did not target socioeconomic needs. Dependence on nonstrategic aid is not an ideal way to reconstruct following civil war, but as the next section demonstrates, dependence on nonstrategic aid can lead to better reconstruction outcomes than dependence on windfall income.

Post-Conflict Reconstruction in Angola versus Mozambique

Mozambique's post-conflict reconstruction has been broader than Angola's. The Angolan government's reconstruction plan was to modernize key areas of the country, particularly the capital, Luanda, with "visible badges of being an important oil state," such as shopping malls, football stadiums, condominiums, skyscrapers, and gated housing compounds for those close to the president (quoted in Soares de Oliveira 2011, 297). The plan was to enrich and broaden the elite while keeping them dependent on the president (Vines, Shaxson, and Rimli 2005, 7). Benefiting the poor was not the focus of the reconstruction efforts. In fact, the poor and their vast shantytowns literally stood in the way of the reconstruction plans in Luanda, and the government took steps to push the poor out of the city (Vines et al. 2005, 6).

Despite calls for greater spending on social services by World Bank officials and other Western donors, especially when oil revenues and gross domestic product increased, expenditures in health and education in Angola reflected no increases following the civil war (IMF 2007, 65). In addition, according to the World Bank, almost all public expenditure, including that directed at health and education, benefited the "urban rich" (World Bank 2006c, 9).[30]

Much of the country continued to lack clean water and drainage systems five years after the war (World Bank 2007b). As a result, epidemics associated with lack of basic utilities, including water and sewer systems and waste collection, affected the country. For example, an outbreak of cholera spread to all but two of Angola's eighteen provinces. Between February 2006 and May 2007, more than 3,000 people died (World Health Organization 2007; LaFraniere 2006). Meanwhile, between 2002 and 2007, corruption remained at the same high level while the government's ability to enforce the law and public respect for the law remained low. In addition, bureaucratic autonomy and effectiveness declined (Political Risk Services Group 2007).

Unlike the Angolan government, Mozambique's government undertook reconstruction projects along with structural adjustment. The latter may have constrained reconstruction in Mozambique by limiting spending on social sectors, fostering corruption, and creating aid dependence (Hanlon 1996; Pitcher 2002). However, some reconstruction appears to have occurred because donors contributed to basic services and infrastructure.

Infant mortality rates declined by 54% more in Mozambique than in Angola within seven years of their respective wars (World Bank 2012a). This is important because infant mortality is highly correlated with attributes of socioeconomic reconstruction, such as education, vaccination coverage, caloric intake, safe drinking water, and general health care (Gerring et al. 2012; Moser, Leon, and Gwatkin 2005; Ross 2006b; Victora et al. 2003). Education, in particular, improves health by offering information on good hygiene and disease prevention. Education can also increase household income, allowing citizens to purchase better food, water, housing, and medical care. As aid to Mozambique increased, so did enrollment in its primary schools, which rose from 38.5% in 1997 to 53.8% in 2000 (United Nations 2000, 118). Cooperatives supported by the United Nations Children's Fund also fostered education. In these cooperatives, women learned how to read and write and how to knit garments for their families and for sale (Hanna 1995). The cooperatives even provided day care for children so that mothers could dedicate themselves to building their skills. A 38-year-old who participated in the cooperatives explained, "The lives of my children have improved because of what I've learned here. I've taken what I've learned and I've gone home and taught it to them. I want my daughters to go to school, continue their education so they can be whatever they want to be. I've learned that women can do whatever men do, and that is good" (quoted in Hanna 1995).

Vaccination campaigns and the availability of food and basic services may also have improved infant mortality rates. Within three years of the civil war, distribution of vaccines to prevent measles, diphtheria, tetanus, and pertussis among children significantly increased (Arndt et al. 2000, 315). Daily caloric intake also increased from 1,680 in 1992 to 2,420 in 1997, while the percent of population with access to safe water increased from 35% in 1995 to 50.2% in 2000 (United Nations 2000, 116). In addition, by 2000 a majority of the population had access to health services, especially primary health care. For example, Africare noted in its evaluation of the clinics it built in the Mozambican town of Chibabava that many of the patients in the new clinics were mothers who had come for postnatal care (Tarragó and Martinelli 1996, 26).

In addition, Mozambique's agriculture sector also improved. Agriculture employed 70% of the population and benefited from the return of millions of refugees, internally displaced persons, and combatants to their homes (Landau 1998, 12).[31] In coordination with the World Bank, the government implemented agriculture programs to help 52,600 farmers by distributing seeds, equipment, and research to expand cultivation (Landau 1998, 23). Because the economy depended on agriculture, the World Bank in particular prioritized reforms that would benefit that sector. After the war, agriculture grew by nearly 7% annually (World Bank 2005b, 18). The agricultural sector also benefited from better transportation, as road rehabilitation specifically aimed to help farmers ship to coastal areas. Cargo transport per kilometer of roads increased from 42.6 million tons in 1993 to 128.7 million in 1996 (Arndt et al. 2006, 93).

More generally, investor contracts and the legal system in Mozambique gained credibility, and the public respect for the rule of law increased (Political Risk Services Group 2007). Mozambique's economic growth became the fastest in Africa at the time. Within ten years, the economy grew by 44% (Heston et al. 2011). More importantly, economic development was broad-based. This post-conflict socioeconomic reconstruction depended on foreign aid.

Summary of Aid Effectiveness in Angola versus Mozambique

So far, the evidence from the two case studies is consistent with my argument. In Angola, nonstrategic donors asked the government to redirect its own wealth to help the poor, but because these donors had little leverage, the government essentially rejected their demands and donors withdrew. The Angolan government also generally did not invest in socioeconomic reconstruction of its own volition. In contrast, the Mozambican government was short on funds following the civil war and had little choice but to commit to nonstrategic donor plans in exchange for aid. The subsequent influx of aid appears to have brought about socioeconomic reconstruction.

It seems plausible that Angolan government officials stonewalled Western donors because the Angolans did not want to lose autonomy over their national budget. My argument predicts that coup-proofing a high-windfall regime actually requires refusing assistance from nonstrategic donors who seek to redirect wealth that the leader uses to hang onto political power. By refusing nonstrategic aid, the leader can use wealth for preventing coups. In the next section, I assess whether Angolan government officials were able to address coup risks by using windfall income to increase security and patronage networks after Angola's civil war. I also consider whether nonstrategic aid facilitated coup-proofing in Mozambique, as the argument predicts it should when a low-windfall government engages productively with nonstrategic donors.

Power Consolidation in Angola

The framework proposed here suggests that the post-conflict Angolan President dos Santos decided that complying with donor conditions was not in his interests because he did not need money from them to survive politically. How did the leader hang onto political power? As Angola analyst Paula Roque said, the dos Santos government was guided by two principles: "control the coffers and control the security apparatus" (Roque 2009, 148). Indeed, defense spending and patronage in the name of regime survival appeared to be the order of the day for the dos Santos administration.

Post-conflict, the Angolan government invested in its internal security infrastructure, as expected of a regime seeking to minimize coup risk. According to the World Bank, the post-conflict budget "seemed to reflect political choices still concerned with the prevalence of a wartime budget" (World Bank 2005a, i). In fact in the decade after the war ended, Angolan armed forces totaled 110,000 men and paramilitary forces totaled 10,000 men (Soares de Oliveira 2011, 292; Roque 2011, 2). As Soares de Oliveira points out, defense expenditures more than doubled, from US$716 million in 2002 to US$2.1 billion in 2010 as nonstrategic aid declined (World Bank 2012a). Soares de Oliveira adds that, with these investments, the Angolan military remained among the most powerful in sub-Saharan Africa, reflecting the Angolan government's interest in domestic and regional security (Soares de Oliveira 2011, 292).

Dos Santos was also able to use available resources for patronage (Roque 2011). While little information is available on the details of the government's patronage networks, in 2003, an independent Angolan newspaper, *Seminario Angolense*, reported that the top twenty wealthiest Angolans possessed more than US$100 million each, and the next thirty-nine on the list possessed at least US$50 million each (Economist Intelligence Unit 2003). Dos Santos topped the list as the wealthiest, and the next nine, in order, included the parliamentary deputy for dos Santos' party, the head of civil affairs in the president's office, an ambassador, a former army chief of staff, the minister of public works, the head of military affairs in the president's office, two businessmen, and a banker. In total, these individuals reportedly possessed at least US$4.19 billion in 2003, 15% of gross domestic product (US$27.5 billion) that year (Heston et al. 2011). This sort of enrichment persisted after 2003, involving not just oil money but also reconstruction funds (Roque 2009). For example, the head of military affairs, seventh in the *Angolense* list, became head of the Office of National Reconstruction with oversight of the China Investment Fund. Reportedly, as of 2008, this office had received billions in U.S. dollars from China, generated very little public information, and had no relationship with the Ministry of Public Works, which is charged with developing Angola's infrastructure (Shaxson et al. 2008). Also, by 2008, generals from the Angolan army had obtained access to large amounts of land in Angola's interior for resource exploitation (Soares de Oliveira 2011, 292).

With a trove of funds from Angolan oil and diamond contracts for revenue, Angolan senior leadership appears to have embarked on a policy to consolidate power by strengthening the security infrastructure and offering payoffs to key elites. If the Angolan government had spent windfall to promote socioeconomic reconstruction, the government might have faced greater coup risk because it would have had less money for security infrastructure and less money for the existing elites, which might encourage them to attempt a coup. Consistent with the low-windfall coup-proofing hypothesis, power consolidation appears to have been the dos Santos regime's primary goal, and the government appears to have used as much windfall income as it could toward this end.

Power Consolidation in Mozambique

All post-conflict leaders seek to prevent coups, but I argue that income structures constrain their choices. Unlike MPLA leadership in Angola, and in keeping with the incentives-based framework I propose, Frelimo consolidated power in Mozambique by using nonstrategic aid to strengthen security and hand out patronage.

Strengthening Security Infrastructure

Following the war, Mozambique's Frelimo leaders enhanced security by rebuilding the government's coercive power. However, the government did not build coercive power by bolstering the strength of the military. Members of Frelimo and Renamo were supposed to share authority within the new military, the Armed Forces for the Defense of Mozambique. The treaty ending the civil war stipulated that the new military would house both parties' troops and equipment

However, Chissano (and Renamo leader Dhlakama) did not invest substantially in the new military. Instead, both Chissano and Dhlakama appear to have invested in "'hidden' armies" (Vines 1996, 158). Dhlakama's, sometimes called the Presidential Guard, based itself in central Mozambique in Catema and Massala, within 40 kilometers of Meringue, Renamo's capital during the war. This army numbered approximately 1,000 soldiers when the United Nations left the country in December 1994 (Agence France Presse 1995; Vines 1996, 158). In addition, as of 1993, Dhlakama controlled approximately 19% of Mozambique (Vines 1996, 3). The peace treaty limited Dhlakama's legal authority in Renamo strongholds: Chissano and Dhlakama agreed that whichever one of them lost the presidential elections would appoint a district administrator where he won a majority and the winner would appoint governors in the provinces overseeing the districts. Chissano won the presidential election in 1994 and could therefore appoint all governors. However, Renamo's military force allowed Dhlakama to overcome the legal limits on his authority and retain control over Renamo strongholds throughout the country. In Dombe, a Renamo stronghold in the central province of Manica, for example, individuals loyal to Dhlakama used force four times in 1995 and 1996 to stop the government's deployment of officials.[32]

Facing potential threats to its rule from outside and inside the state apparatus from Renamo and other potential rivals, Frelimo's hidden army was the police force. Aid allowed Frelimo leaders to reconfigure and strengthen police operations. The government implemented a 1992 law that restructured the police and called it a paramilitary force (Lalá and Francisco 2006, 179, fn32).[33] By the time the United Nations left Mozambique, this force, known as the Rapid Intervention Police, housed 2,000 elite soldiers (United Nations 1994b; Vines 1996, 180, fn18). Even though the government ostensibly intended the unit for crowd control, the police received Frelimo's functioning "heavy weapons" and were given "military training" (quoted in Masimba 1994).[34] A government official acknowledged, "I'm not prepared to tell you that the government kept weapons, but it probably found ways, because it is responsible for law and order. The police remained the only legal body with arms, and it was in the hands of the government. The police were stronger than they had been" (quoted in Fortna 2008, 144). Dhlakama repeatedly complained about the force and the United Nations attempted to monitor it (United Nations 1994b).[35]

After the United Nations left Mozambique, the Frelimo-dominated police remained well equipped, and the size of the force grew with nonstrategic aid. Between 1997 and 2007, the police received steady financial support from Spain, the Netherlands, and other bilateral and multilateral donors (United Nations Development Program 2007). Thus, as nonstrategic aid increased, Frelimo was able to strengthen Mozambique's internal security infrastructure.

Co-opting Elites

Although Renamo had formally agreed to end all hostilities and entered the government as an opposition party, in practice, Renamo still constituted the main threat to Frelimo's ability to consolidate power following the war. Nonstrategic aid offered Frelimo an opportunity to secure its grip on power by enticing Renamo officials with financial incentives in exchange for cooperation.

In Mozambique, it was primarily the nonstrategic donors who directly bought off Renamo leaders at first and integrated the former rebels into the government. These donors did not need to spend very much. The payoffs amounted to less than 2% of total aid to Mozambique even in 1993, as donors sought to incorporate Renamo into Mozambique's first elections. In exchange for payoffs, these donors could achieve a multi-party democracy, a top priority for donors involved in the peace process (Manning and Marlbrough 2010). From the donors' perspective, Chissano had already welcomed multi-party elections leading up to the ceasefire, so the main remaining obstacle to successful elections was

Dhlakama's willingness to participate. As a 1993 European Commission report said, "the most pressing issue concerning the elections is the proper involvement of Renamo—and the other emerging political parties—in the process" (quoted in Manning and Marlbrough 2010, 161–2). Frelimo could not complain about the aid payoffs to Renamo because donors had so much leverage in Mozambique. Also, much of the remaining aid filled up the government's empty coffers, and some of it could be used for patronage. Finally, Frelimo leaders also likely benefited from the elaborate schemes to turn Renamo into a political party because the handouts could incorporate Renamo leaders into a system where Frelimo leaders could dominate and continue to co-opt them.

The payoffs to Renamo leaders began in 1993 when the United Nations provided Renamo with a US$23 million trust fund that included a per-month cash stipend for Dhlakama and his top commanders (Synge 1997, 60; Vines 1996, 152). The fund originated as a deal between the Italian government, Dhlakama, and Chissano to encourage Dhlakama to sign the peace treaty. After the signing, the Italian economy weakened and Italy could not meet its promise to fully finance the trust fund. Dhlakama refused to participate in the ceasefire commissions that would oversee demobilization unless Renamo received the promised funds. As Renamo's chief negotiator explained at the time, "There is no democracy without money" (quoted in Vines 1998, 73). UN officials then decided to coordinate the fund with aid from European governments and the U.S. government. Thus, donors were eager to satisfy Renamo's financial demands in exchange for Renamo's non-violent participation. As put by an Italian diplomat "I had a bag full of cash for eventualities. Demands came at all hours. We needed to be flexible" (quoted in Vines 1998, 73).

Chissano won the winner-take-all election in 1994, and that maintained Frelimo members as the primary aid recipients in Mozambique. Meanwhile, Dhlakama was left with few options to generate income. Renamo candidates won seats in the National Assembly, but Chissano appointed the cabinet and all provincial governors.[36] To ensure Renamo members would remain integrated into the political system and perhaps to reduce coup risk, donors and Frelimo offered more handouts to Renamo members.

Western donors were open to these payouts because they meant Renamo members would remain committed to democracy. Dhlakama appears to have obtained income by convincing donors that his party's buy-in was necessary to sustain democracy. Upon meeting with French President Jacques Chirac, for example, Dhlakama "assured President Chirac" of his determination "to pursue democracy" and "promised he would never go back to violence or war" (quoted in Rádio Mozambique 1998). Between 1995 and 1999, Dhlakama toured European countries such as Italy, Germany, England, Spain, France, Belgium, Switzerland, and Portugal, claiming to need their financial assistance to "consolidate" democracy in Mozambique (Rádio Maputo 1996). Reports of Dhlakama's visit with the Portuguese president in 1997 described the Renamo leader as "moved" by the president's conclusion that "democracy [in Mozambique] must be financed" (quoted in Rádio de Portugal 1997).

Much of the income Renamo leaders received for participation in the second national elections of 1999 came from the countries Dhlakama visited. In total, governmental administration of the 1999 elections cost US$49.23 million, and international donors (especially the European Commission and the United Nations Development Program) footed most of that bill, which amounted to 2.2% of the total aid to Mozambique that year (Pottie 2001, 149). To support political parties and civic education, the U.S. government also promised US$1.17 million and the Swiss, Swedish, and Dutch together posted $1.08 million (Pottie 2001, 149). Political parties received direct funding from the Mozambique government as well as from the national election commission. At the time, the commission had seventeen members: eight from Frelimo, six from Renamo, one from the Democratic Union (a small party led by Renamo defectors), and two government representatives. The commission distributed funds among political parties according to a formula that included the number of parliament members each party had and the number of candidates each was running in the upcoming election (Pottie 2001, 149–50). The elections commission also dispersed money to pay for political activities such as voter registration, civic education, and tallying ballots. Since most of these jobs involved hiring local people, opportunities for patronage were ample. Electioneering work became especially rewarding in Renamo-dominated rural areas with high unemployment (Manning 2001, 147–148).

Renamo members as well as the Frelimo elite also received some of the state largesse.[37] Renamo candidates who won races and became members of parliament received salaries of approximately US$760 per month (21 times the statutory minimum wage in Mozambique) as well as transportation and constituency-support funds (Mozambique News Agency 2002). Renamo members who joined national commissions gained government allowances, cars, and other small benefits (Manning 2002, 31). Frelimo officials seldom objected to such payoffs, likely because the payoffs appeared to foster stability. A former member of the Mozambican cabinet noted, "Now there's no way we would go back to war because . . . no leader in Renamo has the attitude for it. They benefit from being normal citizens, having political power, and being members of society, compared to fearing death."[38] In addition, non-Renamo government officials directly benefited from donor programs, especially from the privatization schemes, which offered leadership roles over private banks and industrial and agricultural companies (Pitcher 2002).

The buying-out process allowed Frelimo's top leaders to consolidate power in Mozambique. The U.S. ambassador to Mozambique during the peace process felt that following the 1994 elections, Frelimo was determined to maintain its monopoly on power. "It believed firmly that elections would do politically what it had been unable to do militarily—eliminate Renamo" (Jett 1999, 103). The strategy to co-opt Renamo with payoffs related to elections and other governmental participation appears to have worked.

Thus, in the case of Mozambique, donors directly bought out the opposition and incorporated it into the political process with nonstrategic aid. Most relevant for this analysis, however, is that nonstrategic aid helped Frelimo consolidate power.

Alternative Explanations

While windfall income plausibly explains differences in the effectiveness of nonstrategic aid in Angola and Mozambique, alternative explanations may also account for the variation between the two cases. Drawing on a careful reading of the history of the two cases and on hundreds of newspaper articles and reports by donors, government agencies, and scholars, I consider nine potentially confounding factors.

Because studies find that aid works best in countries with stronger institutions, I examine whether Mozambique or Angola had stronger institutions when their respective wars concluded. I compare their political administration under colonial rule; their industrialization during colonial rule; their post-independence institutions; and the destruction they experienced after independence. Mozambique's government officials may also have used foreign aid toward socioeconomic reconstruction more than Angola's did because of UN security guarantees in Mozambique; an ongoing unresolved insurgency in Angola; Chissano's need for popularity following the civil war; post-conflict democracy in Mozambique; or the quality of Chissano's leadership.

The evidence suggests that these factors do not explain the variation in aid effectiveness in these two cases as well as the interaction of non-strategic aid and windfall income.

1. *Political Administration under Colonial Rule*

Both Angola and Mozambique had similar political administration under Portuguese rule (Bender 1978; Chabal 2002; Hall and Young 1997; Minter 1972; Newitt 1995). Before independence, Angolans and Mozambicans did not manage any of their own policing, justice systems, or other political administration. As late as the 1950s, Portuguese colonialism prohibited political parties or public assembly, censored media and other literature, and subjected indigenous peoples to arbitrary arrests and prison camps (Minter 1972, 35). By disenfranchising indigenous groups from political activity, the Portuguese significantly limited local capacity in both countries. Given their similar institutional histories prior to independence, the two countries' colonial-era political administration cannot account for their differences in post-conflict reconstruction.

2. *Industrialization during Colonial Rule*

Angola was more industrialized than Mozambique on the eve of independence. This difference raises the possibility that Angolan leaders found it easier than Mozambican leaders to foster socioeconomic reconstruction after the war because Angolans could use the institutional capacity engendered by their country's history of wealth.

Prior to independence, Angola's economy depended mainly on oil, diamonds, iron ore, and agriculture. It promised much to foreign investors who were eager to take advantage of new investment opportunities (El-Khawas 1974). Angola's foreign exchange earnings from minerals alone increased by more than 100% during the 1960s, and constituted 40% of the total by 1971 (El-Khawas 1974, 24).

Mozambique's economy lagged behind Angola's. The same companies that explored and profited from Angola's mineral wealth looked for similar opportunities in Mozambique but found little (El-Khawas 1974, 24). Mozambique's investment opportunities included agriculture (cashews, sugar), which constituted almost 67% of foreign exchange earnings in 1972, labor export to South African mines, and transportation from its coastal port towns to profitable inland areas of southern Africa (El-Khawas 1974, 25; Minter 1972).

The Portuguese faced armed liberation movements in both countries, and investors were equally uncertain about whether the Portuguese would succeed in either country (El-Khawas 1974). However, Angola's resource wealth offset that uncertainty while Mozambique's resources could not do the same. The Angolan colony therefore attracted and maintained substantial investments, which enlarged and industrialized the economy. In 1973, two years before independence, Angola's per-capita gross domestic product was six times greater than Mozambique's (US$2611 versus US$448.74) (Heston et al. 2011). Its exports were also much greater; Angola exported US$2.1 billion in 1970 while Mozambique exported US$786 million (El-Khawas 1974, 23–24).

Thus, Angolan leaders approached the end of civil war with a history of stronger economic performance and industrialization than Mozambique. While MPLA officials were not in charge of the country during its colonial prosperity, they witnessed the industrialization and oversaw the transition of contracts with Portugal to contracts with their new government in Angola. MPLA leaders were therefore in a better position to invest in reconstruction than Frelimo leaders, and that fact makes it potentially challenging to compare the two countries. However, if prewar industrialization affects post-conflict reconstruction, Angola was in a position to outperform Mozambique. Because Mozambique outperformed Angola, differences in prewar industrialization cannot explain differences in these countries' post-conflict reconstruction.

3. Post-Independence Institutions

Following independence, Angola and Mozambique had similarly authoritarian institutions, and their leaders were therefore unaccountable to the population at large. Both leaders implemented single-party authoritarian institutions with control in the hands of the president and central committee and tight constraints on the press. Both parties created legislatures, called the People's Assembly in both cases, that were merely rubber-stamp institutions and met twice a year at most.[39] Also, the government of each country had the power to hold citizens suspected of crimes or political disloyalty, creating a sense of fear among any opposition. In 1975, for example, Frelimo leaders formed a secret police that regularly arrested, tortured, and killed citizens (Human Rights Watch 1992, 148). In Angola, an early and significant politicide occurred after an attempted coup by an MPLA faction leader in 1977. MPLA leaders responded by purging the party: incarcerating and killing many of its members and members of the urban intelligentsia more broadly (Hodges 2004, 50–51).

From the start, leaders in both Angola and Mozambique feared violent internal opposition. To control rural populations, in the late 1970s Frelimo leaders created "communal villages." The government would gather peasants within a certain distance, create a village by giving them a school and a health clinic, and monitor and coordinate their economic activities. Within a few years, Frelimo leaders had grouped almost two million people into 1,266 villages (Human Rights Watch 1992, 67). Peasants who refused to join communal villages suffered attacks by the government, including the burning of their homes (Hall and Young 1997, 103). Although the villages were designed in theory to support communist-style production, Mozambican president Samora Machel admitted at the time that in practice "communal villages are a political instrument because they unite and organise us and thus enable us to exercise power. We must realise that if we are dispersed and disorganized we will not be able to exercise that power" (quoted in Hall and Young 1997, 102). According to the director of communal villages at that time, "When it is said that we are forcing people into communal villages, it is true. . . . Because if we don't, then the enemy will use those people to destroy their own future. These people are being liberated" (quoted in Human Rights Watch 1992, 23). Citizens in urban areas were also vulnerable to being displaced. In the early 1980s, as violence and drought spread throughout rural areas, thousands of people migrated to the major cities. In a move that Frelimo leaders called Operation Production, troops took the urban unemployed to farms in the north—some were farms in name only—in order to purge "underdevelopment" (Hall and Young 1997, 104). Over the next decade, Mozambique's leaders maintained policies to separate, monitor, arrest, and sometimes kill citizens as part of their counter-insurgency strategy.

Similarly, in Angola, MPLA leaders granted governorships to military commanders. Because these local officials were generally isolated, operating in the hinterlands with minimal communication with MPLA leaders in Luanda, the officials were unaccountable to citizens and only loosely accountable to MPLA leaders (Hodges 2004, 68–72). These local officials regularly preyed on the populations they governed. While this might seem puzzling given that these officials might have sought to win hearts and minds in favor of the government, local government officials seemed to have had a greater interest in looting for their short-term wealth and in eliminating potential resources for UNITA leaders.[40] Rank-and-file soldiers ultimately employed a similar strategy throughout Angola as well. While MPLA leaders invested heavily in creating a strong military force, the soldiers themselves were not paid well. Particularly during the 1990s, they were allowed to loot villages for resources (Hodges 2004, 74). Because post-independence leaders in both Angola and Mozambique implemented oppressive, authoritarian institutions, post-independence institutions cannot account for differences between these countries in post-conflict reconstruction.

4. Post-Independence Destruction

Another possibly confounding factor is the degree of war destruction. The development picture was equally catastrophic in the two countries, however. When their respective wars ended, each faced infant mortality rates among the very highest in the world (World Bank 2012a). Approximately 173,427 Angolans were killed in battle during the war between 1975 and 2002 (Lacina and Gleditsch 2005). Also, by the time the Angolan ceasefire was signed in 2002, 4.1 million citizens had been internally displaced and more than 445,000 had become refugees (World Bank 2007a, 1). In Angola, social expenditures had declined during the 1990s such that by the middle of the decade, 70% of Angolans earned less than a dollar a day (Le Billon 2001b, 60). As Angolan finance minister Pedro de Morais said, "political and military conflicts in the region, resulting from the Cold War, made it impossible for its [Angola's] sources of energy to be used for causes such as poverty alleviation" (quoted in Shankleman 2006, 102–3).

Similar to Angola, approximately 171,990 Mozambicans were killed in battle between 1976 and 1992 (Lacina and Gleditsch 2005). Estimates indicate between 5.5 million and 6.5 million Mozambicans were displaced internally or became refugees (United Nations 1994a). Much of the infrastructure—roads, bridges, utilities, health clinics, schools—was destroyed, and public services were in total disrepair.[41] Ninety percent of the population was impoverished at the ceasefire (Human Rights Watch 1992, 103). As Mozambique's war ended, its people continued to suffer from severe droughts, with millions at risk of dying of famine.

In both countries, only a privileged few had access to clean water, sanitation, or electricity. Further, millions of land mines lay unexploded throughout the countryside in both Angola and Mozambique. Both the MPLA in Angola and Frelimo in Mozambique were ill-equipped to deal with these problems. In both countries, government leaders had been dedicated to winning a difficult civil war. The fighting had destroyed much of the infrastructure, and the staffs of both governments had done little to rebuild their countries during the war. As a result, both dos Santos and Chissano faced significant challenges to successful reconstruction. Because their wars were similarly destructive, war-related destruction cannot explain why the government of Mozambique brought about more socioeconomic reconstruction than the government of Angola.

5. United Nations Security Guarantees

A difference between Angola and Mozambique is that Angola's civil war ended decisively, while Mozambique's ended with a negotiated settlement that the United Nations implemented. One might ask whether UN security guarantees might have been enough to foster socioeconomic reconstruction. Such guarantees are promises that the UN makes to punish anyone who violates a ceasefire. These guarantees are intended to create an environment of trust in which combatants can demobilize and share power (Doyle and Sambanis 2006; Fortna 2008; Hartzell 1999; Walter 1997).[42] By helping keep the peace among former combatants, external enforcement of a ceasefire, especially by the United Nations, could also reassure domestic and foreign investors that the coast is clear for renewed economic activity (Kang and Meernik 2005). An increase in investment should create jobs and increase tax revenues, giving the government more funds for reconstruction.

By themselves, however, security guarantees alone don't explain why Mozambique's leaders concluded that reconstruction spending served their interests. The Mozambican government leadership chose to use new income to build roads, promote education, and vaccinate children. It is not obvious by what mechanism the presence of peacekeepers would prompt Mozambique's leaders to tie their own hands and spend on reconstruction, especially after the United Nations departed in 1994.

In the early 1990s, the United Nations also attempted to enforce a ceasefire in Angola. The combatants there signed the Bicesse Accords in May of 1991 and agreed to a ceasefire that MPLA and UNITA members would monitor through a joint political-military commission, the *Comissão Conjunta Politico-Militar*, and by unarmed observers from the United Nations. The agreement called for the demobilization of UNITA rebels and some MPLA military units, the establishment of a new army with both UNITA and MPLA soldiers, and the holding of multiparty elections.

While peacekeepers succeeded in Mozambique, they failed in Angola, giving way to the most violent decade of Angola's civil war. Windfall can help explain the failure in Angola. UN peacekeepers administered Angolan elections on September 29 and 30, 1992 with the hope that elections would integrate both the MPLA and UNITA into the government and allow them to solve future conflict peacefully. Dos Santos won the presidential election but received only 49.6% of the vote, compared to the UNITA candidate Savimbi's 40%, which was not a wide enough margin to avoid a second-round run-off election (Hodges 2004; Roque 2008). Opposition parties, however, claimed that MPLA leaders had committed fraud in the first round, and so the second-round run-off did not occur as war broke out again in Angola.

UNITA rebels resumed fighting immediately. Dos Santos responded by using the government's paramilitary police force, the Rapid Intervention Police, or ninjas, to repress UNITA party members in Luanda. Even during the brief peace before the elections, UNITA had maintained diamond production and increased military equipment, so the rebels were well positioned to fight against the MPLA (Le Billon 2001b). Meanwhile, the MPLA maintained its hold over Luanda and Cabinda's oil, and could therefore continue the fight against UNITA (Sherman 2000).

The different outcomes that security guarantees had in Angola and Mozambique reinforce peacekeeping scholarship, which finds that peace created by UN peacekeepers lasts longer in resource-poor countries than in resource-rich countries (Fortna 2008). Thus, the income structure of governments emerging from war appears to underlie not only aid effectiveness, but also the effectiveness of peacekeeping following civil war.

6. Unresolved Insurgency

In Angola, a small-scale insurgency persisted in the province of Cabinda after the war ended in 2002. One might wonder if this insurgency compelled MPLA leaders to continue to govern with a wartime mentality and avoid reconstruction spending. If so, this might serve as an alternative explanation for why Mozambique outperformed Angola. At this writing, the insurgency involves a group with anywhere from several hundred to 2,000 rebels and has remained peripheral (Porto 2003, 2). The province of Cabinda is a 7,283-square-kilometer area located between the Democratic Republic of the Congo and the Republic of Congo, disconnected from mainland Angola.

Cabinda's importance to the Angolan government had remained significant because Cabinda generates more than half of Angola's total annual oil production. Oil was discovered in the region in 1957. Aware of the wealth at stake, Cabindan nationalists mobilized for independence from Portugal and created the Front for the Liberation of the Enclave Cabinda (FLEC). But the independence agreements that transitioned Angola to postcolonial rule delivered Cabinda to MPLA leaders in Luanda.

To then try to obtain independence from Angola, FLEC rebels targeted MPLA forces in Cabinda as well as foreign workers involved in the oil industry. This insurgency has persisted even after the Angolan military decisively defeated UNITA rebels in 2002. Throughout the war against FLEC rebels, the Angolan government has offered them amnesty and integration, but this has yet to entice the rebel group to give up its low-intensity war.

While civil war persisted in Angola but not in Mozambique, because the war has remained peripheral, it has not affected the Angolan government's ability to spend on the population at large. In fact, Cabindan grievances include the government's failure to transfer much of the Cabinda-generated oil wealth to residents of that region. In sum, it seems unlikely that these differences in the presence of insurgency are sufficient to explain the differences between Angola and Mozambique in reconstruction following war.

7. Need for Post-Conflict Popularity

Another potentially confounding issue is the role of popularity. Perhaps Chissano did not invest in reconstruction in order to secure aid but rather to expand his popularity and that of Frelimo. Leaders with more popularity may be better able to reduce coup risk by reducing grievances or making it harder for elites to coordinate against the leader.

Frelimo's popularity was not widespread when the civil war ended. In the 1994 elections, the first after the civil war, Frelimo candidates barely secured a majority for the national assembly, winning 52% of seats, and winning the presidency with 53.3% of the vote. Eighty percent of registered voters cast their ballots in the election. Out of Mozambique's ten provinces, Renamo candidates won five (see Manning 2001, 146). Thus, Chissano had room to increase Frelimo's popularity.

After overseeing the spending of US$7.8 billion in aid during the five years after the ceasefire, Frelimo managed to expand its appeal as evidenced by survey data collected by the U.S. Agency for International Development in partnership with Mozambique's Eduardo Mondlane University in 1997 and 2001 (USAID 2005). By 2001, 40% more of the respondents believed the government was interested in their needs than respondents in 1997 (USAID 2005, 5). Frelimo was rewarded in the 2004 election, winning 64% of the vote for the presidency and 64% of the assembly seats. Thus, Frelimo leaders appear to have used aid to increase popularity through reconstruction spending.

If popularity were an important factor in coup risk, however, we would expect it to matter for all leaders, not just leaders with low windfall. However, the MPLA's need for popularity did not seem to affect reconstruction spending in Angola. In Angola, reconstruction spending has generally favored the elite, the party, and the military. Meanwhile the MPLA appeared to address any negative consequences of declining popularity with state pressure. For example, the MPLA's waning popularity became evident during the 2008 legislative elections—the first elections in Angola since the end of the war. MPLA candidates defeated UNITA candidates in a landslide with 82% of the vote, but only after deciding to "manufacture the conditions necessary to guarantee its overwhelming victory," as analyst Paula Roque has said (Roque 2009, 143). Specifically, after large rallies turned out to support UNITA candidates and polling demonstrated substantial support for the opposition, MPLA leaders began to question whether their party would win the two-thirds majority in the National Assembly they needed to reform the constitution as they saw fit. In response, MPLA political and security officials became close advisors of the national electoral commission administering the elections (Roque 2009, 146). Thus, the MPLA appears to have used its coercive capacity to ensure a favorable outcome for the party.

Despite the pre-election rallies in 2010 that protested the inequities between rich and poor in Angola, the poor were incapable of directly threatening dos Santos. As a report funded by the United Kingdom's aid agency noted, "Widespread poverty has almost never created a serious challenge to the president's hold on power; this is even more so today than in the war" (Shaxson et al. 2008, 4). Unlike Frelimo in Mozambique, the MPLA in Angola apparently did not spend on reconstruction because it did not perceive broad-based popularity as crucial for political survival.

The observation that popularity does not matter to all post-conflict leaders argues against the idea that popularity is a driving incentive for leaders trying to consolidate power in a country with weak institutions.

Instead, evidence suggests that popularity may be a byproduct of leader efforts to please donors when post-conflict countries have low windfall.

8. Post-Conflict Democracy

One might wonder whether Mozambique's reconstruction outperformed Angola's because Mozambique was more democratic after its war ended than Angola. In Mozambique, the United Nations administered free and fair elections two years after the 1992 ceasefire. Angola, however, did not hold national elections until 2008, six years after the war ended, and then only for the legislature. Because Frelimo election victories depended on appealing to a broad constituency of citizens, the party's calculus for political survival might have included improving living conditions for the population at large. In Angola, the MPLA did not need to appeal to a broad constituency for political survival. Although some have questioned the quality of Mozambique's democracy, few would doubt that Mozambique was more democratic than Angola, particularly in the ten years after their respective ceasefires (Manning 2010; Weinstein 2002). Did Frelimo foster reconstruction to appeal to voters or to appeal to nonstrategic donors? Was the key difference between Angola and Mozambique that post-conflict Mozambique transitioned to democracy faster and to a greater degree than Angola following its civil war?

Unfortunately, the evidence from the two cases does not allow a determination of the merit of one explanation over the other. However, after its own conflict, the Central African Republic implemented democratic institutions like those in Mozambique, also with the help of the United Nations. Like Chissano in Mozambique, a stalemated President Ange-Félix Patassé in the Central African Republic signed agreements with rebels. The January 25, 1997 Bangui Agreements called for elections. In April 1998, the United Nations introduced a multidimensional force in the Central African Republic that was similar to the UN force in Mozambique. Its mandate included supporting the agreements. The first post-conflict elections in the Central African Republic appeared to be free and fair, like the first post-conflict elections in Mozambique. Unlike the government of Mozambique, however, the government of the Centeal African Republic was not desperate for income at the ceasefire because the country was rich in diamonds and other minerals. Five years after the ceasefire, reconstruction remained stagnant in the Central African Republic (Wakabi 2006; World Bank 2012a). Thus, the Central African Republic provides an African post-conflict example with a ceasefire in the 1990s and free and fair UN-administered elections where democracy was not sufficient for reconstruction to occur.

The quantitative analysis described in Chapter 3 accounted for the possibility that democracy explains the variation in reconstruction better than nonstrategic aid by holding democracy levels constant across a broad set of cases. Even when I included this important control variable, the results remained consistent and supported the argument in this book.

9. Post-Conflict Leadership

Differences in leadership abilities present another potentially confounding factor. Mozambique's Chissano is regarded internationally as a strong and good leader who navigated his country through successful ceasefire negotiations and several free and fair democratic elections and served two terms before, crucially, stepping down. He tried to rally support for Western donor programs, particularly during the early 1990s when some members of the Frelimo party in the population at large may have been skeptical about abandoning socialism. A senior Frelimo official commented that following the war,

> [Chissano] had to mobilize throughout the country to make people understand that we needed this change in order to survive. We needed to change from socialism to survive. There was silent opposition from the orthodox in the party but they understood there was no money in the bank to pay salaries. The Central Committee of Frelimo said this is what we have to do . . . . And the World Bank and the IMF had to be used to save the economy as a way to solve our problems.[43]

In 2007, in recognition of his role in transforming Mozambique, Chissano won the inaugural Ibrahim Prize for Achievement in African Leadership, a highly publicized award that is given out by a selection board that includes Nobel Laureates. The award consists of a

US$5 million prize distributed over ten years and then US$200,000 every year for the rest of the recipient's life. According to former UN Secretary General Kofi Annan, who presented the prize to Chissano:

> [T]he Prize celebrates more than just good governance. It celebrates leadership. The ability to formulate a vision and to convince others of that vision; and the skill of giving courage to society to accept difficult changes in order to make possible a longer term aspiration for a better, fairer future.[44]

Dos Santos has received comparatively little praise for his leadership. Since the ceasefire, the international human rights community has widely criticized dos Santos for corruption, for forcibly displacing Luanda's poor, and for treating civilians in Cabinda inhumanely. Thus, we cannot hold "good leadership" constant between the two cases. In a report on corruption in the Angolan government, Human Rights Watch stated that the government has become "a symbol of the depredations of a resource-rich, but unaccountable government" (Human Rights Watch 2010).

It is certainly plausible that Chissano learned from Mozambique's experience with socialism and sought other economic strategies to bring about reconstruction in his country. He may also have worked to improve living conditions because he was desperate for donor money, as I argue here—or several motivations may have shaped Chissano's behavior. The key questions are: Would Chissano have behaved the same way if he had been rich in windfall income when the war ended? Would dos Santos have behaved like Chissano if he had been president of Mozambique and would Chissano have behaved like dos Santos if he had been president of Angola?

While these case studies raise important questions about the impact of leadership on post-conflict outcomes, leadership is potentially endogenous to the environment in which these leaders operate.[45] In other words, perhaps "good" leaders like Chissano emerged because "bad" leaders could not survive in a low-windfall environment. Windfall income is arguably a driving force that restricts the kind of leadership that can be successful: low windfall may set the stage for the emergence of "good" leaders.

Summary

While the findings from the Angola and Mozambique case studies largely mirror what this book's argument would lead us to expect, there may be alternative explanations. Angola and Mozambique demonstrated similarities in political administration during colonial rule, in post-independence institutions, and in post-independence destruction, and these similarities essentially eliminate these factors as potential alternative explanations. The two cases also demonstrated differences in industrialization during colonial rule, United Nations security guarantees, ongoing insurgency, need for post-conflict popularity, post-conflict democracy, and quality of post-conflict leadership. We cannot overlook these differences, but they either bias the comparison in favor of Angola, or their logic and evidence appear to fail to account for the different outcomes in the two cases. Thus, even after considering these alternative possibilities, the case studies appear to support the argument.

In summary, Angola and Mozambique essentially constitute "most similar" cases, except for sources of income. Both succeeded at coup-proofing after civil war, but they did so with very different strategies. While the Angolan government could depend on natural resource rents and some investment from China, the Mozambican government could only turn to nonstrategic donors for income. Consistent with the framework I presented in Chapter 2 and the general findings from the regression analyses in Chapters 3 and 4, the Mozambican government was compelled to undertake reconstruction initiatives to obtain and sustain desperately needed aid from nonstrategic donors, whereas the Angolan government could essentially ignore reconstruction because windfall income was already available to shore up the regime. Nonstrategic aid appeared to work successfully where incentives to use it well existed, despite the lack of strong post-conflict institutions.

While the post-conflict leaders in both countries faced formidable domestic opposition and both appear to have invested heavily in defense and patronage networks, Mozambican leaders chose to spend more on socioeconomic reconstruction than Angolan leaders. However, donors made different demands of Angola because of its resource wealth. In Angola, donors insisted that the government allocate windfall income to socioeconomic reconstruction, whereas in Mozambique, donors were willing to pay for reconstruction themselves. Thus, Angolan leaders were saying "no" to aid from the nonstrategic donors as much as he was saying "yes" to keeping their own significant windfall income. However, because Angolan leaders did not depend on a source of revenue that required socioeconomic reconstruction, they could focus on building patronage networks through direct and indirect payoffs that included investing in reconstruction to benefit the elite and the military. In Angola, it appears that any spending on socioeconomic reconstruction would not offset lost investment in security and payoffs to the elite. As a result, nonstrategic donors could do little to improve the standard of living in Angola, consistent with my argument and the results of the quantitative analyses.

Because Angola and Mozambique share substantial similarities but differ in their windfall income, I investigated whether their differing windfall influenced differences in their post-conflict reconstruction. But in spite of the similarities, Angola and Mozambique differed across four potentially confounding factors that predict that Mozambique would outperform Angola: UN security guarantees; new insurgency; post-conflict democratization; and the quality of post-conflict leadership. I identified why these potential confounding factors, in addition to other alternative explanations, are likely insufficient to account for the marked reconstruction differences between Angola and Mozambique following civil war. Nevertheless, to further investigate the argument and to bypass between-country differences, I also investigate a country with windfall variation over time, where some of these potential confounds are constant and essentially nonfactors in explaining differences in reconstruction. Uganda presents an opportunity to explore a country where, following civil war, the same leader was in power both before and after a change in windfall income status.

6

Same Country, Change in Windfall
Uganda

AS YOWERI MUSEVENI began to rule Uganda in 1986, violence was occurring daily throughout much of the country, including the capital, Kampala. Residents there rushed home by early evening for fear of assaults or being caught in hostilities between government forces and insurgents. Within five years of the start of Museveni's rule, former adversaries governed and patrolled communities together; the government eliminated major threats to its survival as it enforced peace throughout most of the country; and living conditions improved. Citizens could access new health clinics and schools. They could keep more of the income they earned through agriculture and transport their goods using rehabilitated roads. Why and how did reconstruction occur in Uganda following civil war?

As my argument would predict, Museveni's government was essentially desperate for income as Museveni brought an end to civil war in Uganda. At the time, state institutions had collapsed, and the country was both resource-poor and strategically unimportant to most Western donors. Then, when the government discovers natural resources in the neighboring Democratic Republic of the Congo in the mid-1990s, the government's interest in development, and in implementing aid agreements, appears to wane (Reno 2002). Windfall income further increased after December 2001, when the government began to receive strategic aid from the U.S. government as an ally in the War on Terror in the region. In the mid-2000s, oil was discovered within Uganda's borders. I find that the emergence of Uganda's natural and strategic endowments can explain the timing and shift in the government's behavior. Aid stopped being effective after the mid-1990s, but only after the government obtained access to natural resources and then strategic importance to donors.

Uganda thus presents a helpful case for examining the argument within one country. Uganda lacked windfall income following the end of civil war in 1988, then later found windfall. If the argument in this book holds, Uganda will behave as a low-windfall country immediately following its civil war, but after realizing windfall it will behave as a high-windfall country.

In this chapter, I therefore take another step to examine my argument's validity. I corroborate the process that seems to explain differences between Mozambique and Angola in post-conflict reconstruction by investigating the post-conflict dynamics in Uganda before and after the government obtained access to windfall income. By comparing the strategies of the same leader before and after discovering windfall, the analysis minimizes confounding variables and maximizes inference.

Of course, not all confounding factors can be held constant over time in Uganda.[1] Early in his governance, Museveni appears to have been a uniquely good leader with a keen interest in bringing about reconstruction in the country, an interest that was evident when he was a rebel, well before he overthrew the government, and well before he welcomed large amounts of aid to Uganda (Khadiagala 1995; Ng'ethe 1995; Weinstein 2006). Was Museveni's leadership unique, or were there circumstances in Uganda that made it possible for Museveni to exercise good leadership? Why did Museveni's preferences for broad-based development appear to change after the mid-1990s? Was aid effective or did aid create patronage networks that ultimately undermined reconstruction gains from Museveni's early years? I investigate these questions and then, at the end of the chapter, I consider whether leadership explains the variation in Ugandan reconstruction better than windfall.

I organize the chapter around the observable implications of the argument. First, I analyze whether the Ugandan government interacts with donors as the argument predicts: does the government follow through on commitments made to international financial institutions? Do these institutions serve as gatekeepers of other aid? Then, I analyze whether the government uses nonstrategic aid as my argument predicts: for reconstruction, strengthening security, and buying out of elites. If the argument is valid, while the Ugandan government lacks windfall income, Museveni should make choices similar to those of President Chissano of Mozambique. Finally, I ask whether the government of Uganda loses interest in socioeconomic reconstruction (and acted more like the government of Angola) after striking it rich with windfall. I begin with a brief background that demonstrates the fragile nature of government institutions in Uganda when Museveni overthrew the previous government and the power consolidation challenges Museveni faced.

Brief Background: Civil War in Uganda

On January 21, 1979, in a coordinated military effort with Ugandan exiles in Tanzania and Kenya, the Tanzanian army invaded neighboring Uganda to overthrow Idi Amin and end his authoritarian rule. One of the rebels involved was Museveni, a western Ugandan and member of the Ankole, Uganda's second largest ethnic group.[2]

At this moment when it looked as if peace might finally come to Uganda, the country faced a dire need for reconstruction. According to Cherry Gertzel, "Death and exile had depleted the ranks of the civil service, and the lack of resources had by the end of 1978 ground government almost to a halt, so that at liberation Uganda was in some respects a country without a bureaucracy" (Gertzel 1980, 469). According to Jimmy Tindigarukayo, another close observer, "The Ugandan system of government and administration was more disintegrated than ever before. There was both an institutional and a political vacuum, coupled with a state of anarchy as reflected in widespread looting, rape, and armed robberies" (Tindigarukayo 1988, 609). Pockets of the country were stable only in the presence of Tanzanian troops. Unfortunately, conflict would resume and reconstruction would have to wait.

In April 1979, the Tanzania military installed a new Ugandan government led first by Yusuf Lule and then by Godfrey Binaisa. Neither could hold on to power for long. By May 1980, the Ugandan Military Commission that administered the national army took control of the government. The Commission organized national elections for September 30, 1980. Former president Milton Obote returned from exile to run for president on the Ugandan People's Congress ticket and won (Mutibwa 1992, 143).[3] Despite allegations of fraud, he was sworn in on December 5, 1980.

Museveni, a member of the Military Commission, ran against Obote in the election. Apparently motivated by what he considered fraudulent election results, Museveni launched the National Resistance Army, which declared war on the new regime from southern-central Uganda (see Weinstein 2006, 67–69). Another rebel group, the Uganda Freedom Army, joined the fight, supported by Uganda's largest ethnic group, the Baganda, in the south and headed by Lule's former minister of internal affairs, Andrew Kayiira. The Federal Democratic Movement also drew support from the Baganda to fight the regime. In addition, rebel groups organized to fight Obote in western Uganda (Tindigarukayo 1988, 617; Tripp 2010, 151). The Uganda National Rescue Front, organized by Amin's minister of finance, Moses Ali, organized northwest Uganda against Obote. In the West Nile, former members of the Uganda National Army also fought the regime. In the end, Museveni's group grew by incorporating rebel groups, fought effectively, and took from Obote control of large portions of the country (Tindigarukayo 1988, 617; Tripp 2010, 151).

The Tanzanian president withdrew his troops by 1983, which left Obote alone with an undisciplined and divided Ugandan military to fight the rebels. On July 26, 1985, former Obote army commander Tito Okello defeated Obote's forces and took control of Kampala and the presidency. Obote fled into exile once again, but Museveni continued fighting. In August 1985, Kenyan President Daniel arap Moi chaired peace talks between Museveni and the Okello government. The parties signed an agreement in December, but Museveni did not lay down arms and his forces defeated the Okello regime a month later. Museveni was sworn in as president on January 29, 1986, and fighting came to a halt.

To consolidate power, Museveni faced pressure to include a variety of ethnic groups in his regime. Uganda was ethnically fragmented with past political instability expressed along ethnic lines. Museveni was not Muganda, that is, a member of the Baganda, the largest and wealthiest ethnic group and a formidable threat to his power. Museveni therefore needed to diffuse their ability and desire to threaten his rule. Because Obote excluded the Baganda from his regime in the 1960s and acted against their interests, they had violently challenged Obote's rule. However, Museveni had developed strong relationships with the Baganda during the war, and likely believed that he needed to maintain these relationships. To diffuse the threat the Baganda and other ethnic groups posed, Museveni prohibited opposition political parties and instituted the National Resistance Movement system. The system allowed democratic competition between candidates and participation by citizens, but it prohibited groups from organizing. Candidates could only run for public office as individuals, and everyone in theory belonged to the same party, the National Resistance Movement. The Movement system, however, was not enough to eliminate threats, particularly violent ones, to Museveni's rule. A Ugandan government spokesperson explained that, at the time, Museveni faced "a countryside full of gunmen, and a political environment pregnant with anger, mutual suspicion and vengeance. . ." (quoted in Musoke 1991).[4] As I will show in this chapter, Museveni needed to continually buy political support and strengthen his security infrastructure, and this required income.

Low Windfall

When Museveni became president, the country was in disarray. As many as 303,000 Ugandans had died from violence related to civil war between 1980 and 1986 (Lacina and Gleditsch 2005). In addition, the economy was in shambles. As a result of Amin's predatory regime and nearly a decade of civil conflict, the country's coffers were essentially bare when Museveni captured Kampala. Museveni had enough foreign exchange to cover 21 days of imports and faced a debt totaling US$2.5 billion (Dijkstra and van Donge 2001, 851;

Sharer, De Zoysa, and McDonald 1995, 19). According to Museveni's finance minister at the time, in addition to macroeconomic instability, Uganda faced:

> (a) severe shortage of supply of basic necessities like soap, cloth, housing, blankets, sugar and salt; (b) severe bottlenecks involving: shortage of transport; badly damaged roads, both trunk and feeder; malfunctioning power and water supply; lack of agricultural inputs; unutilized capacity in the industrial plants; (c) disruption of life in most parts of the country, leaving behind displaced people, orphans and widows; (d) high level of insecurity. . . (Kiyonga 1987, 1).

The government of Uganda lacked easy-to-access natural resources like oil or diamonds. The country also lacked strategic attractions for foreign donors. A former senior U.S. government official confirmed this view, "I would say that Uganda was not our highest priority by a substantial measure. . . . [O]ur reaction to Museveni was that we were going to take one step at a time and see what we think of his performance in office. We weren't involved in his coming into power, but we didn't block him either."[5] Only the British, who had colonized Uganda, offered small amounts of aid. Although Museveni had expressed Marxist sympathies, Soviet support to the developing world had waned by the early 1980s, and the Ugandan government was not able to extract any aid from the Eastern bloc.

The Ugandan economy failed to recover or generate significant government revenue under Museveni's initial economic program. Following a command-style model, the government subsidized basic commodities, promoted state-run monopolies, and bartered Ugandan goods with communist economies in Cuba, North Korea, and Yugoslavia. But inflation increased dramatically from 120% in May 1986 to 380% in May 1987, and the black market expanded (Botchwey et al. 1998, 89; Brett 1996). The bartering agreements failed, as Ugandans received old or damaged equipment from their trading partners.[6] According to a former Ugandan cabinet member, "The president would get tractors that didn't work or rusty guns. He needed cash."[7] By January 1987, the minimum wage of six dollars per month was insufficient even to pay for two pounds of meat, which sold at seven dollars on the black market (Rule 1987).

Satisfying Gatekeepers of Nonstrategic Aid

As the argument in this book would predict, Western donors were willing to offer aid to Uganda, but only if the government was in good standing with international financial institutions, and that required economic reforms. A Ugandan journalist commented in an interview that "Museveni needed cash. He went to the Eastern bloc—but didn't get anything... He then went to the OECD who said he needed to go first to the IMF and the World Bank, both of which would provide funding with conditionality and structural adjustment."[8]

As in Mozambique and Angola, the Fund and the Bank—the two prominent international financial institutions—were first on the scene to support Uganda financially in exchange for free-market economic reforms and reconstruction policies that aimed to stabilize the economy and reduce poverty. The staffs of the Fund and the Bank specifically asked Ugandan government officials to devalue the currency, remove price controls, end oil subsidies, privatize state-owned enterprises, spend only on essential activities to keep the government running, liberalize the agricultural and industrial sectors, liberalize monetary policy, and embrace donor support for reconstruction of basic services and infrastructure (Lateef 1991).

A former senior U.S. government official indicated that Museveni's standing with the Bank and the Fund was important for American aid disbursement,

> No question about it... [W]e would always make the point, that unless you get with it, with your rescheduling, your arrearages and clear them and so forth, it's not going to be possible for us to do the kinds of things [we do], and so we would point you in that direction. And if people would press back and say 'but aren't you the United States of America, the world's greatest superpower?' We would say 'Yeah, but we have a Congress, and the Congress says 'you gotta pay back...' so it was not hard for us to make that point that people had to pay attention to the IFIs... [T]he IFIs were important and of course they are important.[9]

However, Museveni and his supporters initially associated Western demands for reform with the economic disaster of the Obote regime in the early 1980s. Under Obote, the Ugandan government had agreed (but failed to implement) donor agreements calling for neoliberal economic programs. According to a former Ugandan cabinet member, "The president was in a dilemma. Does he do what [former president] Obote was doing—and risk being associated with the donors—or does he do nothing and stay cash poor? He had tried all other options."[10]

At first, Museveni appointed a strong critic of the international financial institutions to be his first minister of finance (Mugyenyi 1991, 63). But by late 1986, Museveni was essentially desperate for income and sought out the International Monetary Fund. Ugandan officials suggest that the government turned to the Fund because the government needed money. A former Ugandan cabinet member commented that, "the president convinced the cabinet through a series of meetings—where he explained and explained that we meet conditions because we needed the money."[11] Another former cabinet member similarly remarked that, "Donors could bully us with money. No one could challenge the president's political decision."[12] A Ugandan legislator stated that in the late 1980s, the government accepted conditions because "there were external pressures from donors. And there were pressures from within—such as the need for cash to make the government run. Donors were providing access to money."[13] Another legislator from that time period indicated that by complying with conditions, "[Museveni] could say to donors 'I did all you wanted, you got what you wanted, now I get what I want, which is money'."[14] A Ugandan journalist confirmed that the money at stake strongly influenced government officials' discussions on whether to accept the demands of the international financial institutions: "Anyone in the government who would have said to Museveni 'no' would have been crazy. Principled opposition to conditionality in that moment did not matter. The government was operating out of desperation."[15] Donor agencies also note the government's desperation at that time. For example, a group of independent evaluators of the Fund pointed to an internal Fund document from 1988 that "note[d] correctly of this period that 'the [Ugandan] authorities were anxious to rally the support of the donor community'" (quoted in Botchwey et al. 1998, 89).

Ugandan government officials were under explicit pressure from the Fund and the Bank to accept and comply with their policies. According to a former senior official at the Bank, it and the Fund could apply pressure because "we were the 'gatekeepers.' We were the ones who would say [to other donors] the environment is ok, so you can turn on the tap or this government is misbehaving. Squeeze it. The IMF and the Bank were playing that role [in Uganda]. . . . I could sit with Museveni and say, for example, look, if you do some outrageous things. . . there's going to be a reaction."[16]

Perhaps the most striking example of Museveni's sensitivity to the opinion of the international financial institutions was his response to a financial scandal in 1991. To address a budget deficit, the finance minister borrowed from Uganda's central bank in violation of Fund conditions and triggered an increase in inflation. The Fund staff interrupted the lending program as a result. Museveni responded vigorously to restore his standing with the Fund. He told the parliament that "inflation was indiscipline" (quoted in Dijkstra 2002, 843). He fired the finance minister and combined the Ministry of Finance with the Ministry of Planning and Economic Development. He appointed a well-known advocate of Fund programs, Emmanuel Tumusiime-Mutebile, to be permanent secretary of the new Ministry of Finance, Planning, and Economic Development.[17] On Tumusiime-Mutebile's first day in his new position, he convinced the president to adopt a cash budget system, in which "revenues collected in January would place a limit on government expenditures in February."[18] The amount of money ministries received would now depend on whether there was cash in government coffers (Therkildsen 2001). The Fund staff restarted the lending program, and Bank staff expressed enthusiasm for Uganda's prospects (Holmgren et al. 2001, 137).

As was the case for the government of Mozambique, the best available source of income at the ceasefire for the Ugandan government was aid from nonstrategic donors, and this aid appears to have depended on satisfying the staff of the international financial institutions—particularly officials of the Fund and the Bank.

Nonstrategic Aid Increased

Under apparent pressure to secure an income source, Ugandan government officials implemented the programs advocated by the international financial institutions. The strategy worked: nonstrategic donors responded with a steady flow of aid in response to Uganda's good standing with the Fund and Bank. But, as in Mozambique, maintaining nonstrategic aid flows would require continued good standing with the Bank and the Fund and achievement of donors' reconstruction goals.

World Bank officials could "turn off the tap" because they chaired the consultative group meetings where donors decided how much aid to give to Uganda. According to a former senior Bank official, "at the time... we had a reasonably good influence on the other donors, and, of course, the mechanism we used was the consultative group meetings."[19] On June 12, 1987, a senior official at the World Bank chaired a consultative group for coordinating Ugandan aid that included representatives from Britain, France, West Germany, Japan, and the United States, as well as the Fund, the African Development Bank, the European Economic Community, and the Saudi Development Bank (BBC 1987). These donors agreed to give Uganda US$533 million. The group met again in November 1988 and, according to the British Broadcasting Corporation, "The meeting reviewed progress made under Uganda's economic recovery programme and... [the] participants commended the government for its courage and persistence in restoring order and creating a bold programme of economic reform..." (BBC 1988). The group allocated an additional US$908 million to Uganda. In 1990, donors disbursed US$980 million more. The British Broadcasting Corporation said that at the 1990 meeting, "Delegates noted with satisfaction the progress in stabilising the economy over the past three years and expressed strong support for the planned programme of structural reforms" (BBC 1991). Thus, total development assistance to Uganda more than doubled between 1986 and 1990, from US$411 million to US$960 million (OECD 2012).

Post-conflict Reconstruction

The government of Uganda depended on funds from nonstrategic donors when the civil war ended in 1988. With aid funds, rehabilitation projects began in earnest throughout the country except in the north, where ongoing violence made donor access difficult. A report prepared for the United Kingdom's aid agency noted that, "as various rebel movements were 'put down' further areas of the country were opened up and accessible for government and non-government activity" (Carlson 2004, 2). The focus of donor aid during this period was, according to the World Bank, "reconstruction and rehabilitation," even if "this is not readily apparent from the project titles. . .or from some of the project documentation" (Kreimer et al. 2000, 24).

Nonstrategic donors determined the nature and target of the spending. As in Mozambique, there was little difference between donor reconstruction plans and Uganda's reconstruction strategy. Uganda's national reconstruction plans reflected donor priorities and demands.[20] A health worker from a nongovernmental organization in Uganda at that time remarked:

> Donors could do whatever they wanted in the immediate 'post'-conflict period. The government said 'yes' to EPI [Uganda National Expanded Program on Immunization], 'yes' to the rehabilitation of hospitals, 'yes' to the rehabilitation of Mulago [hospital], 'yes' to CDD [Control of Diarrheal Diseases]. There was no attempt to redirect programmes because there was no central health policy.[21]

According to a report prepared for the United Kingdom's aid agency, "UNICEF [United Nations Children's Fund] was seen as the 'alternative' Ministry of Health, due to the amount of national health policy driven by the UNICEF director" (Carlson 2004, 4).

Donors directed the spending priorities in Uganda because donors funded Uganda's budget. "Where else would ministries get money?," asked a former Ugandan cabinet member, "Our ministries needed cash for equipment. We needed road construction, school restoration, scholastic materials, hospitals, medicine."[22] Another former Ugandan official said, "every project in my budget was funded by donors."[23] The World Bank, for example, funded new railroads and telecommunications (World Bank 2012b). Germany and the United Nations funded the rehabilitation of 130 kilometers of roads and Japan offered equipment to maintain roads (Ministry of Planning and Economic Development 1990, 105). According to the 1990 report by Uganda's Ministry of Planning and Economic Development, aid workers from the United Nations, Shelter Afrique, and the Danish government's aid agency expanded low-cost housing and improved slums. The U.S. government funded new housing. Donors also funded projects to increase the availability of safe drinking water in Uganda. A large group of donors, including the United Nations and the official aid agencies of the United States, Denmark, Canada, France, India, Italy, Yugoslavia, and Germany, funded 85% of rural water projects in 1989 and 1990, while the World Bank and the African Development Bank funded 66% of urban water projects. Over two years, the projects succeeded at installing nearly 2,000 new pumps. Donors also trained Ugandans to maintain the equipment. In addition to infrastructure, donors funded communications technology and community development. As a Ugandan senior official said, "Money from donors helped greatly."[24]

Additional and substantial amounts of donor-led reconstruction also occurred "off-budget," particularly in the area of health. Off-budget expenditures refer to projects financed and implemented directly by the aid community that did not appear in Uganda's government budget. Off-budget spending occurred because Fund staff insisted on ceilings for ministry expenditures as one component of achieving macroeconomic stability. According to a former senior World Bank official,

> I remember having this conversation with Museveni, where he asked 'What can we do? We have limited resources and are under the watchful eye of the IMF' and I said I think what you need to do is. . . partner with these other informal. . . sources of support, particularly civil society, foundations and others to try to get more resources that could be channeled to addressing this issue of poverty in the social sectors.[25]

A report prepared for the UK aid agency notes "The Ministry of Health ceiling has led to a number of anomalies as some donors who wish to put more into health services turn to project aid to circumvent MOFPED [Ministry of Finance, Planning, and Economic Development] limits" (Carlson 2004, 3). Thus, spending on health provision, according to the report, "was a key element of many aid programmes, though this was not mirrored by development of national health policy. . ." (Carlson 2004, 2). Some examples of off-budget programs include UNICEF's programs to reduce child mortality; the Danish aid agency funding a program to distribute medicine; and the U.S. Agency for International Development funding family planning (Carlson 2004, 2). Regardless of whether spending on health occurred through ministry budgets or off-budget, health services reached the population at large because donors were engaged and the government faced incentives to maintain that engagement.

After significant spending on Uganda's needs, the country experienced reconstruction. Within five years of the 1988 ceasefire, per capita income had increased by 14%, expanding in rural areas by 10.5% (Heston et al. 2011; Sharer et al. 1995, 14). By 1999, agricultural output, which constituted approximately 24% of GDP in 1989, had increased by 6% annually and benefited smallholder farmers (Holmgren et al. 2001, 125). Manufacturing also grew by 13% annually between 1989 and 1999, decreasing Uganda's dependence on the agriculture sector (Holmgren et al. 2001, 125; Sharer et al. 1995).

Socioeconomic conditions improved. With donor support, full immunization rates increased by 58% between 1988 and 1995 (Botchwey et al. 1998). Between 1988 and 2000, infant mortality declined by 21% (World Bank 2012a). Some aid targeted infant mortality directly through vaccination while some targeted other attributes of reconstruction correlated with infant mortality, such as health clinics, education, clean water, and sanitation. One example is the U.S. Agency for International Development's Child Survival Project in the districts of Semuto and Butuntumula. According to project documentation, "[The goal] was to improve the health of the people, particularly those under 5 years of age, and pregnant women in Semuto and Butuntumula. . . through sustainable community based strategies in health and child welfare" (Okoth and Subin 1995, 1). Aid workers created and trained community health groups, recruited and trained community health workers, offered vaccinations and oral rehydration treatments, and offered mosquito bed nets and family planning services. By 1995, 45.5% of children younger than one year of age in the target districts received essential vaccinations, representing a 24% increase since 1993 when the project began, 52.3% of cholera cases were receiving oral rehydration therapies, a 39.4% increase since 1993, and 38.1% were aware of the importance of bed nets for malaria prevention, an increase from 9% in 1993 (Okoth and Subin 1995, 6).

As in Mozambique, a puzzling aspect of Uganda's reconstruction is that it occurred even though the country complied with demands for structural adjustment. As I have said, critics argued by the late 1980s that those structural changes were insensitive to the needs of the poor because they emphasized a lean state and cut government spending on health and education (Cornia et al. 1987). Perhaps if the international financial institutions had promoted spending on the social sectors in Uganda, reconstruction spending (and subsequent reconstruction) might have been greater. If structural adjustment indeed inhibits reconstruction spending, Uganda's reconstruction might have been even stronger had structural adjustment not been part of donor demands. But it is also plausible that the amount of reconstruction spending would have remained the same, with more of it "on-budget" and less "off-budget."

Why did the Ugandan government go to great lengths to comply with donor reconstruction objectives? Why did government officials not siphon away much of the aid that donors brought into Uganda for reconstruction, as the "aid curse" notion expects, particularly those governing weak states, will do? Why did the government under Museveni choose to foster reconstruction in the late 1980s and early 1990s? In the next section, a close look at the case reveals that nonstrategic aid helped the government consolidate power. Specifically, nonstrategic aid appears to have helped Museveni consolidate power by allowing him to do two things: increase internal security and increase payoffs to supporters and potential rivals. Thus, Museveni faced strong incentives to meet donor reconstruction goals in order to secure aid flows that could help him consolidate power.

Power Consolidation

In 1986, within days of capturing Kampala and becoming president, Museveni restored order to the city. According to a senior Ugandan official at the time, "There was no more popcorn, no more shots heard at night" there.[26] Similarly, a former Ugandan cabinet member remarked:

> [Museveni] became president on a Sunday. On that Monday night, he called on us to meet with him at his house. Our meeting lasted

past midnight. During the night, two shots were fired. Each time, he picked up the phone and called someone to find out who. I was shocked by this: there were always many shots in Kampala. Now there was a shot and he could call and ask who? When the meeting was over, we were concerned about getting home safely. The president said it would be ok, but we insisted on escorts, and he provided them. Thursday night of that week, we came over again to meet with him. That night, we forgot to ask for an escort.[27]

This sense of security was short-lived. Within months, Museveni's rule came under threat, even in Kampala.[28] Facing these threats, Museveni needed resources he could access quickly and easily to strengthen his regime's defenses. "Otherwise," according to a Ugandan journalist, "someone would have replaced him."[29] A former Ugandan cabinet member said, "For two years, there was a decline in money to run anything. . . . Where was money for defense going to come from? How do we survive and minimize enemies?"[30] According to another former cabinet member, "It was imperative to have resources in order to have government. At the very least, roads, equipment, and military funding was needed for security, and to make up for bad equipment."[31] While my argument focuses on threats to the leader from within the state apparatus, Museveni faced threats both inside and outside the state apparatus.

But the Ugandan government lacked easy-to-access natural resources, the economy was too poor to offer significant tax revenue, and Uganda had no strategic importance to market in exchange for aid. Thus, the only plausible option was nonstrategic aid. After signing agreements with international financial institutions in May 1987, the government received large amounts of aid. The influx of money appears to have allowed the government to finance ongoing expenses for security infrastructure.

While nonstrategic aid did not include large-scale military assistance, it funded policing and other aspects of domestic security, aid that essentially allows a government to spend more on internal security by freeing up money from other areas (Feyzioglu, Swaroop, and Zhu 1998; Pack and Pack 1993). As a former senior Ugandan official said, "once money came into the country, the president could do anything he wants with it. And the money could go to military expenditures, to president's office expenditures and to state house [official residence of the president] expenditures."[32] According to a Ugandan journalist, "Donors didn't question what the government did with the money—so long as [the government] did something with it. You implement primary education, you make donors happy, you make the public happy, and then you get the money that oils the machinery that helps you keep power."[33]

Museveni's government publicly announced that a large portion of its federal budget would be used for security expenditures. The finance minister, Crispus Kiyonga, explained this decision in a budget forecast he delivered to the parliament on July 24, 1987: "The National Resistance Army is still a new army which needs to be fully equipped in order to increase its operational capacity and also to ensure that it will promptly and effectively deal with any future threats to the security of the country. It is therefore necessary to devote relatively more resources in the security area" (Kiyonga 1987, 11).

Museveni thus increased the size of military from between 5,000 and 14,000 soldiers in 1986 to between 70,000 and 100,000 by 1992 (Economist Intelligence Unit 1993, 8; Tripp 2010, 147). Although those who fought alongside Museveni in the early 1980s remained leaders of the government's military, the rank and file largely consisted of the various rebel groups that the government incorporated (Tripp 2010, 52). A 1987 amnesty offer, for example, prompted 40,000 rebels and soldiers from previous regimes to join Museveni's army (Tripp 2010, 140). As a Ugandan journalist said, Museveni "could rule using carrots and sticks. He would cripple the rebels then integrate them through cooptation. Aid made this process possible."[34] The government's overwhelming military strength—based on aid—allowed it to strengthen the security infrastructure and offer peace throughout most of the country for the first time in decades.

Even donors who typically resist using aid for security expenditures accepted government officials' reasoning that they would be unable to meet donor reconstruction goals without establishing security first. A team of independent external evaluators for the Fund remarked on the expansion of the military: "By 1987, the government had gained widespread support for restoring peace to the country, and although isolated cases of fighting still continued, the policy of amnesty to the vanquished forces had brought about a great deal of reconciliation and improved the security situation, even if it had to bear the cost of a vastly increased army..." (Botchwey et al. 1998, 89).

In addition to using nonstrategic aid to strengthen internal security, Museveni could use it to buy and maintain political support. From the moment that he seized the capital, he appears to have focused on building coalitions. In his first cabinet in 1986, ten out of thirty-three ministers belonged to the rival Democratic Party, two belonged to the Ugandan People's Congress, and three were leaders of rebel armies (Kampala New Vision 2007; Tripp 2010, 48–9).

With nonstrategic aid inflows, the Ugandan government was also able to fund a large cabinet that could hold opposition leadership (Khadiagala 1995; Langseth et al. 1995). That is, to consolidate power, Museveni brought rivals (e.g., opposition politicians, rebel leaders) into the government where continued co-optation was feasible. Supported by aid, the cabinet grew from thirty-three members in 1986 to forty-four by 1990, and continued to grow (Mwenda and Tangri 2005, 459).[35] Museveni explained in 1988: "The groups which are threatening me would bring me a list of twenty bad people, and in order to preserve peace, I would have to choose two or three of the least bad of them [to serve in the government]" (quoted in Kiyaga-Nsubuga 2004, 106, fn 7). A member of the Democratic Party described Museveni's strategy of coalition building: "[Former president] Obote wanted to kill parties by violence. Museveni, being a tactician, wants to kill them by kindness—giving us ministerial posts" (quoted in Rwegayura 1992).

Not all combatants chose to take advantage of the amnesties or offers of integration into the government. The majority of those who rejected the government's offer belonged to the Holy Spirit Movement or to the Ugandan People's Democratic Army (formerly Ugandan National Liberation Army). The remnants from these groups joined a new group from the Acholi region of northern Uganda, the Lord's Resistance Army (LRA), under Joseph Kony. This rebel group has largely fled from northern Uganda into neighboring countries as of this writing. Kony's goals remain unclear, but he appears to favor turning the Ugandan government into a theocracy guided by apocalyptic Christianity and tribal traditions.

Why did the Ugandan government not succeed at buying out Kony or crushing the LRA rebels with its increasing military strength in the early 1990s? This is a complicated question, but there appear to be four ways in which the LRA differed from the other rebel groups. First, the LRA consisted of those who rejected Museveni's first amnesty offer. Those who joined Kony were therefore less likely to accept Museveni's subsequent offers than members of other rebel groups. Second, unlike other rebel leaders, Kony received substantial material support from Sudan, including bases for his operations. Sudanese support transformed Kony's force from "a motley group of rebels into a coherent, well-supplied, military enterprise" (Van Acker 2004, 338). Third, the LRA involves cult ideology. The ideology appears to help Kony compel LRA rebels to reject material benefits from the government. LRA rebels come to view Museveni as "Satan" and Museveni's agenda as "impure" (Titeca 2010, 66). Fourth, since the early 1990s, Museveni appears to use the war against Kony to justify continually using nonstrategic aid for defense. As journalist Andrew Mwenda said, "[The war] provided [Museveni] with an important justification for increasing the defence budget" (Mwenda 2010, 50).[36] Thus, paradoxically, maintaining the low-intensity war against the LRA may serve Museveni's interests in obtaining funds to bolster internal security for coup proofing. A final possibility is that Museveni's commanders directly benefit from the war, eliminating their incentive to end the conflict. Top commanders of Museveni's army have been accused of stealing funds directed at the conflict by inventing "ghost soldiers" or even selling weapons to LRA rebels (Tripp 2010, 170).

Museveni was successful at eliminating threats to his rule despite the LRA's resistance. During the first five years of his rule, Museveni expanded the security infrastructure, incorporated more than half-a-dozen rebel groups into the National Resistance Army, and granted cabinet posts to opposition leaders, which combined to help him consolidate power. This process of strengthening security and buying out the opposition appears to have been made possible by nonstrategic aid.

Striking it Rich: Newfound Natural Resources and Strategic Importance

In the mid-1990s, Ugandan soldiers apparently began looting diamond, gold, and other mineral wealth from the collapsed Democratic Republic of the Congo (Reno 2002; Tripp 2010, 174; United Nations 2002). Between 1995 and 1997, Uganda's gold exports increased from US$15.89 million to US$133.8 million, making gold Uganda's second-leading export after coffee (Reno 2002, 424). As Will Reno points out, this occurred despite the fact that Uganda itself contains little gold. Then, in 2003, Uganda discovered oil deposits in the Lake Albert region of Western Uganda, near the Congo. By 2007, all twelve drills in the country were successful, and conservative estimates indicated that 500 million barrels had been discovered (some estimate as much as 2.5 billion barrels) (Vokes 2012). Uganda is expected to produce 200,000 barrels per day, equivalent to Chad, and generate US$1.7 billion annually. Many foreign companies have applied to the Ugandan government for exploration rights. Meanwhile, corruption scandals have widened in the country, as the prime minister, other ministers, and other senior Ugandan politicians have been accused of receiving millions of U.S. dollars in bribes from oil companies (Vokes 2012). According to data from the International Country Risk Guide, governmental corruption in Uganda increased in 1996, returning to pre-1988 levels, and has remained at the same high level through 2007 (the last year with available data) (Political Risk Services Group 2007). As the nongovernmental organization Global Witness said, "the risk of the resource curse phenomenon taking hold in Uganda cannot be ignored" (quoted in Kron 2011).

In addition, after 2001, Uganda became strategically important to the U.S. government in its War on Terror. In December 2001, the U.S. government declared the LRA a terrorist organization and offered funds to help the Ugandan government protect the population from the threat posed by the rebel group. Strategic aid continued to pour into Uganda to advance U.S. interests against Sudan, which was on the U.S. list of state sponsors of terror; to support the U.S.-backed government in Somalia; to fight against al-Shabaab, the al-Qaeda cell in Somalia; and to generally counteract al-Qaeda activities in east Africa. Because Uganda became strategically important to donors, particularly the U.S. government, aid increased by 27% from 2001 to 2009 (and by 58% since 1995) even as the Ugandan government let its commitment to nonstrategic donor goals slip (OECD 2012).

As windfall income increased, the government of Uganda appears to have become less concerned with nonstrategic donor priorities and developed an adversarial relationship with nonstrategic donors (Branch 2011). By 2004, World Bank consultants noted that "The achievements of the first decade of the Museveni regime have been steadily eroded..." (quoted in New Times 2005). Ugandan journalist Andrew Mwenda similarly noted that "the government's liberalization drive...has waned" (Mwenda 2006, 7).

By the mid-2000s, Museveni appeared willing to forego some nonstrategic aid. Specifically, Museveni resisted calls for term limits, creating concern among nonstrategic donors (Girod et al. 2009). In 1995, Uganda's government issued a constitution that set term limits for the presidency, and under its provisions, Museveni could not run for office after the 2001 election. But in 2003, his party began advocating for an amendment to the constitution to allow the president to run indefinitely (Barkan et al. 2004; Tangri 2006).

Nonstrategic donors threatened to cut aid if parliament repealed term limits, but Museveni persisted, and on July 12, 2005, Uganda's parliament eliminated the limits. In response, Norway immediately cut one-third of its budget-support aid to Uganda, explaining, "The reason for the cuts is a growing awareness related to the negative development in the Ugandan government's handling of democracy, human rights and the fight against corruption" (quoted in Mutumba 2005). Other nonstrategic donors followed. By the time of the election, nonstrategic donors had withheld anywhere from 5% to 60% of their budget-support assistance (Girod et al. 2009). The fact that the Ugandan government's commitment to the agenda of nonstrategic donors changed after Uganda acquired windfall income suggests that changes in a government's resource base alter the government's will to invest in reconstruction.

Since the government's commitment to donors' development agenda began to decline, the rate of change in infant mortality flattened. While the annual percent change in infant mortality improved by 0.16% on average between 1988 and 2000, it worsened between 2001 and 2009, slightly increasing by 0.01% on average (World Bank 2012a).

Some might argue that natural resources and strategic importance did not change the government's incentive structure. Instead, they might say that the government's change is consistent with the "aid curse" and that in an environment of weak institutions, aid must have fostered corruption and hindered reconstruction. Museveni, in other words, might have started out as a good leader, but aid flows may have allowed him to create patronage networks that undermined the progress of his early years in office.

Changes in the Uganan government's access to natural resources and strategic aid, however, do seem to explain reconstruction outcomes in Uganda better than sheer increases in any aid do. The government experienced enormous aid increases during Museveni's early years, as well as after the mid-1990s. But as noted earlier, corruption declined during Museveni's early years, and then increased after windfall was discovered. The aid curse cannot account for this variation. The case study of Uganda thus appears to support this book's argument by demonstrating that the aid curse does emerge in countries with weak institutions, but only under certain circumstances. Aid appears to stop being effective in Uganda once the government was no longer desperate for income, when the government obtained access to windfall from natural resources and strategic importance to donors.

Was it Good Leadership?

Another way to explain the reconstruction in Uganda is to say that Museveni was an exceptionally skillful leader and keenly dedicated to improving living conditions in his country (Khadiagala 1995; Ng'ethe 1995). That is, even if the right structural conditions are in place for coup-proofing and reconstruction spending via nonstrategic aid, a good leader may be needed to identify an opportunity, convince other politicians and the public of the right course of action, and then implement the plan. Indeed, Museveni was able to overthrow the Ugandan government with a disciplined military effort that relied on no outside help (Weinstein 2006). Regarding Museveni's rebel group, a senior member of the rival Democratic Party commented that "part of what was remarkable was the civility of the soldiers. Where did that come from? There was a lot of discussion about becoming a different kind of army, about having a different attitude."[37] Before becoming president, Museveni drafted a Ten-Point Program that called for reconstruction, human rights protection, and transparency. According to the senior member of the Democratic Party, "It seemed that soldiers knew the plan well while in the bush."[38] So, was leadership or income structure the key to Museveni's reconstruction spending?

After all, Obote led the same country, with the same low levels of strategic importance and resource rents, and he also became president after a civil war. Although Obote's government complied with several macroeconomic conditions that the international financial institutions required, Obote (unlike Museveni) failed to convince the international community that he was committed to reconstruction. Within a year after Obote's rule began, donors were already concerned with rampant corruption in Uganda, as well as looting and physical insecurity. As a British diplomat said, "When you give five Land-Rovers to an emergency food program, and a week later you see. . . soldiers tearing around town in them, how can you think seriously about bringing in a mountain of money?" (quoted in Jaynes 1981). During a two-week period in 1981, diplomats and aid workers lost 23 vehicles (Worrall 1981). Over time, indiscipline and corruption by soldiers became extreme and Obote appears to have done little to assuage donor concerns (Brittain 1985). Western donors were disenchanted with Obote's government and offered less than half of what the government received during Museveni's first five years in office (OECD 2012).

Initially, Museveni appears to have governed more responsibly than Obote, investing more in basic services than Obote. Obote's government ultimately received less foreign aid than Museveni's government and was subsequently less capable of coup-proofing the regime. Clearly, the fact that bad leaders may underperform supports this book's argument.

Crucially, though, the Ugandan government under Museveni seems to have behaved differently under different circumstances of windfall. Assuming that leadership qualities and preferences stay reasonably constant, a leader should remain a "good" leader even in the presence of windfall income. Although Museveni's leadership style may have had a role in the early successes of his presidency, his style appears to have been unable to satisfy donors after the Ugandan government gained access to windfall in the 1990s. As a director of an aid organization said, "The Museveni of the 1980s would not recognize the Museveni of 2005. They would fight each other. He has done a complete turnaround."[39]

Museveni's "turnaround" makes it hard to interpret Uganda's story as a story about leadership quality. Without the right conditions, even good leadership is unlikely to be good enough. In other words, what drives reconstruction may not be the quality of leadership but rather the income structure.

Summary

Uganda emerged from civil war in the mid-1980s with empty state coffers and little capacity to produce revenues. The aid curse predicts that aid should not have helped the country because its institutions were so weak. But the government met donor reconstruction objectives and subsequently managed to reconstruct the country. Museveni's strong leadership—an alternative explanation for Uganda's positive reconstruction outcomes—does not appear to account well for the Ugandan experience because the Ugandan government became less successful at meeting donor reconstruction goals as Uganda's income sources changed, even though Museveni remained president during both periods.

The case of Uganda therefore supports this book's argument that leaders with low windfall choose to spend aid on reconstruction following civil war because they desperately need continued income from nonstrategic aid to sustain the government. By securing a steady source of revenue from nonstrategic donors in the early years of his rule, the government of Uganda was able to strengthen defense and buy political support. This likely enabled Museveni to prevent any coups. Nonstrategic donors were willing to accept security improvements and payoffs to elites. Like the cases of Mozambique and Angola, the case of Uganda suggests that senior government officials were aware of these relationships.

7

Improving Aid Effectiveness after Civil War

THE ARGUMENT THAT I have developed to explain differences in post-conflict reconstruction emphasizes the incentives that different sources of government income create. Because the governments of post-conflict Uganda and Mozambique lacked windfall income from resource rents or strategic aid, they faced strong incentives to accept nonstrategic aid in exchange for carrying out reconstruction projects. They appear to have agreed to spend much of the aid on reconstruction because the alternative was a government with very little income. In contrast, post-conflict leaders with windfall income face a different calculus. For them, what they would gain by implementing aid agreements appears not to be worth the loss of budgetary control.

These incentives imply the two linked hypotheses that predict the conditions under which aid fosters reconstruction and the mechanism by which that happens. To reiterate, my nonstrategic-desperation hypothesis argues that states emerging from civil war use aid effectively to bring about reconstruction when these states lack windfall income. My low-windfall coup-proofing hypothesis explains this trend by arguing that leaders in low-windfall states implement the aid agreements because doing so reduces their risk of coup.

In other words, reconstruction occurs as a by-product of leaders seeking to promote the survival of their regimes. I have used data on socioeconomic reconstruction and on coups and offered three case studies of countries with varying income sources to demonstrate when and why foreign aid indeed fosters post-conflict reconstruction in countries that meet one specific criterion: lack of windfall income.

These findings have important policy implications for donors. The fundamental argument of this book is that countries with low windfall face incentives to direct aid toward reconstruction projects following civil war. In particular, aid only appears to foster reconstruction in these low-windfall countries when they are accountable to donors who are primarily interested in reconstruction. Paradoxically, these are the cases where donors have the least at stake. The findings presented here also point to the complementary conclusion that donors seeking to foster reconstruction after civil war cannot reasonably expect to succeed in strategically important or resource-rich countries because the incentives are not compatible with meeting donor reconstruction objectives.

While the findings appear to be robust, I decided to examine them further against additional cases. I begin this concluding chapter by presenting five additional low-windfall governments that brought about successful socioeconomic reconstruction with nonstrategic aid. By adding these cases, I don't have to rely on Mozambique and Uganda alone to support the argument. I then present five exceptional cases, cases that do not fit the argument in this book. Two lacked windfall but failed to bring about reconstruction of their states. The three additional cases each possessed a wealth of windfall income but managed successful socioeconomic reconstruction. The dynamics of these cases reveal my argument's limitations.

The three cases of high windfall yet successful socioeconomic reconstruction let me answer the question of whether there is any hope for post-conflict countries with high windfall. I also examine the strategies donors have recently employed in high windfall countries to improve reconstruction. Unfortunately, existing policies have yet to counter the curse of windfall income. I conclude the chapter by discussing the lessons this research holds for donors seeking to support reconstruction and avenues for future research.

Supportive Cases

The following are the success stories of five additional post-conflict, low-windfall countries, all of which qualify as Phoenix States. All their governments managed to bring about socioeconomic reconstruction in spite of weak institutions and reliance on aid. In all cases, their aid was nonstrategic.

El Salvador

El Salvador lacked windfall after its civil war ended in 1992.[1] Backed by the United States, the army and paramilitary death squads fought rebels seeking to address longstanding inequality (Wood 2001, 869). Civil war ended with intervention by the United Nations, which facilitated a peace accord between the parties (Stanley and Holiday 1997). At the ceasefire, El Salvador lacked access to rents from natural resources that take little labor or capital to extract. And with the end of the Cold War, the country lost much of its strategic importance to the United States (Wood 2001, 869). El Salvador therefore was desperate for income after its civil war ended.

The post-conflict reconstruction tasks were daunting in part because the decade-long war had been significantly destructive, with over 75,000 Salvadoran casualties (Karl 1992, 147), one-quarter of the population displaced, and a loss of over US$2.2 billion in infrastructure. In addition, much governmental spending during the war had focused on the military rather than on social services (del Castillo 2001, 1972; Karl 1992, 150–51).

Because the government was desperate for income, the international community had leverage. Much like the governments of Mozambique and Uganda, the government of El Salvador exceeded the expectations of the international financial institutions as it brought about macroeconomic stability and designed plans to reconstruct the country (del Castillo 2001, 1975–76; Stanley and Holiday 1997). Donors eagerly financed Salvadoran president Alfredo Cristiani's reconstruction efforts (Wood 2001, 883–84), disbursing US$5 billion in the ten years following the end of the war (OECD 2012). With foreign aid, the government rehabilitated national infrastructure, redistributed land to peasants, invested in human capacity, provided social services, reintegrated combatants, and promoted economic growth (del Castillo 2001).

Guatemala

As in El Salvador, the Guatemalan government lacked windfall income from natural resources or strategic aid when civil war ended in 1996, after 36 years of fighting.[2] Also as in El Salvador, before the civil war, the right-wing Guatemalan government targeted left-wing and centrist groups, giving rise to rebellion (Carothers 1991, 58–59; Economist Intelligence Unit 2006, 5). The civil war was also heavily destructive, with more than 200,000 people killed and approximately 400,000 displaced (United Nations Development Program 2009, 6).

Following the war, President Alvaro Arzú Irigoyen launched socioeconomic reconstruction initiatives financed by international assistance (Economist Intelligence Unit 2006, 5). In the ten years following civil war, Guatemala received US$4.3 billion for reconstruction (OECD 2012). Desperate for income, the Guatemalan government implemented reconstruction programs, some of which reached the population at large, and began to improve human development throughout the impoverished country (United Nations Development Program 2009; World Bank 2009a). Specifically, in cooperation with donors, the government increased social-sector expenditures by 60% between 1996 and 2000 (World Bank 2009a, xi), and in the next six years, poverty declined by 5% while net enrollment in primary education increased by 11.2% and in secondary education by 6.5% (World Bank 2009a, vii and xii). Meanwhile, per capita income and life expectancy increased (World Bank 2009a, ix).

Bosnia

Bosnia also lacked windfall income when its civil war ended in 1995 because it lacked both strategic importance to donors and natural resource wealth (Pugh, Cooper, and Goodhand 2004, 143).[3] The civil war had caused significant loss of human and physical capital. Ethnic cleansing was a common strategy as Bosnian Muslims, Croats, and Serbs tried to control territory during the war (Economist Intelligence Unit 2005, 4–5). Fighting ended when Bosnian Muslims and Croats joined forces and, with backing from the United States and the North Atlantic Treaty Organization, defeated the Bosnian Serbs.

External actors directly implemented reconstruction efforts in Bosnia—offering US$11.2 billion in the ten years following the war

(OECD 2012). Some of the external actors included the United Nations, the Organization for Security and Cooperation in Europe, the European Union, the IMF, the World Bank, and nongovernmental organizations (Pugh 2002, 467). Because the country lacked windfall, it depended heavily on these external actors for financial support (Götze 2004, 671). As was the case in Mozambique, Uganda, El Salvador, and Guatemala, local actors in Bosnia lacked leverage in deciding how to spend the aid money (Economist Intelligence Unit 2005, 17). International assistance financed reconstruction efforts throughout the country, including the rehabilitation of infrastructure destroyed during the war, such as the rail network, roads, telecommunications, and electricity (Economist Intelligence Unit 2005, 24–26 and 33).

Rwanda

Rwanda also emerged resource poor following the civil war that ended in 1994.[4] The war was extremely destructive, involving the genocide of up to one million people and the internal displacement of another million. Two million left the country as refugees (Economist Intelligence Unit 2004, 11; Obidegwu 2003, 1). As a result of the war, GDP and government revenues collapsed while inflation soared (Obidegwu 2003, 10). The war ended when rebels decisively captured Rwanda's capital, Kigali.

Lacking strategic importance to donors or rents from natural resources, the post-conflict government was desperate for income (Prunier 1995, 327–328). As a World Bank economist put it, "Rwanda's economic recovery depended on the generosity of external assistance" (Obidegwu 2003, 10). The international community offered large amounts of money for reconstruction (US$6.3 billion in the ten years following the war) in part because the government agreed to implement policies regarding good governance, poverty reduction, trade, privatization, and investment (OECD 2012; Obidegwu 2003, 39–40). Dependent on this nonstrategic aid, the government used much of it to rebuild the country, and the socioeconomic reconstruction has been astonishing. According to the Bank economist, the government of Rwanda "resettled over 3 million people displaced by the genocide, re-established peace, law and order within its territory, rehabilitated social and economic infrastructure, restored economic stability and revived economic growth. Poverty has been gradually reduced" (Obidegwu 2003, 39).

Cambodia

Finally, Cambodia represents another case consistent with my argument.[5] The country's political instability ended with a coup that brought Hun Sen to power in 1997. The coup was preceded by decades of civil war between rebels fighting a communist government that had toppled the Khmer Rouge regime in the late 1970s (Gottesman 2003). The war originally ended in 1992 when the United Nations intervened with a multidimensional peacekeeping operation, which supported the national elections that occurred the following year. However, the elections failed to keep long-term peace (Economist Intelligence Unit 2008a, 5).

The international community responded to the 1997 coup by withdrawing support for the government (Economist Intelligence Unit 2008a, 5; Hendrickson 2001, 103). Meanwhile, the country remained extremely underdeveloped with much of the infrastructure in disrepair after decades of political violence (Economist Intelligence Unit 2008a, 12). Desperate for income, Cambodia permitted national elections in order to reassert the government's legitimacy and restart foreign aid (Economist Intelligence Unit 2009a, 5). The government also complied with conditions specified by the IMF and the World Bank (World Bank 2009b, i). With foreign aid constituting nearly half of the national budget by 2005, the government quickly became dependent on that aid and spent it to satisfy some donor goals (Chanboreth and Hach 2008, 3). Specifically, reconstruction efforts have benefited transportation infrastructure, telecommunications, and the construction sector (Economist Intelligence Unit 2008a, 3, 13, and 17). The government has also increased manufacturing and improved social service provision (World Bank 2009b, i). Meanwhile, Cambodia experienced solid economic growth and broad-based development between 1997 and 2009, with per capita income soaring by 96% and infant mortality declining by 52% (Heston et al. 2011; World Bank 2012a).

These five cases from different regions indicate that the pattern I presented with statistics and examined with regard to Mozambique and Uganda can also explain the dynamics in a number of other low-windfall post-conflict countries.

Exceptional Cases with Low Windfall

Counting Mozambique, Uganda, and the five additional countries discussed here, I evaluated 35 low-windfall countries (across 372 country years) that experienced civil war during the last four decades. While 75% of low-windfall countries with high levels of nonstrategic aid realized socioeconomic reconstruction and so support my argument, 25% fell short of expectations and failed to bring about socioeconomic reconstruction. These cases are not the norm, and the quantitative results across a large sample in Chapters 3 and 4 support the argument of this book. But because these cases challenge the argument, I have examined them in order to assess what might be missing from the analysis offered here.

Equatorial Guinea

Armed conflict erupted in Equatorial Guinea as a result of the extreme brutality of the country's dictator, Francisco Macias Nguema Biyogo.[6] Nguema became dictator when the country achieved independence from Spain in 1968. He promptly centralized power, looted national coffers, and assaulted, killed, or expelled much of the opposition, including ethnic groups outside his Esangui clan (Economist Intelligence Unit 1997a, 31 and 34). Estimates indicate that between 25% and 50% of the population fled, were exiled, or were killed (Economist Intelligence Unit 1997a, 34; McSherry 2006, 25). Meanwhile, Spanish and Nigerian expatriates fled, which halted cocoa production and resulted in a steep decline in GDP (McSherry 2006, 25). Armed conflict between Nguema and his nephew, Teodoro Obiang Nguema M'basogo, ended when Obiang overthrew Nguema in 1979 (Klitgaard 1990, 20).

When Obiang's rule began, Equatorial Guinea lacked windfall income from natural resources or strategic aid. Yet, the government failed to dramatically improve socioeconomic conditions. Instead, Obiang appears to have maintained the same patronage system as his uncle, which gave his family control over all governmental institutions and allowed them to enrich themselves (Economist Intelligence Unit 1997a, 34). Thus, even if the government lacked access to windfall income, country experts describe the regime as "lacking in domestic political will and therefore not very successful" at rehabilitating the economy (Economist Intelligence Unit 1997a, 40). Unlike Mozambique, Uganda, and the five supportive cases discussed earlier, the Obiang government chose not to take steps to open the gates to large amounts of nonstrategic aid.

Why did the government of Equatorial Guinea forego opportunities to reconstruct the state? The government appeared to lack capacity to implement reconstruction efforts, but then so did many other governments examined in this book. A more compelling explanation is that the country's leadership relied on illicit money and was therefore not desperate for income from the international community. Instead, the country became a "classic criminal state" where elites obtained rents from "toxic waste dumping, drug trafficking, pirate fishing, arms and aircraft smuggling, and forced labor of children" (McSherry 2006, 25). With illicit money, a shadow form of windfall income, the government lacked incentives to comply with aid agreements and potentially lose access to this wealth.

Haiti

As was the case with Equatorial Guinea, Haiti lacked natural resource wealth and strategic importance following the political instability and coup that ousted Jean-Bertrand Aristide in 1991.[7] Also as in Equatorial Guinea, Haiti failed to bring about socioeconomic reconstruction. Throughout the 1990s and 2000s, Haitian physical infrastructure remained in collapse (Economist Intelligence Unit 2001, 44; Farmer 1994). Human capital was depleted and the economy was one of the poorest in the Western hemisphere, with high rates of infant mortality, much of the population malnourished, and the health care infrastructure in poor condition (Economist Intelligence Unit 2001, 42–43).

A main reason for Haiti's inability to invest in reconstruction with nonstrategic aid is that political instability and a lack of leadership have persisted. As was the case in Cambodia, the West disapproved of the coup in 1991 and cut foreign aid (Dupuy 1997; Economist Intelligence Unit 2001, 39). But even as foreign aid began to become available again in the 1990s, instability continued to break out, making it difficult to implement any aid program or reconstruction effort.

Thus, the cases of Equatorial Guinea and Haiti demonstrate reasons that certain cases fail to fit the argument proposed in this book. In Equatorial Guinea, contraband and other illicit activities essentially created a form of windfall income, such that the government was actually relatively rich in windfall income during the 1980s, even if that wealth did not come through legal exports of natural resources. Haiti appears to have struggled to implement reconstruction initiatives because severe instability (even if not all-out war) continued to inhibit these efforts. Other low-windfall governments that appear inconsistent with the argument of this book (perhaps Somalia after 2006) may also be rich in windfall from illicit networks or may confront sufficient instability that hinders reconstruction activities. These cases add nuance to my argument, emphasize the crucial role of political stability in reconstruction, and show that illicit activity can be a form of shadow windfall income. Windfall income from illicit activities may provide the same disincentives towards post-conflict reconstruction as windfall income from natural resources or from strategic aid.

Exceptional Cases with High Windfall

Cases of successful socioeconomic reconstruction in spite of high windfall can show us how these countries' leaders overcame disincentives for reconstruction. Those that succeeded potentially provide policy lessons, and to discern those lessons, I consider three cases: Oman after 1975, Azerbaijan after 1994, and Liberia after 2003.

Oman

A separatist, communist insurgency in the poverty-stricken southern Dhofar province of Oman ended in 1975, after twelve years of civil war (Gardiner 2006; Hughes 2009; Peterson 2007).[8] By 1970, the rebels controlled most of Dhofar (DeVore 2012, 149–50). But the British intervened by leading local groups in a counterinsurgency campaign that also involved spending on development (DeVore 2012, 144–45).

At the time, Oman possessed large amounts of oil wealth and the government was strategically important to the British, which resulted in a total windfall of US$5089.87 per capita in 1975. Located on the Persian Gulf, Oman offered the British access to India by sea. The British thus held the country as a protectorate and maintained significant influence over its government after granting Oman full independence in 1951 (O'Reilly 1998, 72). With British help, Sultan Qaboos bin Said took power from his father, Sultan Said bin Taimur, in a bloodless 1970 coup and ultimately fought (and ended) the southern insurgency. The British backed the coup in the first place because they blamed Sultan Said bin Taimur for refusing to promote development that promised to end the insurgency (DeVore 2012, 150–51).

In spite of the windfall income available to the government, Sultan Qaboos continued to promote socioeconomic reconstruction after the civil war ended (Owtram 2008, 97–142). Indeed, the Sultan is widely viewed as a leader with a vision for socioeconomic reconstruction (O'Reilly 1998, 71). Consistent with British logic at the time, the Sultan appears to have believed that by rebuilding physical infrastructure and strengthening state capacity, he would not only help end the insurgency but also obtain popularity throughout the country (Looney 2009, 4–5). Oman's reconstruction following the war was extraordinary, especially given the regime could have opted to extract windfall revenues for patronage and security while ignoring citizens' needs. Instead, the government invested in improving its own efficiency; distributing revenues across the country; giving impoverished regions a greater share; rehabilitating and expanding the country's physical and human capital; expanding sectors unrelated to oil, including (for example) manufacturing and agriculture; and promoting the private sector (Looney 2009, 5–6).

The case of Oman thus raises good leadership (discussed in the cases of Mozambique and Uganda) as a plausible explanation for reconstruction success. While we earlier concluded that good leadership in high-windfall countries appears to be insufficient for reconstruction efforts, in the case of resource-rich Oman, good leadership was aligned with British strategic interests and local stability. If the Sultan had been able to maintain stability and security without investing in reconstruction, he may have been able to get away with keeping more of the rents for his private use while maintaining British strategic support. Another lesson from this case is that external actors may succeed at turning development into part of the strategic-importance agenda, particularly when development is clearly linked to stability. The fact that the British withdrew support from the previous Sultan who refused to invest in development may have pressured Sultan Qaboos to promote reconstruction efforts. Thus, a lesson that emerges out of this case is that external actors might succeed at development in resource-rich states where they back a leader who values socioeconomic development or if they can somehow credibly commit to withdraw aid if agreements are not met.

Azerbaijan

Azerbaijan represents another case of surprisingly successful reconstruction in an oil-rich state.[9] As in Oman, Azerbaijan's war was confined to a specific disputed area of the country, Nagorny Karabakh. The main parties to the war over the territory (which is majority ethnic Armenian), included the government of Azerbaijan versus ethnic Armenian separatists and the Armenian Army (Economist Intelligence Unit 2008b, 5–6). The war displaced approximately 10% of Azerbaijan's population and generated 800,000 refugees (Economist Intelligence Unit 2008b, 6). It also affected Azerbaijan's economy, as the agriculture and industrial sectors suffered declines (Economist Intelligence Unit 1997b, 50).

As in Oman, Azerbaijan after its 1994 ceasefire possessed significant oil and gas wealth and strategic importance to Western powers, all of which added up to a total windfall of US$204 per capita. Azerbaijan was strategically important to the United States because it bordered Iran, cooperated in anti-terrorism activities, and allowed the United States rights to fly over the central Asian territory to fight in Afghanistan (Economist Intelligence Unit 2008b, 16).

Also as in Oman, the government of Heydar Aliyev (and that of his son, who succeeded him in 2003) fostered economic reconstruction. The government promoted macroeconomic stability and economic diversification, especially by investing in the services sector (Economist Intelligence Unit 2008b, 29; World Bank 2003, 1). Meanwhile, windfall income was used to promote physical and human capacity throughout the country. The UN Development Program points out that the government used revenues from hydrocarbons, as well as from its broader economic growth, to benefit the population at large by building infrastructure, addressing extreme poverty, reducing hunger and tuberculosis, increasing the quality of maternal and child nutrition, and offering universal primary education (United Nations Development Program 2013). Within fifteen years of the ceasefire, the World Bank asserted that the country represented one of the "top ten reformers" in the world (Doing Business 2009).

The Aliyevs may have invested heavily in socioeconomic reconstruction as a way to maintain popularity while keeping their authoritarian hold on power intact (Guliyev 2009, 4). Corruption remains a problem while leaders enrich themselves with windfall rents. While the reason behind Oman's success may be strong, visionary leadership, the reason behind Azerbaijan's success may be a strategy to avoid popular unrest. Again, external actors might achieve greater success in post-conflict reconstruction if they back leaders who already face domestic pressures to invest in reconstruction.

Liberia

A third case of surprising socioeconomic reconstruction in a country with access to wealth from natural resources is Liberia in the 2000s.[10] War ended in 2003, after President Charles Taylor agreed to be exiled as part of a peace accord (Hegre, Østby, and Raleigh 2009, 11). Elections in 2005 gave way to victory by Ellen Johnson Sirleaf, who focused on building a broad-based government that included technocrats and that focused on reconstruction.

When the civil war ended in 2003, Liberia faced extensive destruction with hundreds of thousands of Liberians displaced (Economist Intelligence Unit 2008c, 7). In spite of access to diamonds, timber, and rubber, the government invested in socioeconomic reconstruction in a number of ways. It improved the quality of governance by reforming the legal system, the police, and the military (Economist Intelligence Unit 2008c, 8–9). Meanwhile, donors partnered with the government to implement reconstruction projects throughout the country (Economist Intelligence Unit 2008c, 12). Electricity and water were rehabilitated with some success after the war. In addition, the combination of public reconstruction projects and individuals improving their homes expanded the construction sector (Economist Intelligence Unit 2008c, 18).

One plausible explanation for Liberia's reconstruction is strong leadership. Johnson Sirleaf is widely considered to be a great leader, genuinely interested in improving the welfare of Liberians (Economist Intelligence Unit 2008c, 3). A 2011 Nobel Peace Prize winner prior to becoming president, Johnson Sirleaf served for five years as Director of the Regional Bureau for Africa of the United Nations Development Program, where she worked toward the same economic principles that she implemented as president (Nobel Prize 2013).

Another plausible explanation for Liberia's successful socioeconomic reconstruction is that Liberian resources could no longer generate rents as they once did. The country faced sanctions on diamond and timber exports, its two primary sources of rents prior to the end of the war (Economist Intelligence Unit 2008c, 20). Effectively, the government of Liberia became resource poor. Because sanctions have been an important policy to counteract the resource curse in Liberia, I later evaluate the merit of sanctions across a broader set of cases.

The examples presented here demonstrate how leadership can matter in both positive and negative ways towards reconstruction following civil war. The examples of Equatorial Guinea and Haiti show that leaders can forego reconstruction even if the conditions for using nonstrategic aid for reconstruction appear favorable. In contrast, the examples of Oman, Azerbaijan, and Liberia show the enormous potential impact of backing post-conflict leaders who are genuinely interested in the welfare of their people, regardless of windfall income. However, my empirical analyses suggest that such leaders may be rare following civil war, and the case study of Uganda shows that even a government with a "good" leader may ultimately be driven by the incentives and disincentives attributable to having or not having windfall income.

Policies to Counteract the Windfall Curse

The windfall curse remains a challenge for donors and recipients, in spite of heroic efforts to design policies specifically to overcome both the resource curse and the aid curse. External actors have attempted five strategies to persuade resource-rich governments or governments rich in strategic aid to reduce poverty in their countries: (1) sanctions;

(2) the Kimberley Process Certification Scheme; (3) revenue management funds; (4) transparency initiatives; and (5) bypassing governments.

Sanctions

To accompany the carrot of aid, sanctions from donor countries provide a stick to compel cooperation. Sanctions commonly are economic, including trade embargoes and restrictions on financial transactions. They can either target an entire country (Iraq during the 1990s) or particular sectors, companies, or individuals (Cortright and Lopez 2002; Tostensen and Bull 2002). In theory, sanctions can directly affect resource wealth: country A's economy might depend on whether country B imports its commodity. If country B imposes sanctions on country A, prohibiting it from exporting that commodity, country A's government revenues should suffer. The government would effectively become resource poor and therefore subject to donor pressure.

However, sanctions have failed to induce reform in many high-profile post-conflict countries rich in natural resources. Sanctions frequently fail because resource-rich governments can easily access new markets and continue accumulating much-needed resource revenues. Basically, if the product is desirable enough, a willing buyer likely exists. Thus, even if external actors specifically sanction sectors that fuel war (such as Angola's diamond sector in the late 1990s), they will find it hard to stop internal actors from seeking out alternative markets or means to export the commodity. For example, despite sanctions, Angola's UNITA rebels continued to export diamonds using routes through the Democratic Republic of the Congo, Zambia, and Congo (Grant and Taylor, 389).

Recent sanctions against Sudan further illustrate the problem. Sudan represents a fragile state with a history of civil war. In 1997, the Clinton administration imposed sanctions on its government because of its association with terrorist groups, its human rights violations, and suspicions that it was involved in a failed coup attempt against Egyptian president Hosni Mubarak. Sudan was already on the U.S. list of state sponsors of terror, which means that it was already blocked from receiving foreign aid or U.S. exports related to defense. The 1997 sanctions went so far as to embargo all trade with the United States, freeze the assets of more than 100 Sudanese companies with stakes in U.S. markets, and prohibit U.S. companies from doing business with the Sudanese government.

In 1999, Sudan began oil production, thanks to a pipeline the Chinese built and financed. At the same time, war erupted in the Sudanese region of Darfur, along with allegations that paramilitary troops were committing genocide in the region. In response, the United States expanded its sanction program in 2000 to suspend all business dealings with Sudan's oil company, Sudapet, and the Sudanese Greater Nile Petroleum Consortium.

The situation in Darfur continued to worsen. In April 2006, the Bush administration froze the assets of specific Sudanese officials involved in the Darfur conflict. In September, the U.S. government accused Sudan's government of genocide. The U.S. government and the United Nations called for a peacekeeping operation, but the Sudanese government rejected that intervention. In May 2007, the U.S. government reinforced its efforts by beefing up enforcement of existing sanctions and expanding the list of blocked companies to include thirty-one additional businesses, most of which were oil-related and run by the Sudanese government. By cutting these companies out of the U.S. banking system, the sanctions were supposed to make it more difficult for Sudanese elites to obtain revenues from oil.

Five weeks after the 2007 sanctions were imposed, the Sudanese government announced it would double its oil production with the opening of a second oil terminal on the Red Sea. Despite sanctions, the U.S. Treasury Department reported in January 2009 that ". . .central U.S. policy goals of stability and peace have not yet been secured. . ." (Office of Foreign Assets Control 2009, 7). Sudan's oil industry continued to flourish. By 2007, it was producing nearly 500,000 barrels per day (IMF 2008).

U.S. sanctions failed to meet their objectives in Sudan because the United States is not a major importer of Sudanese oil. With China sponsoring development of the oil infrastructure and willing to purchase Sudan's oil, U.S. sanctions amounted to an inconvenience. Sanctions are likely to fail at turning a resource-rich country into a resource-poor country when the targeted country can still sell its natural resources to other interested buyers. Even if the sanctions against Sudan had been perfectly enforced, with the Chinese government a willing buyer the Sudanese government could have continued to ignore international pressure over Darfur. The effective use of sanctions to promote reconstruction following civil war remains elusive.

Kimberley Process Certification Scheme

Peer-evaluated certification schemes are similar to sanctions in providing a stick to compel cooperation with aid agreements. The Kimberley Process Certification Scheme was designed to stop the sale of diamonds mined in conflict zones and thereby cut off funding to warring groups. Civil society organizations pressured diamond-rich governments and the diamond industry to agree to the initiative by conducting an international shaming campaign that spread information about violence committed during civil wars fueled by diamond wealth in places like Angola and Sierra Leone. Under the Kimberley Scheme, the diamond industry and diamond-rich governments signal that that they are not selling or trading "blood diamonds" that originate from areas of violent conflict.

Nongovernmental organizations raised awareness of the problem when they noticed that diamonds were funding violent conflict in several African countries. In 1996, the British nongovernmental organization Global Witness revealed that the diamond industry was buying diamonds from UNITA rebels, essentially sponsoring UNITA's continuing fight against the MPLA government in Angola. To blunt the diamond trade, in 1998 the UN Security Council imposed sanctions on UNITA diamonds. UNITA's diamond trade nevertheless survived because it was able to route its diamond exports through neighboring countries. However, the experience engendered a global conversation about conflict diamonds among nongovernmental organizations, the United Nations, and the diamond industry, which led to a 2000 meeting between all the stakeholders in Kimberley, South Africa, to discuss the problem.[11] The UN General Assembly then passed a resolution asking the group to design an international certification scheme. The stakeholders acted on this request and unveiled the Kimberley Process Certification Scheme in 2002. Under the Scheme, a country can become a "certified" diamond dealer if a government body within the country administers the certification scheme, the country passes national laws against the trade of conflict diamonds, and the country provides a certificate that indicates the origin of all of its diamonds. In support of the process, in July 2003 U.S. President George W. Bush signed the Clean Diamond Trade Act into law, which states that the United States, the world's leading diamond importer, will only import certified diamonds (Grant and Taylor 2004).

Whether the Kimberley Process realized its goals is an open question. The launch of the initiative preceded the end of several conflicts, including the wars in Angola and Sierra Leone, where diamond revenues had been a major source of military funding. It is difficult to say how significant a role the Kimberly Process played in ending these conflicts. National diamond industries, which are not transparent, provide the guarantees voluntarily and countries who fail to comply do not seem to suffer any ill effects. By December 2011, Global Witness declared that it could no longer vouch for the Kimberley Process, citing lack of compliance by Cote d'Ivoire, Venezuela, and Zimbabwe (Global Witness 2011). Many in the international community nevertheless hold out hope for this model.[12]

Revenue Management Funds

Revenue management funds represent a repository for resource rents that can be allocated for poverty reduction under the purview of an independent panel. When Chad needed a pipeline to export its oil reserves in 2000, the government signed an agreement with the World Bank and other external actors: donors would finance the US$4.8 billion pipeline and the government of Chad would adopt a revenue management fund. The Chad government was to deposit royalties in an offshore account, and an independent panel would monitor expenditures to make sure they contributed to the country's reconstruction.

Once oil revenues started pouring in, however, Chad's government officials reneged. The government declared that it would offer less to the special account in order to increase its general budget and increase military spending. The World Bank was forced to agree to a softer version of the program that left Chad government officials with much more discretion over oil revenues than the Bank initially desired. In particular, the new agreement allowed Chad officials to increase military spending and abandon a fund meant to store oil revenues to benefit future generations. But even this program failed in

2008, when the Chadian government declared that it would not comply with the conditions. Once Chad government officials were able to receive large amounts of resource rents, they no longer had an incentive to bear the costs of international discretion over their revenues. In fact, these officials had every reason to redirect those funds from poverty reduction to military spending. After a lengthy civil war, Chad is again embroiled in civil conflict and its president, Idriss Déby, has survived at least three coup attempts (Powell and Thyne 2011). It is likely that Déby senses insecurity about his future and fears that if he fails to use oil wealth to co-opt or repress as needed, one of his rivals may overtake the regime and its control over oil revenue. The revenue management funds approach failed in Chad, at least in part because the incentives favored compliance early in the agreement, but not after officials received windfall.

Transparency

Some of the latest initiatives by donors to address the resource curse emphasize transparency. A 2008 assessment of the World Bank and International Monetary Fund aid programs conducted jointly by the Bank Information Center and Global Witness focused on this issue (Bank Information Center and Global Witness 2008). However, it is not yet clear what transparency alone can do to promote good governance. Take, for example, the case of Angola. In 2001, a spokesperson from British Petroleum agreed in a public interview with Global Witness to reveal what it paid the Angolan government on an annual basis.[13] Sonangol chief executive Manuel Vicente sent a letter to British Petroleum threatening that if the company released the data, Angola would terminate its contracts. The government of Angola must have found transparency threatening. Soon after, the Angolan government passed three new laws designed to limit information, which researchers from Human Rights Watch concluded were effective. In particular, the group said, the state security bill "criminalizes possession of documents that the government considers sensitive," including "data on oil revenues, IMF documents, or other documents that should be in the public domain in order to further public oversight" (Human Rights Watch 2004). Angola's anti-transparency campaign appears to have worked. *The New York Times* reported three years later that oil executives still avoided the media because "they do not want to risk offending the government" (LaFraniere 2007).

In 2004, after Angola had become the target of an international transparency campaign, Angolan officials changed course and agreed to release some information about government revenues. The Angolan government began publishing monthly data on diamond and oil production and income. The government put this information on its ministry of finance website, along with its annual budget. However, this increased financial transparency has not improved basic living conditions for most Angolans (Human Rights Watch 2010). So what does transparency do? Transparency without institutions that increase the accountability of leaders may have only negligible effects on government spending. In regard to Angola's transparency efforts, the World Bank reported that "resistance to change in other areas notwithstanding, the authorities have moved to enhance transparency in oil revenues, but the improvement has not led yet to a clear decline in corruption, at least as captured by perception-based measures" (World Bank 2007a, viii). As of 2011, according to the International Monetary Fund, the Angolan government could not account for US$27.8 billion that went missing between 2007 and 2010 (Human Rights Watch 2010; IMF 2011, 9).

One reason for this apparent failure is that even if all budgeting were truly transparent, transparency alone represents only a half measure. Fiscal transparency without concomitant political accountability cannot ameliorate the curse of windfall income. Some observers conclude that countries like Angola will only become less corrupt if mechanisms can be put in place to hold government officials accountable. In resource-rich states, there is a correlation between representative legislatures operating systems of checks and balances and greater fiscal responsibility (Humphreys and Sandbu 2007).

The Extractive Industries Transparency Initiative (EITI) is an example of a program that may have potential to drive real reform because it squarely addresses both transparency and accountability. Started by the British government in 2002, EITI is a consortium of oil companies, civil society organizations, and governments that have agreed to promote the disclosure of company payments and government receipts relating to resource revenues. Member governments agree to publish all available information on receipts from oil and gas companies, and member companies agree to reveal what they pay. In this way, EITI promotes transparency. EITI is unique in that it emphasizes monitoring of government revenues. The government, civil society, and the private sector appoint EITI validators to check whether company payments match government receipts, and whether government revenues are allocated for development. If a government fails to report revenues or to allocate them for development, that government loses its EITI accreditation. In this way, EITI promotes accountability of government spending. The potential impact of EITI is still not known, and continued research is needed to determine why some countries decide to comply while others do not. It also remains to be seen whether the existence of EITI will successfully encourage reform in resource-rich countries.[14]

In summary, sanctions, the Kimberley Process, revenue management funds, and transparency initiatives have not proved fruitful in incentivizing recipient countries to meet donor guidelines by fostering socioeconomic development. This demonstrates how difficult it is for donors and other external actors to pressure a resource-rich government plagued by weak institutions to undertake systemic reform and spend money on development. There is little reason to implement agreements or to concede to external leverage if a country's leader genuinely does not need the money. From this perspective, these policy alternatives may have failed because they rely on convincing the governments of resource-rich fledgling countries to behave in a way that is counter to their interests in controlling their own income.

Bypass Governments

Bypassing governments altogether is another possible way to overcome the windfall curse.[15] In countries with strategic importance to donors, fostering reconstruction is difficult. For example, in Afghanistan and Iraq, the United States has been addressing the aid curse by bypassing the government altogether and targeting communities directly—with some success. These two cases are instructive.

Afghanistan is among the world's most besieged countries. The Soviet invasion of 1979 led to civil violence that continued until the U.S. military and allies of the U.S. government overthrew the Taliban government in 2001. The US government initiated Operation

Enduring Freedom after the September 11 terrorist attacks on the basis of the Taliban's support for al-Qaeda. While the ostensible goals of this mission were to disable al-Qaeda and capture its leader, Osama bin Laden, the U.S. government also found itself in the position of having to rebuild Afghanistan (see Dobbins et al. 2003).

The United Nations quickly passed a resolution to guide post-conflict reconstruction in Afghanistan, which essentially called upon the international community to offer a peacekeeping force and large amounts of development assistance. The U.S. government led this effort by offering the largest amount of aid, coordinating efforts among donors, and providing advice to Afghan President Hamid Karzai. Documents and regular public statements by U.S. government officials show that, as lead donors, U.S. government officials wanted to encourage political and economic development and markedly reduce corruption in Afghanistan (Chandrasekaran 2009).

More than ten years and billions of dollars later, however, meaningful reconstruction has not occurred in Afghanistan. Health centers and schools have not been constructed in nearly sufficient numbers. But some government officials have built luxurious new homes, presumably enriching themselves through aid scams and drug trafficking. It was reported in 2009 that the chief of police in Kabul owned a home that cost US$10,000 per month, eighteen times Karzai's monthly salary. As *The New York Times* put it, "The state. . . now often seems to exist for little more than the enrichment of those who run it" (Filkins 2009).

If Karzai was failing to meet U.S. reconstruction goals, why did the American government continue to support him? The administration of President George W. Bush appears to have believed that reducing support for the Karzai regime might allow Afghanistan to fall back into the Taliban's hands. Starting in 2002, the Taliban reconstituted itself, recaptured territory, and launched attacks throughout the country, including attempts on Karzai's life. Given that the U.S. government had an interest in Karzai's survival (Bush and Karzai had biweekly video conferences), the U.S. government could not credibly threaten to withdraw support, even if Karzai ignored the reconstruction agenda. Aid to Afghanistan was indisputably strategic. Numerous states that the U.S. government deems critical players in the war on terror fit a similar profile. They receive large amounts of strategic

U.S. aid in exchange for access to their territories and assistance in identifying terrorist networks.[16] While senior U.S. officials may genuinely want to encourage reconstruction, they have security concerns that trump reconstruction goals. As of 2009, senior U.S. officials had been unable to threaten "or else" when calling for meaningful reform in Afghanistan under the presidencies of both George W. Bush and Barack Obama (Cooper 2009). The risk that the Taliban would recapture Afghanistan, for example, appears to have compelled American officials to continue bilateral assistance, despite corruption in the Afghan government. And as long as Afghan government officials and other aid recipients believed they would receive aid regardless of their efforts on the reconstruction front, they lacked an incentive to use aid to achieve reconstruction goals.

The question is whether external actors like the U.S. government can encourage reconstruction in countries where, for strategic reasons, those actors are unwilling to withdraw support. This is particularly critical in countries like Afghanistan, with very high strategic value or mineral wealth. As the statistical analysis in Chapter 3 shows, foreign aid under these circumstances can have negative, unintended consequences if channeled through traditional routes. In such cases, donors may improve reconstruction outcomes by seeking other modalities for aid delivery, such as increasing direct control over ministries (World Bank 2011).

Another option is to funnel aid through nongovernmental organizations instead of through the government itself. Under this scenario, regardless of how motivated a state may be to carry out reconstruction projects, it would experience reconstruction as the result of extragovernmental spending. Indeed, since 2001, donors with a strategic interest in a country with a weak government appear to have given more assistance to nongovernmental organizations in that country than to the central government (Bermeo 2008). Of course, governmental support for these efforts in the recipient country should also improve their effectivetiveness.

The U.S. government has also pursued extragovernmental aid disbursement in Afghanistan and Iraq as part of its counterinsurgency strategy (U.S. Army/Marine Corps 2006). After years of failure at reconstructing either country, the U.S. government issued a counterinsurgency strategy in 2006 that called for a different type of aid disbursement—U.S. security forces, along with donors, were to bypass the government and directly disburse aid for small-scale projects that targeted specific community needs. Evidence from the Commander's Emergency Response Program in Iraq, where Coalition and Iraqi commanders directly funded the small-scale projects, suggests that such aid improved basic services, although the findings from other similar programs are less conclusively positive (Berman, Shapiro, and Felter 2011).[17]

From the perspective of the U.S. military, this aid disbursement strategy was meant to "win hearts and minds" and thereby reduce support for the insurgency. But from a broader perspective, what is striking about this project is that this form of aid actually improved living conditions in a strategically important (and resource rich) country. Programs that bypass governments may result in greater reconstruction than simply giving cash to corrupt leaders, even if such programs have less impact without the support of those leaders. Bypassing governments may be the model for future aid disbursement in countries that are strategically important to donors. The governmental support these programs need to thrive, however, may be difficult to obtain because of the negative incentives of windfall income.

Future Research

This book raises four questions for future research: (1) How far can non-strategic donors push cash-poor recipients? (2) How far can cash-poor recipients push donors? (3) What are the implications of power consolidation after civil war for authoritarian institution building? (4) How do post-conflict countries "get to Denmark"?

Future research should analyze how far leaders in countries with no source of income other than aid will go to secure aid agreements. In Mozambique, donors imposed tough demands for democratization and the Mozambican government complied (Manning and Marlbrough 2010). In Uganda, donors did not call for democracy in the immediate aftermath of the civil war, and the political system did not become a full multi-party electoral system. Given that Ugandan government officials were initially eager to comply with donor demands, they may have implemented a more fair democracy if donors called for it. Using a thorough understanding of how government income sources inform post-conflict leaders' decision making, donor countries and international financial institutions could potentially leverage more reform for their money.

It is also worth considering how much money rivals of the government can obtain as payoffs from nonstrategic donors. In Mozambique, Renamo received millions of U.S. dollars in direct payoffs from donors who were eager to see Renamo leaders participate in national elections as a political party. However, the amount of aid that donors disbursed as payoffs was relatively small. One wonders if Renamo could have received even more from donors, particularly in the lead-up to the 1994 elections. Dhlakama may have wondered this himself. When asked by the press after the 1994 elections whether he was "spoiled" by donor assistance, Dhlakama responded: "Renamo was a political and military movement that was transformed into a political party. It contested the elections. It received aid from the international community. One should not complain about whether that aid was too little or not. We used that aid for food and fuel. The money is gone, but we have not created an economic power base to survive as a political party" (quoted in Televisão de Moçambique 1995). When rebel participation in the government is very important to donors, how much might rebel groups conceivably charge their leaders or donors for integrating into the political system? Under what circumstances are rebel groups likely to receive higher or lower payoffs from donors (or from their governments)?

One might also ask how much defense spending recipient governments can get away with when negotiating with nonstrategic donors (see Boyce 2007). Governments that depend on nonstrategic aid spend some portion of their aid on security infrastructure. Donors let this happen (and sometimes directly fund the security apparatus) because security appears to be necessary for reconstruction. Across developing countries that are not emerging from war, however, donors view defense spending as detrimental to macroeconomic stability. The question therefore remains: at what point will security spending prompt nonstrategic donors to withdraw on the grounds that this spending reduces development potential?

This research also suggests a new set of questions about the influence of power consolidation strategies following civil war. Natural resources appear to fuel authoritarianism following civil war in countries like Angola (Roque 2009; Soares de Oliveira 2011). Does the coup-proofing that nonstrategic aid facilitates also enable authoritarian institution-building in low-windfall countries? Socioeconomic reconstruction may benefit citizens for decades after the civil war, as it has in Mozambique, in Uganda to a lesser degree, and in other low-windfall post-conflict countries, such as Rwanda. But power consolidation has given way to authoritarian practices within each of these countries. With a strong internal security apparatus and patronage, some of these leaders are able to weaken the opposition even before election campaigning begins. As a result, elections can fail to move beyond minimum international requirements of freedom and fairness, as has been the case in resource-rich countries (Soares de Oliveira 2011).

Uganda's Museveni, for example, is extremely powerful after governing Uganda and establishing patronage networks and internal security since 1986. As of this writing, there are no signs that he intends to step down. Similarly, Mozambique has arguably become a one-party state, as Frelimo has won every election since the ceasefire (Manning 2010; Weinstein 2002). In fact, Frelimo has maintained or expanded its significant control with each election. Thus, dependence on nonstrategic aid may help reconstruction, but at best, create only minimally democratic post-conflict regimes. This possibility should be explored across a broad set of cases, especially as external actors continue to invest to achieve democracy after civil war (see Zürcher et al. 2013; Dresden 2014).

Lastly, the evidence provided in this book can explain socioeconomic reconstruction following civil war, but these Phoenix States remain dependent on donor aid for their survival. Finding techniques for helping these post-conflict success stories to become autonomous actors in domestic reconstruction is an important area for future research. The ultimate goal is to help post-conflict countries "get to Denmark" by creating legitimate governments that deliver high-quality public services to the vast majority of their populations.

Conclusion

In this book, I developed an incentive-based argument for understanding post-conflict reconstruction. I then rigorously tested the hypotheses that emerged from this framework with statistics and examined them further with case studies.

The results support the nonstrategic-desperation hypothesis, in that aid is more likely to foster post-conflict reconstruction if the recipient has low windfall income (i.e. lacks resource rents and holds only low strategic importance to the donor). Further, the results also support the low-windfall coup-proofing hypothesis, in that following civil war, the interaction of low windfall, nonstrategic aid, and reconstruction, reduces coup risk. A subset of leaders chose socioeconomic reconstruction following civil war because it reduces their risk of coup. The test cases of Angola, Mozambique, and Uganda combine to explain how income drives choices to reconstruct or to not reconstruct following civil war.

Findings suggest that donors will see an increase in reconstruction from nonstrategic aid following civil war only in countries that have no windfall from natural resources and, paradoxically, no strategic interest for the donor. This occurs because only governments that meet these conditions are desperate enough to comply with aid agreements. With continued aid, these leaders can consolidate power and reduce their risk of coup. If aid flows are halted, these low-windfall leaders become more vulnerable to a coup. In contrast, for leaders with windfall income following civil war, external pressures, whether conditions, sanctions, or certifications, fail to drive recipients towards compliance with aid agreements because the increase in aid revenue does not replace the redirection of windfall revenue to the general population. More importantly, reconstruction may not decrease their risk of coup.

The argument and analyses provided here reinforce the notion of the resource curse and demonstrate that the aid curse is conditional, at least following civil war. For post-conflict countries lacking windfall income from natural resources or strategic aid, nonstrategic aid can bring about measurable post-conflict reconstruction even if institutions are weak.

NOTES

Acknowledgments
1. Parts of this book appear in Girod (2012); Girod (n.d.).

Prologue
1. Personal communication, July 2012.
2. All dollar values in the book are in constant 2005 U.S. dollars unless otherwise indicated.
3. For a review, see Wright and Winters (2010).

Chapter 1
1. Organski and Kugler (1980) use the term "Phoenix Factor" to refer to the return to pre-war economic performance for countries that fight in international wars. By "Phoenix States," I refer to countries that experience successful socioeconomic reconstruction in the aftermath of civil war.
2. In this book, post-conflict reconstruction refers to socioeconomic reconstruction, a broad-based improvement in living conditions for the majority of citizens following civil war. Note that I use the terms socioeconomic reconstruction, reconstruction, and development interchangeably throughout the book.
3. Institutions in this book represent the government's capacity and will to respond to citizen needs (Boyce and Forman 2010; Iqbal and Starr 2008; Krasner 2004; Murshed 2010). This definition of institutions does not include "islands of efficiency" that do not serve the population at

large (Hertog 2010, 28–29). For example, Angola had a relatively strong military during the 2000s when the government decisively ended civil war, but it lacked strong institutions to serve citizens. Institutions to serve citizens remained fragile even as Angola's national oil company maintained elaborate and sophisticated arrangements with multinational oil companies, banks, and foreign governments (Soares de Oliveira 2007).

4. For a review of the fiscal sociology on how nontax revenues shape governance, see Moore (2004) and also Morrison (2009).

5. For the landmark study behind this argument, see Burnside and Dollar (2000). Their findings have been debated, but there is some consensus in the literature that aid is more effective when recipient institutions are strong. See McGillivray et al. (2006) and Wright and Winters (2010).

6. Institutional fragility often plagues post-conflict states because states with fragile governmental and fiscal institutions are more likely to experience civil war in the first place (Fearon and Laitin 2003; Naudé, Santos Paulino, and McGillivray 2011). Civil war exacerbates fragility because civil war destroys the already sparse infrastructure, formal economy, and any governmental capacity present prior to the conflict. To look at two metrics associated with institutional fragility, in countries that experienced civil war between 1970 and 2009, infant mortality was 45% higher than the rest of the world and per capita income was 64% lower (Heston, Summers, and Aten 2011; World Bank 2012a).

7. As scholar and practitioner Graciana del Castillo has said, "issues related to post-conflict economic reconstruction are addressed only tangentially or as an afterthought, and with little economic rigor, specificity, or comprehensiveness" (del Castillo 2008, 20). Scholars have focused mainly on post-conflict peace and democracy (Doyle and Sambanis 2006; Fortna 2008; Fortna and Huang 2012; Hartzell, Hoddie and Rothchild 2001; Howard 2008; Paris 2004; Ponzio 2011; Toft 2010; Walter 1997; Wantchekon 2004; Wood 2001; Zürcher et al. 2013). Case studies detail the rich possibilities for aid in fostering socioeconomic reconstruction, as well as problems that aid creates for socioeconomic reconstruction (Call 2008; Caplan 2005; Chetail 2009; del Castillo 2008; Dobbins et al. 2003; Kumar 1997; Paris and Sisk 2009; Stewart and Fitzgerald 2001).

8. The few cross-national studies on post-conflict economic growth find that successful growth depends on preexisting institutional strength (Collier and Hoeffler 2004a; Flores and Nooruddin 2009) or on "economic fundamentals" (Kang and Meernik 2005).

9. Like the aid curse, the resource curse presents a "paradox of plenty," wherein an abundance of money from natural resources fails to flow to the people who need it, resulting in poor development (Karl 1997; Ross 2012). Many post-conflict countries confront the resource curse because dependence on natural resources can be associated with the outbreak of war (Collier and Hoeffler 2004b; Fearon and Laitin 2003; Humphreys 2005; Ross 2004; Ross 2006a).

10. For a similar argument applied to democracy promotion, see Dunning (2004).
11. The extant literature gives an answer to the puzzle of why countries in general (including both post-conflict countries and countries that have not experienced conflict) manage to bring about broad-based development when they lack access to windfall income. Under these circumstances, leaders depend on taxes and popular support and must therefore spend on development to increase tax revenues and popularity via improved economic opportunities for citizens (Bueno de Mesquita and Smith 2010). But as a group, post-conflict countries are different from other countries because institutions are generally fragile after civil war. The general argument is therefore less applicable to them. Given that building a tax administration that can generate meaningful sums of revenue is quite difficult in a weak institutional context, the question remains: why are some post-conflict countries able to bring about successful reconstruction?
12. Other donors, such as the Soviet Union, China, Saudi Arabia, and Venezuela, are not included because they offer minimal data on their aid disbursements. A new source—AidData—offers data on aid commitments for some of these donors. See AidData (2012).
13. In addition, OECD donors operate both through and alongside a large and complex network of other donors; including international organizations (like the World Bank), faith-based organizations (like Catholic Relief Services), and secular private organizations (like Save the Children), all of which also raise their own funds. I analyze these non-state donors in the book only to the extent that they influence or implement aid efforts funded by the OECD donors.

Chapter 2

1. Some scholars argue that the international community should stay home, because external actors are likely to fail and make things worse (Brownlee 2007; Englebert and Tull 2008; Herbst 2004; Weinstein 2005).
2. I have deliberately simplified the relationship between leaders, their rivals, and donors here in order to generate hypotheses that can help explain why only some post-conflict countries develop. This simple argument focuses on the key decisions leaders make regarding development while minimizing threats to self-preservation following the end of civil war. These decisions are likely to be influenced by leader income sources.
3. For a review of coup-proofing studies, see Belkin and Schofer (2003) and Powell (2012).
4. Leaders generally appear to be concerned with political survival (Bueno de Mesquita et al. 2003; Goemans 2008). But the logic of the argument presented here is the same whether one emphasizes aid recipients' interests in political survival or personal enrichment (Bratton and van de Walle 1997).

5. Powell and Thyne define coup attempts as "illegal and overt attempts by the military or other elites within the state apparatus to unseat the sitting executive" (2011, 252).
6. Powell and Thyne (2011, 250).
7. See for example Biddle and Zirkle (1996); Pilster and Böhmelt (2011); Quinlivan (1999).
8. See Smith (2008) and Banks (2011).
9. See Roessler (2011). As the case of Uganda will show, the resumption of war may actually allow the leader to convince donors to permit (or fund) greater security expenditures than the leader would otherwise be able to allocate (Barkan et al. 2004; Mwenda 2010; Tripp 2010). Thus, paradoxically, the resumption of civil war may help a low-windfall leader obtain resources to stay in power.
10. The argument does not make specific predictions about who is likely to receive government handouts. Likely coup plotters may come from supporters or from opponents, so either group could receive handouts.
11. Natural resources and foreign aid in general appear to stabilize regimes in distress (Nielsen et al. 2011; Savun and Tirone 2012). The influence of this income on regime stability (in samples including all countries) depends on whether the regime is autocratic or democratic and on the leader's time horizon (Kono and Montinola 2009; Licht 2010; Morrison 2009; Wright 2008).
12. Strategic interests tend to trump the development interests of the democratic donors from the OECD because democracies seek to benefit their own citizens with aid disbursements. See Bueno de Mesquita and Smith (2007). For examples from the War on Terror, see Byman (2006).
13. In fact, donors sometimes disburse more than they commit to strategically important recipients (Desai and Kharas 2010).
14. Personal communication, July 2012.
15. Studies find this problem across developing countries (Bearce and Tirone 2010; Stone 2010). For a similar conclusion regarding foreign aid's influence on democratization in Africa, see Dunning (2004).
16. See also Callaghy (1984) and Reno (1998).
17. The regime survival literature lumps strategic and nonstrategic aid together, but disaggregation is important because strategic aid is free from credible threat of withdrawal, while nonstrategic aid is not (e.g., Ahmed 2012; Bueno de Mesquita and Smith 2010; Morrison 2009; Smith 2008).
18. Donors also promote democratic reform (Widner 1994). To ensure the effect of nonstrategic aid on coup risk is not confounded by democracy, I later test the empirical model both including and excluding democracy.
19. Nonstrategic donors also support post-conflict security through peacekeeping operations. As with nonstrategic aid, the goal of these operations is stability, not power consolidation by one side. Peacekeeping operations generally aim to achieve stability by offering security

guarantees in addition to aid to combatants (Doyle and Sambanis 2006; Fortna 2008; Harzell and Hoddie 2003; Walter 1997; Wantchekon 2004).

20. Nonstrategic donors seek budgetary control over the internal spending of the recipient (World Bank 2006a). In states that are desperate for income, nonstrategic donors have funded most if not all development expenditures. For example, external financing supported nearly all development expenditures over the three years following the 1994 ceasefire in Rwanda (National Bank of Rwanda 2004, 164). In addition, donors fund projects outside of the government's budget (i.e., "off-budget"). Leaders stand to lose some budget autonomy by complying with nonstrategic aid agreements, but putting the national budget in the hands of donors may make a low-windfall leader less susceptible to a coup because fewer rewards are readily available to successful coup plotters. See Grossman (1992).
21. Personal communication, July 2012.
22. Personal communication with IMF economist, July 2012.
23. Do leaders actually "choose" the abstract concept of development that is under study in this book? Leaders certainly choose whether or not to implement specific development assistance agreements, each of which addresses some component of broad-based development. Implementing development initiatives requires coordinating the efforts of many individuals, each of whom face opportunities for corruption or mistakes, so leaders also choose whether to punish noncompliance and reward compliance. Leaders also sign off on government budgets that allocate money in ways that enrich the population at large or foster kleptocracy. Indeed, leaders make dozens of decisions daily that can aggregate up to socioeconomic reconstruction.
24. Social spending appears to contribute to broad-based development (Ghobarah, Huth, and Russett 2004; Lake and Baum 2001). Similarly, infrastructure rehabilitation appears to help broad-based development (Esrey et al. 1991; Ingram and Fay 2008).
25. According to a senior World Bank official, for example, "in every single adjustment operation that I ever was involved in, and there were a lot of them [including many in the 1980s], there were conditions on the maintenance of social spending. . . . Now sometimes the huge proportion of civil servant salaries and phantom workers were in health and education. So there might have been some effort to do that [i.e., cut those expenditures]. But in general from very early on, people were conscious that having kids not going to school because of the budget was a pretty bad thing. . . . It didn't take even the sort of serious macroeconomists very long to figure that out" (Personal communication, July 2012).
26. Personal communication, September 2012.
27. See also Gibson et al. (2005, 89) and Schmidtchen (1999).
28. For a review, see Wright and Winters (2010).

29. Personal communication, September 2012.
30. Personal communication, July 2012.
31. Note that this hypothesis makes no specific predictions about the average influence of windfall on coup risk. While windfall could reduce coup risk by providing an immediate source of income to use against potential rivals (Smith 2008), windfall could increase coup risk by sufficiently increasing the size of the prize for successful coup plotters (Collier and Hoeffler 2004b; Grossman 1992). Similarly, my hypothesis is mute regarding the average effects of nonstrategic aid and of reconstruction on coup risk.

Chapter 3

1. The start date is inclusive and the end date is exclusive.
2. Data availability on the variables of interest limits the sample size in some of the regressions.
3. The Online Appendix is available at http://www9.georgetown.edu/faculty/dmg78/.
4. Experiments and quasiexperiments focused on post-conflict settings include Blattman (2009), Fearon, Humphreys, and Weinstein (2009), and Paluck and Green (2009).
5. Unlike mortality rates, data on growth are susceptible to single-year aberrations (Forbes 2000; Navia and Zweifel 2003). The data on growth is therefore presented averaged over three- and five-year periods and come from Heston et al. (2009). For a similar approach, see Murdoch and Sandler (2004). The data on other indicators of socioeconomic reconstruction come from the World Bank (2012a).
6. Donor-recipient voting at the United Nations General Assembly (UNGA) has been used as a measure of foreign-policy affinity (Thacker 1999). This measure is not included here because it seems to be an ambiguous measure of strategic importance (Stone 2010). Including UNGA voting altered few observations, so the hypothesis is supported with or without UN voting affinity (Online Appendix Table 5, model 1). Data on UNGA voting range from –1 (lowest affinity) to 1 (highest affinity) and come from Gartzke (2006).
7. See also Bermeo (2008) and Neumayer (2003).
8. The Cold War period is measured between 1970 and 1989.
9. I take the logarithm of nonstrategic aid and of windfall.
10. I code the variable dichotomously in some parts of the analysis because low and high windfall represent simplifying categories that help the reader link the result to the argument. However, most models rely on the continuous coding of windfall to maximize the amount of information provided by the variable. Measuring windfall as an interval offers an additional way to conceptualize and test the influence of increasing windfall on post-conflict reconstruction. The results remain consistent

when windfall is measured as an interval variable, with each interval representing a quartile of the windfall data (see Online Appendix Table 5, model 3).
11. Results remain consistent when I include battle-related violence after the war (the logarithm of *Postwar Deaths*) as a control using data from Lacina and Gleditsch (2005). Results also support the hypothesis when I include *Incumbent Tenure*, the number of years the incumbent is in power, as a control using data from Cheibub, Gandhi and Vreeland (2010). The results also remain consistent when I include a control for whether the leader's entry into office was irregular (e.g., coup or revolution), *Irregular Entry*. The data on irregular entry come from Goemans, Gleditsch. and Chiozza (2009), and the variable is coded as "1" if the leader's entry was irregular and "0" otherwise (Online Appendix Table 6, model 1).
12. I use data from the World Bank (2010).
13. The data on ethnic fractionalization come from Fearon and Laitin (2003). Results also support the hypothesis when I control for other demographic factors that may correlate with development. I include a control for *Population Density* because, if citizens are dispersed, governments may be unable to offer health care and other goods to the whole population (Ross 2006b). The data come from Heston et al. (2011) and Rose (2005). I also control for *malaria* ecology using data from Sachs (2003) because a population facing greater incidences of malaria may face higher infant mortality rates and be less able to engage in productive economic activities (Gallup and Sachs 2001). See Online Appendix Table 6, model 2.
14. The instrument is relevant to aid (statistically significant at the 99% level with an F-statistic of 75.76).
15. Social scientists have become increasingly skeptical of instrumental variables. For example, Randall Morck and Bernard Yeung argue that "Useful instrumental variables are, we fear, going the way of the Atlantic cod" and call for careful historical analysis as a better approach to identifying causal relationships (Morck and Yeung 2011, 50).

Chapter 4
1. Technically, the dependent variable is coup occurrence because coup risk is unobserved.
2. The results remain consistent when using rare events logistic regression (Tomz, King, and Zeng 2003) (Online Appendix Table 12, model 1).
3. As in the previous analysis, the results remain consistent when strategic aid is measured using UNGA voting or using Cold War aid only. See Online Appendix Table 12, models 2 and 3.
4. I impute missing data using Amelia (Honaker, King, and Blackwell 2011).
5. UN security guarantees cannot be included as a control variable because no coups occur in the data after the UN offered security guarantees.

6. A concern with split-panel data is that the split data do not share a common intercept. Dawson and Richter (2006) developed a technique for calculating the common intercept that allows a direct comparison of slopes in three-way interactions. Using this technique with countries with high levels of nonstrategic aid and increasing development, I find a statistically significant difference between high- and low-windfall slopes, supporting Figure 4.1.
7. Calculated using *Clarify* (King, Tomz, and Wittenberg 2000; Tomz, Wittenberg, and King 2003). While windfall moderates the relationship between nonstrategic aid, development, and coup risk, having windfall is not sufficient to prevent coups (Online Appendix Table 14). Perhaps windfall's effects on coup reduction wash out its effects on increasing coup risk. As windfall increases, leaders have more money to buy out rivals and strengthen security. However, leaders with greater windfall also face rivals with more to gain from a successful coup. As the prize of a successful coup increases, so does the incentive for both the coup leader and the followers to launch a coup (Arriola 2009; Collier and Hoeffler 2004b; Grossman 1992).
8. See Chapter 3 for an explanation of the instrument. The instrument is relevant to aid (statistically significant at the 99% level with an F-statistic of 54.85).

Chapter 5

1. On similarities between Angola and Mozambique, see Minter (1994), Scott (1988), and Young (1988).
2. On Mozambique's post-independence political economy, see Cahen (1987), Hall and Young (1997), Hanlon (1991), Newitt (1995), Ottaway (1988), and Saul (1985). On Angola's, see Messiant, Lachartre and Cahen (2008), Hodges (2004), and Chabal and Vidal (2008).
3. These data are unavailable—partly because the Chinese government has not been transparent with aid disbursements, and partly because Chinese aid is not universally considered foreign development assistance as defined by the OECD (Lum et al. 2009, 1).
4. See Chilcote (1967) and Marcum (1969).
5. On Angola's civil war, see Bender (1983), James (1992), and Minter (1994).
6. See Legum (1976).
7. On Mozambique's civil war, see Chingono (1996), Finnegan (1992), Hall and Young (1997), Minter (1994), Synge (1997), and Vines (1996).
8. Personal communication, August 2012.
9. Personal communication, September 2012.
10. Personal communication, August 2012.
11. See also Pawson (2007).
12. See Costa (2007).

NOTES TO PAGES 67–69   157

13. The aid associated with humanitarian projects could reach individuals in need because donors, not the government, disbursed it directly. However, the government's lack of support for the aid—for instance, not expediting payment of port fees—appears to have reduced the aid's effectiveness.
14. Although Bank officials welcomed Mozambican government input into some policy discussions, as became common practice in all Bank operations during the 1990s (Buur, Baloi, and Tembe 2012; Pitcher 2002), Bank officials still generally administered aid programs from Washington. For example, Mozambique's health ministry staff took an active role in designing a health plan that would allow the ministry to keep some of its existing policies (Hanlon 1996). Despite the collaborative process to create some ministry policies, however, ministry staff still ultimately depended on the Bank for money and for oversight. The health program was effectively "run from Washington and not Maputo" (Hanlon 1996, 48). Donors' dominance over development policy in Mozambique is heavily criticized, particularly on the grounds that this dominance hinders local capacity development. For more on this argument, see for example Hanlon (1996) and Pfeiffer (2003).
15. Of course, not all nonstrategic aid agreements to Mozambique included strong, explicit enforcement teeth. In particular, bilateral donors may not have monitored specific agreements but appeared to have been responsive to signals sent by multilateral donors. Also, governments may be able to spend some types of aid more freely than other types. For example, budget support aid may be spent more freely than project aid because project aid targets specific needs of a project (materials, staff, and the like), while budget support is intended for broad government priorities. Grant aid may be spent more freely than aid that comes as loans because loans need to be repaid. However, leaders' dependence on nonstrategic donors seems to have influenced how freely leaders can actually use budget support or grants. Aware that they need to satisfy donors in order to keep aid flowing, Mozambique's leaders complied with policies regardless of the nature of the aid.
16. Hanlon (1996) quotes the World Bank official in the context of criticizing the Bank for dominating policy dialogue in Mozambique with potentially inappropriate policies for the country.
17. Author interview, September 2005, Maputo.
18. Author interview, September 2005, Maputo.
19. Author interview, September 2005, Maputo.
20. Author interview, September 2005, Maputo.
21. Saul (1991) points out that Chissano made this statement in the context of criticizing Mozambique's structural adjustment program.
22. Personal communication, September 2012.
23. Personal communication, August 2012.

24. Personal communication, August 2012.
25. Personal communication, August 2012.
26. Personal communication, September 2012.
27. On similar dynamics in post-conflict Tajikistan, see Driscoll (2012).
28. Pfeiffer (2003) criticizes the collaboration, arguing that it weakened local capacity for health management.
29. See Pfeiffer (2003) for example.
30. See also Soares de Oliveira (2011), 297.
31. See Manning and Marlbrough (2010) on how bilateral donors contributed to the reintegration of combatants.
32. The press cites confusion over whether these were *regulos*, who are armed and loyal to Dhlakama, or Renamo soldiers who did not demobilize. See Agence France Presse (1995).
33. The parties did not address the police force with the General Peace Accord negotiations.
34. See also Lalá and Francisco (2006, 165); and U.S. State Department (1995).
35. According to a Carter Center representative in Mozambique, "There were suspicions that demobilized soldiers were secretly being transferred... and trained [in violation of the accords]. This was discovered by the UN; things were called what they were" (quoted in Fortna 2008, 144–45).
36. Chissano successfully rejected pleas by Dhlakama for positions in the cabinet or the authority to appoint governors in the provinces where Renamo members won a majority.
37. Renamo members did not enter the civil service in large numbers (especially in rural areas) because of intimidation from Renamo veterans (Manning 1998, 184).
38. Author interview, September 2005, Maputo. See also Harare Financial Gazette (1998).
39. In the early 1990s, during a ceasefire attempt in Angola that failed, the international community sponsored an election wherein UNITA candidates won seats in the newly created parliament. But even these members seemed to fear losing state patronage if they challenged the MPLA, so UNITA leaders not in parliament could not count on their parliamentary members. This new parliament appears to have operated as a rubber stamp. See Hodges (2004).
40. See Jerry Bender's analysis cited in Hodges (2004).
41. On the socioeconomic impact of the destruction, see Pfeiffer (2003) and Cliff and Noormahomed (1993).
42. On the influence of learning between peacekeeping operations, see Howard (2008).
43. Author interview, August 2005, Maputo.
44. Quoted in Mo Ibrahim Foundation (2007).
45. For a similar treatment of leadership, see Weinstein (2006).

Chapter 6

1. One might ask if Uganda's slight democratization by the mid-1990s also confounds hypothesis testing. Uganda was slightly more democratic when the government discovered windfall than when he ended the war. But as discussed in the previous chapters, democracy is expected to bring about reconstruction. Uganda's democratization therefore increases the likelihood that successful reconstruction would occur, creating a harder test for finding a negative effect of windfall on reconstruction after the mid-1990s.
2. On Uganda's civil war (1981–1986), see Karugire (1988) and Odongo (2000). On Museveni's National Resistance Army, see Weinstein (2006).
3. See also Uzoigwe (1983).
4. The spokesperson offered this description in the context of defending the regime's decision to rule with a large cabinet that included many potential rivals, a decision that I discuss later in this chapter.
5. Personal communication, July 2012.
6. Author interview, July 2005, Kampala. See also Brett (1996).
7. Author interview, July 2005, Kampala.
8. Author interview, August 2005, Kampala. See also McEwen (1986a) and McEwen (1986b).
9. Personal communication, July 2012.
10. Author interview, July 2005, Kampala.
11. Author interview, July 2005, Kampala.
12. Author interview, July 2005, Kampala.
13. Author interview, August 2005, Kampala.
14. Author interview, July 2005, Kampala.
15. Author interview, August 2005, Kampala.
16. Personal communication, September 2012.
17. For more on Tumusiime-Mutebile's relationship with Museveni and with donors, see Mallaby (2004).
18. Author interview, senior government official, August, 2005, Kampala.
19. Personal communication, September 2012.
20. Author interview, July 2005, Kampala.
21. Quoted in Macrae, Zwi, and Gilson (2006), 1103.
22. Author interview, July 2005, Kampala.
23. Author interview, July 2005, Kampala.
24. Author interview, August 2005, Kampala.
25. Personal communication, September 2012.
26. Author interview, August 2005, Kampala.
27. Author interview, July 2005, Kampala.
28. Author interview, August 2005, Kampala. Factions from the Ugandan People's Defense Army, which Museveni had just overthrown, reformed under the banner of the Holy Spirit Movement and achieved quick

military victories across northern and eastern Uganda. Meanwhile, six other, smaller insurgencies erupted as well: the Ugandan National Rescue Front in the northwest, the National Army for the Liberation of Uganda in the west, the Former Uganda National Army in the north, the Ugandan People's Army (former president Obote's supporters) in the east, and the Uganda Freedom Movement and Federal Democratic Movement of Uganda in south-central Uganda (Amaza 1998; Brett 1995). Some estimate as many as 27 rebel groups rose to challenge Museveni between 1986 and 1988 (Tripp 2010, 151).
29. Author interview, August 2005, Kampala.
30. Author interview, July 2005, Kampala.
31. Author interview, July 2005, Kampala.
32. Author interview, July 2005, Kampala.
33. Author interview, July 2005, Kampala.
34. Author interview, August 2005, Kampala.
35. When donors demanded that the government cut down the cabinet's size, the number of ministers declined from forty-four in 1990 to twenty-one, including six opposition members, in 1991. Counting deputy ministers and ministers of state, twelve out of forty-two belonged to the opposition in 1991, keeping the proportion of opposition members to the total cabinet about the same.
36. See also Barkan et al. (2004) and Tripp (2010).
37. Author interview, July 2005, Kampala.
38. Author interview, July 2005, Kampala. See also Weinstein (2007, 70).
39. Author interview, July 2005, Kampala.

Chapter 7

1. Data on windfall used throughout this chapter are described in Chapter 3. For more analysis of this case, see Boyce (1996); Holiday and Stanley (1993); Johnson (1993); Johnstone (1995); Karl (1988); Paige (1997); Paus (1996); Stanley (1996); Stanley and Call (1997); Stanley and Loosle (1998); Truth Commission for El Salvador (1993); United Nations (1995); Weiss-Fagen (1996); Williams (1994); Wise (1986); Wood (1996); Wood (1999); (Wood 2000).
2. For more analysis of this case, see Castañeda (1994); Child (1992); Dosal (1995); Dunkerley (1994); Farer (1996); Gramajo Morales (1997); Schirmer (1998); Spence et al. (1998); Stanley (1999); United Nations (1998).
3. For more analysis of this case, see Andreas (2004); Chesterman (2004); Cox (2001); Donais (2003); Donais (2005); Pugh (2004). Pugh, Cooper and Goodhand (2004) suggest Bosnia held some strategic importance to Western donors due to its location in Western Europe (143). Relative to other priorities facing Western donors during this time, however, Bosnia appears to have been peripheral to Western interests (Daadler 2000).

4. For more analysis of this case, see Hintjens (1999); Kuperman (2001); Mamdani (2001).
5. For more analysis of this case, see Jackson (1992); Kiernan (1996).
6. For more analysis of this case, see Bayart, Ellis and Hibou (1999); Frynas (2004); Karl and Gary (2003); Liniger-Goumez (1989); Wood (2004).
7. For more analysis of this case, see Dupuy (1989); Fass (1988); Horblitt (1995); Trouillot (1990); Trouillot (1994).
8. For more analysis of this case, see Akehurst (1982); Al-Yousef (1995); Allen (1987); Allen and Rigsbee (2000); Pimlott (1985); Ray (2008); Thwaites (1995).
9. For more analysis of this case, see Aliev (1998); Franke, Gawrich, and Alakbarov (2009); Heradstveit (2001); Hoffman (2000); Najman and Raballand (2007).
10. For more analysis of this case, see Ellis (2001); Fearon et al. (2009); Howe (1996/97); Liebenow (1987); Moran (2008); Sesay (1996).
11. On the origins and components of the Kimberley Process, see Grant and Taylor (2004).
12. In July of 2010, the U.S. government passed the Dodd-Frank Act, which demands that mining companies listed with the U.S. Securities and Exchange Commission release information on how much they pay foreign governments. The effects of this law are still not well understood. However, the law has come under criticism for creating poverty in resource-rich areas by eliminating resource-extraction jobs. See Seay (2012).
13. See Human Rights Watch (2004).
14. Another idea would be to pay oil rents directly to citizens. Governments could tax that income in exchange for public services (Birdsall and Subramanian 2004; Morrison 2007). The idea of direct transfer to citizens is similar to remittances (Adida and Girod 2011). It has been found that citizens provide their own public services when given direct income via remittances. The effects of this dynamic on governance are ambiguous, and further research is required to determine whether citizens are freeing up the government to be more corrupt or complementing its activities (Abdih et al. 2008).
15. On this strategy, see Dietrich (2013).
16. The United States has also offered strategic aid to states where local security problems are believed to impact the U.S. War on Terror, such as Ethiopia and the Philippines (Byman 2006).
17. See also Crost and Johnston (2010) and Beath, Christia, and Enikolopov (2012).

BIBLIOGRAPHY

Abdih, Yasser, Ralph Chami, Jihad Dagher, and Peter Montiel. 2008. "Remittances and Institutions: Are Remittances a Curse?" Washington, DC: International Monetary Fund.

Adida, Claire L., and Desha M. Girod. 2011. "Do Migrants Improve Their Hometowns? Remittances and Access to Public Services in Mexico, 1995–2000." *Comparative Political Studies* 44(1): 3–27.

Agence France Presse. 1992. "Mozambique Could Become 'Next Somalia': U.N. Representative." September 15.

Agence France Presse. 1995. "RENAMO Denies that Troops Still Armed." July 25.

Ahmed, Faisal Z. 2012. "The Perils of Unearned Foreign Income: Aid, Remittances, and Government Survival." *American Political Science Review* 106(1): 146–65.

AidData. 2012. "AidData: Open Data for International Development." Accessed October 5, 2012. http://www.aiddata.org.

Akehurst, John. 1982. *We Won a War: The Campaign in Oman, 1965–1975*. Wilton, UK: Michael Russell.

Al-Yousef, Mohamed bin-Musa. 1995. *Oil and the Transformation of Oman, 1970–1995*. London: Stacey International.

Alesina, Alberto, and David Dollar. 2000. "Who Gives Foreign Aid to Whom and Why?" *Journal of Economic Growth* 5(1): 33–63.

Aliev, Heydar. 1998. *Azerbaijan Oil in the World Policy*. Baku: Azerbaijan Publishing House.

Allen, Calvin H., Jr. 1987. *Oman: The Modernization of the Sultanate*. Boulder, CO: Westview Press.

Allen, Calvin H., Jr., and W. Lynn Rigsbee, II. 2000. *Oman Under Qaboos: From Coup to Constitution, 1970–1996*. London: Frank Cass.

Amaza, Ondoga Ori. 1998. *Museveni's Long March: From Guerilla to Statesman*. Kampala: Fountain Publishers.

Andersen, Jørgen Juel, and Michael L. Ross. 2014. "The Big Oil Change: A Closer Look at the Haber-Menaldo Analysis." *Comparative Political Studies* 47(7): 993–1021.

Andreas, Peter. 2004. "Criminalized Conflict: The Clandestine Political Economy of War in Bosnia." *International Studies Quarterly* 48(1): 29–51.

Arndt, Channing, Henning Tarp Jensen, and Finn Tarp. 2000. "Stabilization and Structural Adjustment in Mozambique: An Appraisal." *Journal of International Development* 12(3): 299–323.

Arndt, Channing, Sam Jones, and Finn Tarp. 2006. "Aid and Development: The Mozambique Case." Discussion Papers, Department of Economics, University of Copenhagen.

Arriola, Leonardo. 2009. "Patronage and Political Stability in Africa." *Comparative Political Studies* 42(10): 1339–62.

Bank Information Center and Global Witness. 2008. "Assessment of International Monetary Fund and World Bank Group Extractive Industries Transparency Implementation." Washington, DC.

Banks, Arthur S. 2011. "Cross-National Time Series Data Archive." Binghamton, NY: Computer Systems Unlimited.

Barkan, Joel, Saillie Simba Kayunga, Njuguna Ng'ethe, and Jack Titsworth. 2004. "The Political Economy of Uganda." Washington, DC: The World Bank.

Bates, Robert H. 2008. *When Things Fell Apart: State Failure in Late-Century Africa*. New York: Cambridge University Press.

Bayart, Francois, Stephen Ellis, and Beatrice Hibou. 1999. *The Criminalization of the State in Africa*. Bloomington: Indiana University Press.

BBC. 1987. "Aid Donors Announce Extra Assistance for Uganda." June 23.

BBC. 1988. "Uganda; Foreign Aid in 1989." November 8.

BBC. 1991. "Uganda; Creditors' Meeting in Paris Agrees Commitments for Forthcoming Year." April 2.

Bearce, David H., and Daniel C. Tirone. 2010. "Foreign Aid Effectiveness and the Strategic Goals of Donor Governments." *Journal of Politics* 72(3): 837–51.

Beath, Andrew, Fotini Christia, and Ruben Enikolopov. 2012. "Winning Hearts and Minds through Development: Evidence from a Field Experiment in Afghanistan." MIT Political Science Working Paper No. 2011–14.

Belasco, Amy. 2009. "The Cost of Iraq, Afghanistan, and Other Global War on Terror Operations Since 9/11." Washington, DC: Congressional Research Service.

Belkin, Aaron, and Evan Schofer. 2003. "Toward a Structural Understanding of Coup Risk." *Journal of Conflict Resolution* 47(5): 594–620.

Bender, Gerald. 1983. "The Continuing Crisis in Angola." *Current History* 82: 482.

Bender, Gerald J. 1978. *Angola Under the Portuguese: The Myth and the Reality*. Berkeley: University of California Press.

Berman, Eli, Jacob N. Shapiro, and Joseph H. Felter. 2011. "Can Hearts and Minds Be Bought? The Economics of Counterinsurgency in Iraq." *Journal of Political Economy* 119: 766–819.

Bermeo, Sarah Blodgett. 2008. "Aid Strategies of Bilateral Donors." New Haven, CT: Department of Political Science, Yale University.

Biddle, Stephen, and Robert Zirkle. 1996. "Technology, Civil-Military Relations, and Warfare in the Developing World." *Journal of Strategic Studies* 19(2): 171–212.

Biden, Joe. 2008. "Afghanistan. Pakistan. Forgotten." *The New York Times*, March 2.

Birdsall, Nancy, and Arvind Subramanian. 2004. "Saving Iraq From its Oil." *Foreign Affairs* 83(4): 77–89.

Blattman, Christopher. 2009. "From Violence to Voting: War and Political Participation in Uganda." *American Political Science Review* 103(2): 231–47.

Bobba, Matteo, and Andrew Powell. 2007. "Aid and Growth: Politics Matters." Inter-American Development Bank: Washington, DC.

Boone, Peter. 1996. "Politics and the Effectiveness of Foreign Aid." *European Economic Review* 40: 289–329.

Borst, Barbara. 1993. "Mozambique: Donors Back Peace Process with One Billion Dollars." *Inter Press Service*, December 8.

Botchwey, Kwesi, Paul Collier, Jan Willem Gunning, and Koichi Hamada. 1998. "Report of the Group of Independent Persons Appointed to Conduct an Evaluation of Certain Aspects of the Enhanced Structural Adjustment Facility." Washington, DC: International Monetary Fund.

Boyce, James K., ed. 1996. *Economic Policy for Building Peace: The Lessons of El Salvador*. Boulder, CO: Lynne Rienner.

Boyce, James K. 2007. "Public Finance, Aid and Post-Conflict Recovery." University of Massachusetts, Amherst, Department of Economics.

Boyce, James K., and Shepard Forman. 2010. "Financing Peace: International and National Resources for Postconflict Countries and Fragile States." World Development Report 2011: Background Paper. Washington, DC: The World Bank.

Brambor, Thomas, William Roberts Clark, and Matt Golder. 2006. "Understanding Interaction Models: Improving Empirical Analyses." *Political Analysis* 14(1): 63–82.

Branch, Adam. 2011. *Displacing Human Rights: War and Intervention in Northern Uganda*. New York: Oxford University Press.

Bratton, Michael, and Nicolas van de Walle. 1997. *Democratic Experiments in Africa: Regime Transitions in Comparative Perspective*. New York: Cambridge University Press.

Bräutigam, Deborah A., and Stephen Knack. 2004. "Foreign Aid, Institutions, and Governance in Sub-Saharan Africa." *Economic Development and Cultural Change* 52: 255–85.

Brett, E. A. 1995. "Neutralising the Use of Force in Uganda: The Rise of the Military in Politics." *Journal of Modern African Studies* 33(1): 129–52.

Brett, E. A. 1996. "Uganda." In *Limits of Adjustment in Africa: The Effects of Economic Liberalization, 1986–94*, eds. Poul Engberg-Pedersen, Phil Raikes, and Lars Udsholt. Copenhagen: Centre for Development Research in association with James Currey, 309–46.

Brittain, Victoria. 1985. "The Divisions that Tore Uganda Apart: The Political Tensions Behind the Military Coup." *The Guardian*, June 29.

Brownlee, Jason. 2007. "Can America Nation-Build?" *World Politics* 59(2): 314–40.

Buchanan, James M. 1975. "The Samaritan's Dilemma." In *Altruism, Morality, and Economic Theory*, ed. Edmund S. Phelps. New York: Russell Sage Foundation, 71–85.

Bueno de Mesquita, Bruce, Alastair Smith, Randolph M. Siverson, and James D. Morrow. 2003. *The Logic of Political Survival*. Cambridge, MA: MIT Press.

Bueno de Mesquita, Bruce, and Alastair Smith. 2007. "Foreign Aid and Policy Concessions." *Journal of Conflict Resolution* 51(2): 251–84.

Bueno de Mesquita, Bruce, and Alastair Smith. 2010. "Leader Survival, Revolutions, and the Nature of Government Finance." *American Journal of Political Science* 54(4): 936–50.

Burnside, Craig, and David Dollar. 1998. "Aid, the Incentive Regime, and Poverty Reduction." Policy Research Working Paper. Washington, DC: The World Bank.

Burnside, Craig, and David Dollar. 2000. "Aid, Policies, and Growth." *The American Economic Review* 90(4): 847–68.

Buur, Lars, Odele Baloi, and Carlota Mondlane Tembe. 2012. "Mozambique Synthesis Analysis: Between Pockets of Efficiency and Elite Capture." DIIS Working Paper, Copenhagen.

Byman, Daniel. 2006. "Remaking Alliances for the War on Terrorism." *The Journal of Strategic Studies* 29(5): 767–811.

Cahen, Michel. 1987. *Mozambique: La Révolution Implosée: Études Sur 12 Ans d'Indépendance, 1975–1987*. Paris: L'Harmattan.

Call, Charles T., ed. 2008. *Building States to Build Peace*. Boulder: Lynne Rienner Publishers.

Callaghy, Thomas M. 1984. *The State-Society Struggle: Zaire in Comparative Perspective*. New York: Columbia University Press.

Campos, Indira, and Alex Vines. 2008. "Angola and China: A Pragmatic Partnership." Washington, DC: Center for Strategic and International Studies.

Caplan, Richard. 2005. *International Governance of War-Torn Territories: Rule and Reconstruction*. Oxford; New York: Oxford University Press.

Carlson, Cindy. 2004. "Review of Health Service Delivery in Uganda: General Country Experience and Northern Uganda." London: DFID Health Systems Resource Centre.

Carothers, Thomas. 1991. *In the Name of Democracy: U.S. Policy Toward Latin America During the Reagan Years*. Berkeley: University of California Press.

Carroll, Rory. 2002. "Famine in Africa: After the Flood." *The Guardian (London)*, November 30.
Carter, David B. 2009. "The Compellence Dilemma: Non-Domestic Disputes with Violent Groups." Pennsylvania State University: State College, PA.
Carter, David B., and Curtis S. Signorino. 2010. "Back to the Future: Modeling Time Dependence in Binary Data." *Political Analysis* 18(3): 271–92.
Castañeda, Jorge. 1994. *Utopia Unarmed: The Latin American Left After the Cold War*. New York: Vintage.
Chabal, Patrick. 2002. *A History of Postcolonial Lusophone Africa*. London: Hurst.
Chabal, Patrick, and Nuno Vidal. 2008. *Angola: The Weight of History*. New York: Columbia University Press.
Chanboreth, Ek, and Sok Hach. 2008. "Aid Effectiveness in Cambodia." Washington, DC: Brookings Institution.
Chandrasekaran, Rajiv. 2009. "Administration Is Keeping Ally at Arm's Length." *The Washington Post*, May 6.
Chaudhry, Kiren Aziz. 1989. "The Price of Wealth: Business and State in Labor Remittance and Oil Economies." *International Organization* 43(1): 101–45.
Cheibub, Jose Antonio, Jennifer Gandhi, and James Raymond Vreeland. 2010. "Democracy and Dictatorship Revisited." *Public Choice* 143(1–2): 67–101.
Chesterman, Simon. 2004. *You, The People: The United Nations, Transnational Administration, and State-Building*. Oxford: Oxford University Press.
Chetail, Vincent, ed. 2009. *Post-Conflict Peacebuilding: A Lexicon*. Oxford: Oxford University Press.
Chilcote, Ronald H. 1967. *Portuguese Africa*. Englewood Cliffs, NJ: Prentice-Hall.
Child, Jack. 1992. *The Central American Peace Process: Sheathing Swords, Building Confidence*. Boulder, CO: Lynne Rienner.
Chingono, Mark F. 1996. *The State, Violence and Development: The Political Economy of War in Mozambique, 1975–1992*. Aldershot: Avebury.
Cliff, Julie, and Abdul Razak Noormahomed. 1993. "The Impact of War on Children's Health in Mozambique." *Social Science & Medicine* 36(7): 843–48.
Coghlan, Benjamin, Valerie Nkamgang Bemo, Pascal Ngoy, Tony Stewart, Flavien Mulumba, Jennifer Lewis, Colleen Hardy, and Richard Brennan. 2007. "Mortality in the Democratic Republic of Congo: An Ongoing Crisis." New York: International Rescue Committee.
Collier, David, Anke Hoeffler, and Måns Söderbom. 2008. "Post-Conflict Risks." *Journal of Peace Research* 45(4): 461–78.
Collier, Paul. 1999. "On the Economic Consequences of Civil War." *Oxford Economic Papers* 51: 168–83.
Collier, Paul, and Anke Hoeffler. 2004a. "Aid, Policy, and Growth in Post-Conflict Societies." *European Economic Review* 48(5): 1125–45.
Collier, Paul, and Anke Hoeffler. 2004b. "Greed and Grievance in Civil War." *Oxford Economic Papers* 56(4): 563–95.
Cooper, Helene. 2009. "In Leaning on Karzai, U.S. Has Limited Leverage." *The New York Times*, November 12.

Cornia, Giovanni Andrea, Richard Jolly, and Frances Stewart. 1987. *Adjustment with a Human Face*. Oxford: Clarendon Press.

Cortright, David, and George A. Lopez, eds. 2002. *Smart Sanctions: Targeting Economic Statecraft*. Lanham, MD: Rowman & Littlefield.

Costa, Luis. 2007. "Angola Cancela Consultas com Fundo Monetário." *Jornal de Angola*, March 13.

Cox, Marcus. 2001. "State Building and Post-Conflict Reconstruction: Lessons from Bosnia." Geneva: Centre for Applied Studies in International Negotiations.

Crost, Benjamin, and Patrick B. Johnston. 2010. "Aid Under Fire: Development Projects and Civil Conflict." Belfer Center Discussion Paper. Cambridge, MA: Harvard University.

Daalder, Ivo H. 2000. "The United States, Europe, and the Balkans." The Brookings Institution, Washington, D.C.

Dabla-Norris, Era, Camelia Minoiu, and Luis-Felipe Zanna. 2010. "Business Cycle Fluctuations, Large Shocks, and Development Aid: New Evidence." Washington, DC: IMF Working Paper WP/10/240.

Dawson, Jeremy F., and Andreas W. Richter. 2006. "Probing Three-Way Interactions in Moderated Multiple Regression: Development and Application of a Slope Difference Test." *Journal of Applied Psychology* 91(4): 917–26.

de Ree, Joppe, and Eleonora Nillesen. 2009. "Aiding Violence or Peace? The Impact of Foreign Aid on the Risk of Civil Conflict in Sub-Saharan Africa." *Journal of Development Economics* 88(2): 301–13.

de Renzio, Paolo, and Joseph Hanlon. 2007. "Contested Sovereignty in Mozambique: The Dilemmas of Aid Dependence." Global Economic Governance Programme. Oxford: University College.

DeYoung, Karen. 2008. "U.N.'s Envoy to Afghanistan Sees Threats to Progress." *The Washington Post*, April 29.

del Castillo, Graciana. 2001. "Post-Conflict Reconstruction and the Challenge to International Organizations: The Case of El Salvador." *World Development* 29(12): 1967–85.

del Castillo, Graciana. 2008. *Rebuilding War-Torn States: The Challenge of Post-Conflict Economic Reconstruction*. Oxford: Oxford University Press.

Desai, Raj, and Homi Kharas. 2010. "The Determinants of Aid Volatility." Global Economy and Development. Washington, DC: Brookings Institute.

Devarajan, Shantayanan, David Dollar, and Torgny Holmgren. 2001. *Aid and Reform in Africa: Lessons From Ten Case Studies*. Washington, DC: The World Bank.

DeVore, Marc R. 2012. "A More Complex and Conventional Victory: revisiting the Dhofar Counterinsurgency, 1963–1975." *Small Wars and Insurgencies* 23(1): 144–73.

Dietrich, Simone. 2013. "Bypass or Engage? Explaining Donor Delivery Tactics in Foreign Aid Allocation." *International Studies Quarterly* 57(4): 698-712.

Dijkstra, A. Geske, and Jan Kees van Donge. 2001. "What Does the 'Show Case' Show? Evidence of and Lessons from Adjustment in Uganda." *World Development* 29(5): 841–63.

Dijkstra, A. Geske. 2002. "The Effectiveness of Policy Conditionality: Eight Country Experiences." *Development and Change* 32(2): 307–34.

Dobbins, James, John G. McGinn, Keith Crane, Seth G. Jones, Rollie Lal, Andrew Rathmell, Rachel Swanger, and Anga Timilsina. 2003. *America's Role in Nation-Building: From Germany to Iraq*. Santa Monica, CA: RAND.

Doing Business. 2009. "Most Improved in Doing Business 2009." World Bank. Accessed December 3, 2013. http://www.doingbusiness.org/reforms/top-reformers-2009.

Donais, Timothy. 2003. "The Political Economy of Stalemate: Organised Crime, Corruption and Economic Deformation in Post-Dayton Bosnia." *Conflict, Security & Development* 3(3): 359–82.

Donais, Timothy. 2005. *Political Economy of Peacebuilding*. New York: Routledge.

Dosal, Paul J. 1995. *Power in Transition: The Rise of Guatemala's Industrial Oligarchy, 1871–1994*. Westport, CT: Praeger.

Doyle, Michael W., and Nicholas Sambanis. 2006. *Making War and Building Peace: United Nations Peace Operations*. Princeton, NJ: Princeton University Press.

Dreher, Axel, Jan-Egbert Sturm, and James Raymond Vreeland. 2009a. "Global Horse Trading: IMF Loans for Votes in the United Nations Security Council." *European Economic Review* 53(7): 742–57.

Dreher, Axel, Jan-Egbert Sturm, and James Raymond Vreeland. 2009b. "Development Aid and International Politics: Does Membership on the UN Security Council Influence World Bank Decisions?" *Journal of Development Economics* 88(1): 1–18.

Dresden, Jennifer Raymond. 2014. "From Combatants to Candidates: Electoral Competition and the Legacy of Civil War." Presented at the Annual Meeting of the International Studies Association. Toronto, ON.

Driscoll, Jesse R. 2012. "Exiting Anarchy: Militia Politics after the Post-Soviet Wars." University of California, San Diego

Dunkerley, James. 1994. *The Pacification of Central America*. London: Verso.

Dunning, Thad. 2004. "Conditioning the Effects of Aid: Cold War Politics, Donor Credibility, and Democracy in Africa." *International Organization* 58(2): 409–23.

Dunning, Thad. 2008. *Crude Democracy: Natural Resource Wealth and Political Regimes*. New York: Cambridge University Press.

Dupuy, Alex. 1989. *Haiti in the World Economy: Class, Race, and Underdevelopment Since 1700*. Boulder, CO: Westview Press.

Dupuy, Alex. 1997. *Haiti in the New World Order: The Limits of the Democratic Revolution*. Boulder, CO: Westview Press.

Easterly, William. 2001. *The Elusive Quest for Growth: Economists' Adventures and Misadventures in the Tropics*. Cambridge, MA: MIT Press.

Easterly, William. 2003. "Can Foreign Aid Buy Growth?" *Journal of Economic Perspectives* 17(3): 23–48.
Economist Intelligence Unit. 1993. "Country Profile: Uganda." London: Economist Publications.
Economist Intelligence Unit. 1997a. "Country Profile: Gabon, Equatorial Guinea, 1996–1997." London: Economist Publications.
Economist Intelligence Unit. 1997b. "Country Profile: Georgia, Armenia, Azerbaijan, 1996–1997." London: Economist Publications.
Economist Intelligence Unit. 2001. "Country Profile: Dominican Republic, Haiti, Puerto Rico." London: Economist Publications.
Economist Intelligence Unit. 2003. "The Political Scene: The Press Reports New Scandals." Country Report: Angola. London: Economist Publications.
Economist Intelligence Unit. 2004. "Country Profile: Rwanda." London: Economist Publications.
Economist Intelligence Unit. 2005. "Country Profile: Bosnia and Hercegovina." London: Economist Publications.
Economist Intelligence Unit. 2006. "Country Profile: Guatemala." London: Economist Publications.
Economist Intelligence Unit. 2008a. *Country Profile: Cambodia*. London: Economist Publications.
Economist Intelligence Unit. 2008b. "Country Profile: Azerbaijan." London: Economist Publications.
Economist Intelligence Unit. 2008c. "Country Profile: Liberia." London: Economist Publications.
El-Khawas, Mohamed A. 1974. "Foreign Economic Involvement in Angola and Mozambique." *Issue: A Quarterly Journal of Africanist Opinion* 4(2): 21–28.
Ellis, Stephen. 2001. *The Mask of Anarchy: The Destruction of Liberia and the Religious Dimension of an African Civil War*. New York: New York University Press.
Englebert, Pierre, and Denis M. Tull. 2008. "Postconflict Reconstruction in Africa: Flawed Ideas about Failed States." *International Security* 32(4): 106–39.
Eriksson, John, Alcira Kreimer, and Margaret Arnold. 2000. *El Salvador: Post-Conflict Reconstruction*. Washington, DC: World Bank.
Esrey, S. A., J. B. Potash, L. Roberts, and C. Shiff. 1991. "Effects of Improved Water Supply and Sanitation on Ascariasis, Diarrhoea, Dracunculiasis, Hookworm Infection, Schistosomiasis, and Trachoma." *Bulletin of the World Health Organization* 61(5): 609–21.
European Union. 2009. "EU Engagement in Afghanistan." Brussels.
Farer, Tom, ed. 1996. *Beyond Sovereignty: Collectively Defending Democracy in the Americas*. Baltimore, MD: Johns Hopkins University Press.
Farmer, Paul. 1994. *The Uses of Haiti*. Monroe, ME: Common Courage Press.
Fass, Simon M. 1988. *Political Economy in Haiti: The Drama of Survival*. New Brunswick, MD: Transaction Publishers.
Fearon, James D., and David D. Laitin. 2003. "Ethnicity, Insurgency, and Civil War." *American Political Science Review* 97(1): 75–90.

Fearon, James D., Macartan Humphreys, and Jeremy M. Weinstein. 2009. "Can Development Aid Contribute to Social Cohesion after Civil War? Evidence from a Field Experiment in Post-Conflict Liberia." *American Economic Review: Papers and Proceedings* 99(2): 287–91.

Fearon, James D. 2010. "Governance and Civil War." Background Paper, World Bank. Washington, DC: The World Bank.

Feyzioglu, Tarhan, Vinaya Swaroop, and Min Zhu. 1998. "A Panel Data Analysis of the Fungibility of Foreign Aid." *World Bank Economic Review* 12(1): 29–58.

Filkins, Dexter. 2009. "Bribes Corrode Afghans' Trust in Government." *The New York Times*, January 2.

Finnegan, William. 1992. *A Complicated War: The Harrowing of Mozambique*. Berkeley: University of California Press.

Flores, Thomas Edward, and Irfan Nooruddin. 2009. "Democracy Under the Gun: Understanding Postconflict Economic Recovery." *Journal of Conflict Resolution* 53(3): 3–29.

Forbes, Kristin J. 2000. "A Reassessment of the Relationship Between Inequality and Growth." *American Economic Review* 90(4): 869–87.

Fortna, Virginia Page. 2008. *Does Peacekeeping Work? Shaping Belligerents' Choices after Civil War*. Princeton, NJ: Princeton University Press.

Fortna, Virginia Page, and Reyko Huang. 2012. "Democratization after Civil War: A Brush-Clearing Exercise." *International Studies Quarterly* 56(4): 801–08.

Foster, Vivien, William Butterfield, Chuan Chen, and Nataliya Pushak. 2008. *Building Bridges: China's Growing Role as Infrastructure Financier for Africa*. Washington, DC: The World Bank.

Franke, Anja, Andrea Gawrich, and Gurban Alakbarov. 2009. "Kazakhstan and Azerbaijan as Post-Soviet Rentier States: Resource Incomes and Autocracy as a Double 'Curse' in Post-Soviet Regimes." *Europe-Asia Studies* 61(1): 109–40.

Frynas, Jedrzej George. 2004. "The Oil Boom in Equatorial Guinea." *African Affairs* 103(413): 527–46.

Gallup, John Luke, and Jeffrey D. Sachs. 2001. "The Economic Burden of Malaria." *American Journal of Tropical Medicine and Hygiene* 64(1, 2): 85–96.

Gardiner, Ian. 2006. *In the Service of the Sultan: A First-Hand Account of the Dhofar Insurgency*. Barnsley, UK: Pen and Sword.

Gartzke, Erik. 2006. "The Affinity of Nations Index, 1946–2002." Columbia University, New York.

George, Alexander L., and Andrew Bennett. 2005. *Case Studies and Theory Development in the Social Sciences*. Cambridge, Mass.: MIT Press.

Gerring, John, Strom C. Thacker, and Rodrigo Alfaro. 2012. "Democracy and Human Development." *Journal of Politics* 74(1): 1–17.

Gertzel, Cherry. 1980. "Uganda after Amin: The Continuing Search for Leadership and Control." *African Affairs* 79(317): 461–89.

Ghobarah, Hazem Adam, Paul Huth, and Bruce Russett. 2003. "Civil Wars Kill and Maim People—Long After the Shooting Stops." *American Political Science Review* 97(2): 189–202.

Ghobarah, Hazem Adam, Paul Huth, and Bruce Russett. 2004. "Comparative Public Health: The Political Economy of Human Misery and Well-Being." *International Studies Quarterly* 48(1): 73–94.

Gibson, Clark C., Krister Andersson, Elinor Ostrom, and Sujai Shivakumar. 2005. *The Samaritan's Dilemma: The Political Economy of Development Aid.* Oxford: Oxford University Press.

Girod, Desha M., Stephen D. Krasner, and Kathryn Stoner-Weiss. 2009. "Governance and Foreign Assistance: The Imperfect Translation of Ideas into Outcomes." In *Promoting Democracy and the Rule of Law: American and European Strategies*, eds. Amichai Magen, Michael A. McFaul, and Thomas Risse. New York: Palgrave Macmillan Press, 61–92.

Girod, Desha M. 2012. "Effective Foreign Aid Following Civil War: The Nonstrategic-Desperation Hypothesis." *American Journal of Political Science* 56(1): 188–201.

Girod, Desha M. n.d. "Reducing Postconflict Coup Risk: The Low Windfall Coup-Proofing Hypothesis." *Conflict Management and Peace Science.*

Girod, Desha M. and Meir R. Walters. 2012. "Elite-Led Democratisation in Aid-Dependent States: The Case of Mauritania." *Journal of North African Studies* 17(2): 181–193.

Gleditsch, Nils Petter, Peter Wallensteen, Mikael Eriksson, Margareta Sollenberg, and Håvard Strand. 2002. "Armed Conflict 1946–2001: A New Dataset." *Journal of Peace Research* 39(5): 615–37.

Global Witness. 2011. "Global Witness Leaves Kimberley Process, Calls for Diamond Trade to Be Held Accountable." December 5.

Goemans, H.E. 2008. "Which Way Out?: The Manner and Consequences of Losing Office." *Journal of Conflict Resolution* 52(6): 771–94.

Goemans, Hein, and Nikolay Marinov. 2011. "Foreign Pressure and Elections after the Coup." New Haven, CT, and Rochester, NY: Yale University and University of Rochester.

Goemans, Henk E., Kristian Skrede Gleditsch, and Giacomo Chiozza. 2009. "Introducing Archigos: A Data Set of Political Leaders." *Journal of Peace Research* 46(2): 269–83.

Gottesman, Evan. 2003. *Cambodia after the Khmer Rouge: Inside the Politics of Nation Building.* New Haven, CT.: Yale University Press.

Götze, Catherine. 2004. "Civil Society Organizations in Failing States: The Red Cross in Bosnia and Albania." *International Peacekeeping* 11(4): 664–82.

Government of Mozambique. 1994. "Special Program of Assistance Status Report for Mozambique." Maputo, Mozambique.

Gramajo Morales, Héctor. 1997. "Political Transition in Guatemala, 1980–1990: A Perspective from Inside Guatemala's Army." In *Democratic Transitions in Central America*, eds. Jorge I. Domínguez and Marc Lindenberg. Gainesville: University Press of Florida, 111–38.

Grant, J. Andrew, and Ian Taylor. 2004. "Global Governance and Conflict Diamonds: The Kimberley Process and the Quest for Clean Gems." *The Round Table* 93(375): 385–401.

Grossman, Herschel I. 1992. "Foreign Aid and Insurrection." *Defence Economics* 3(4): 275–88.

Guliyev, Farid. 2009. "Oil Wealth, Patrimonialism, and the Failure of Democracy in Azerbaijan." *Caucasus Analytical Digest* 2: 2–5.

Habyarimana, James, Macartan Humphreys, Daniel N. Posner, and Jeremy M. Weinstein. 2007. "Why Does Ethnic Diversity Undermine Public Goods Provision?" *American Political Science Review* 101(4): 709–25.

Hall, Margaret, and Tom Young. 1997. *Confronting Leviathan: Mozambique Since Independence*. Athens: Ohio University Press.

Hamilton, Kirk, and Michael Clemens. 1999. "Genuine Savings Rates in Developing Countries." *The World Bank Economic Review* 13(2): 333–56.

Hanlon, Joseph. 1991. *Who Calls the Shots?* Bloomington: Indiana University Press.

Hanlon, Joseph. 1996. *Peace Without Profit: How the IMF Blocks Rebuilding in Mozambique*. Oxford: James Currey.

Hanna, Mike. 1995. "The Next 50 Years, Part 9: The Women." *Cable News Network*, October 22.

Harare Financial Gazette. 1998. "Dhlakama Says His Main Concern is Mozambique's Development." May 21.

Hartzell, Caroline A. 1999. "Explaining the Stability of Negotiated Settlements to Intrastate Wars." *Journal of Conflict Resolution* 43(1): 3–22.

Hartzell, Caroline A., Matthew Hoddie, and Donald Rothchild. 2001. "Stabilizing the Peace after Civil War: An Investigation of Some Key Variables." *International Organization* 55(1): 183–208.

Harzell, Caroline, and Matthew Hoddie. 2003. "Institutionalizing Peace: Power Sharing and Post-Civil War Conflict Management." *American Journal of Political Science* 47(2): 318–22.

Hegre, Håvard, Gudrun Østby, and Clionadh Raleigh. 2009. "Poverty and Civil War Events: A Disaggregated Study of Liberia." *Journal of Conflict Resolution* 53(4): 598–623.

Hendrickson, Dylan. 2001. "Globalisation, Insecurity and Post-War Reconstruction: Cambodia's Precarious Transition." *IDS Bulletin* 32(2): 98–106.

Heradstveit, Daniel. 2001. "Democratic Development in Azerbaijan and the Role of the Western Oil Industry." *Central Asian Survey* 20(3): 261–88.

Herbst, Jeffrey. 2004. "Let Them Fail: State Failure in Theory and Practice." In *When States Fail: Causes and Consequences*, ed. Robert I. Rotberg. Princeton, NJ: Princeton University Press, 302–18.

Hertog, Steffen. 2010. *Princes, Brokers, and Bureaucrats: Oil and the State in Saudi Arabia*. Ithaca, NY: Cornell University Press.

Heston, Alan, Robert Summers, and Bettina Aten. 2009. "Penn World Table Version 6.3." Center for International Comparisons of Production, Income and Prices at the University of Pennsylvania, Philadelphia, PA.

Heston, Alan, Robert Summers, and Bettina Aten. 2011. "Penn World Table Version 7.0." Center for International Comparisons of Production, Income and Prices at the University of Pennsylvania, Philadelphia, PA.

Hintjens, Helen M. 1999. "Explaining the 1994 Genocide in Rwanda." *The Journal of Modern African Studies* 37(2): 241–86.

Hodges, Tony. 2004. *Angola: Anatomy of an Oil State*. Bloomington: Indiana University Press.

Hodges, Tony, and Roberto Tibana. 2005. *The Political Economy of the Budget Process in Mozambique*. Oxford: Oxford Policy Management.

Hoffman, David I. 2000. "Azerbaijan: The Politicization of Oil." In *Energy and Conflict in Central Asia and the Caucasus*, eds. Robert Ebel and Rajan Menon. Lanham, MD: Rowman and Littlefield Publishers, 55–78.

Holiday, David, and William Stanley. 1993. "Building the Peace: Preliminary Lessons from El Salvador." *Journal of International Affairs* 46(2): 415–38.

Holmgren, Torgny, Louis Kasekende, Michael Atingi-Ego, and Daniel Ddamulira. 2001. "Uganda." In *Aid and Reform in Africa: Lessons from Ten Case Studies*, eds. Shantayanan Devarajan, David Dollar, and Torgny Holmgren. Washington, DC: The World Bank, 101–63.

Honaker, James, Gary King, and Matthew Blackwell. 2011. "Amelia II: A Program for Missing Data." *Journal of Statistical Software* 45(7): 1–47.

Horblitt, Stephen. 1995. "Barriers to Nonviolent Conflict Resolution." In *Haitian Frustrations: Dilemmas for U.S. Policy*, ed. Georges A. Fauriol. Washington, DC: Center for Strategic and International Studies, 129–42.

Howard, Lise Morjé. 2008. *UN Peacekeeping in Civil Wars*. New York: Cambridge University Press.

Howe, Herbert. 1996–97. "Lessons of Liberia: ECOMOG and Regional Peacekeeping." *International Security* 21(3): 145–76.

Hughes, Geraint. 2009. "A 'Model Campaign' Reappraised: The Counter-Insurgency War in Dhofar, Oman, 1965–1975." *The Journal of Strategic Studies* 32 (2): 271–305.

Human Rights Watch. 1992. *Conspicuous Destruction: War, Famine and the Reform Process in Mozambique*. New York: Human Rights Watch.

Human Rights Watch. 2004. "Some Transparency, No Accountability: The Use of Oil Revenue in Angola and Its Impact on Human Rights." Accessed May 5, 2008. http://www.hrw.org/reports/2004/angola0104.

Human Rights Watch. 2010. "Transparency and Accountability in Angola: An Update." Accessed April 13, 2012. http://www.hrw.org/sites/default/files/reports/angola0410webwcover_1.pdf.

Humphreys, Macartan. 2005. "Natural Resources, Conflict, and Conflict Resolution: Uncovering the Mechanisms." *Journal of Conflict Resolution* 49(4): 508–37.

Humphreys, Macartan, and Martin E. Sandbu. 2007. "The Political Economy of Natural Resource Funds." In *Escaping the Resource Curse*, eds. Macartan Humphreys, Jeffrey D. Sachs, and Joseph E. Stiglitz. New York: Columbia University Press.

Humphreys, Macartan, and Jeremy M. Weinstein. 2009. "Field Experiments and the Political Economy of Development." *Annual Review of Political Science* 12: 367–78.

IMF. 1998. "Republic of Mozambique: Selected Issues." IMF Staff Country Report No. 98/59. Washington, DC: International Monetary Fund.

IMF. 2001. "Republic of Mozambique: Selected Issues and Statistical Appendix." IMF Country Report No. 01/25. Washington, DC: International Monetary Fund.

IMF. 2007. "Angola: Selected Issues and Statistical Appendix." IMF Country Report No. 07/355. Washington, DC: International Monetary Fund.

IMF. 2008. *"Sudan: First Review of Performance under the 2007–08 Staff-Monitored Program."* IMF Country Report No. 08/174. Washington, DC: International Monetary Fund.

IMF. 2009. "Angola: Request for Stand-By Arrangement." IMF Country Report No. 09/320. Washington, DC: International Monetary Fund.

IMF. 2011. "Angola—Fifth Review Under the Stand-By Arrangement, Request for Waiver of Applicability of Performance Criteria, and Request for Modification of Performance Criteria—Staff Report; Supplement; Press Release on the Executive Board Discussion; and Statement by the Executive Director for Angola." IMF Country Report No. 11/346. Washington, DC: International Monetary Fund.

Ingram, Gregory K., and Marianne Fay. 2008. "Physical Infrastructure." In *International Handbook of Development Economics*, eds. Amitava Krishna Dutt and Jaime Ros. Cheltenham, UK: Edward Elgar, 301–15.

Iqbal, Zaryab, and Harvey Starr. 2008. "Bad Neighbors: Failed States and their Consequences." *Conflict Management and Peace Science* 25(4): 315–31.

Iqbal, Zaryab. 2010. *War and the Health of Nations*. Stanford, CA: Stanford University Press.

Jackson, Karl D., ed. 1992. *Cambodia, 1975–1978: Rendezvous with Death*. Princeton, NJ: Princeton University Press.

James, W. Martin. 1992. *A Political History of the Civil War in Angola, 1974–1990*. New Brunswick, NJ: Transaction Publishers.

Jaynes, Gregory. 1981. "In Post-Amin Uganda, Dreams Keep Dying." *The New York Times*, April 7.

Jett, Dennis C. 1999. *Why Peacekeeping Fails*. New York: St. Martin's Press.

Johnson, Kenneth Lance. 1993. "Between Revolution and Democracy: Business Elites and the State in El Salvador During the 1980s." Ph.D. Dissertation. Tulane University.

Johnstone, Ian. 1995. *Rights and Reconciliation: UN Strategies in El Salvador*. Boulder, CO: Lynne Rienner.

Kampala New Vision. 2007. "Uganda: Fortunes of the First NRM Cabinet." January 27.

Kang, Seonjou, and James Meernik. 2005. "Civil War Destruction and the Prospects for Economic Growth." *Journal of Politics* 67(1): 88–101.

Karl, Terry. 1988. "Exporting Democracy: The Unanticipated Effects of U.S. Electoral Policy in El Salvador." In *Crisis in Central America: Regional*

Dynamics and U.S. Policy in the 1990s, eds. Nora Hamilton, Linda Fuller, Jeffry Frieden, and Pastor Jr., Manuel. Boulder, CO: Westview Press, 173–91.

Karl, Terry, and Ian Gary. 2003. "The Bottom of the Barrel: Africa's Oil-Boom and the Poor." Baltimore, MD: Catholic Relief Services.

Karl, Terry Lynn. 1992. "El Salvador's Negotiated Revolution." *Foreign Affairs* 71(2): 147–64.

Karl, Terry Lynn. 1997. *The Paradox of Plenty: Oil Booms and Petro-States*. Berkeley: University of California Press.

Karugire, Samwiri Rubaraza. 1988. *The Roots of Instability in Uganda*. Kampala: New Vision.

Keller, Bill. 1993. "Peace From Chaos—A Special Report: Mozambique's Outlook Brightens As Truce Holds and Drought Ends." *The New York Times*, February 22.

Khadiagala, Gilbert M. 1995. "State Collapse and Reconstruction in Uganda." In *Collapsed States: The Disintegration and Reconstruction of Legitimate Authority*, ed. I. William Zartman. Boulder, CO: Lynne Rienner Publishers, 33–47.

Kiernan, Ben. 1996. *The Pol Pot Regime: Race, Power, and Genocide in Cambodia under the Khmer Rouge, 1975–79*. New Haven, CT: Yale University Press.

Kimenyi, Mwangi S., and John M. Mbaku. 1993. "Rent-Seeking and Institutional Stability in Developing Countries." *Public Choice* 77(2): 385–405.

King, Gary, Michael Tomz, and Jason Wittenberg. 2000. "Making the Most of Statistical Analyses: Improving Interpretation and Presentation." *American Journal of Political Science* 44(2): 347–61.

Kiyaga-Nsubuga, John. 2004. "Uganda: The Politics of 'Consolidation' under Museveni's Regime, 1996–2003." In *Durable Peace: Challenges for Peacebuilding in Africa*, eds. Taisier M. Ali and Roger O. Matthews. Toronto: University of Toronto Press, 86–112.

Kiyonga, Crispus. 1987. "Budget Speech." Kampala: Government of Uganda.

Klitgaard, Robert. 1990. *Tropical Gangsters: One Man's Experience with Development and Decadence in Deepest Africa*. New York: Basic Books.

Kono, Daniel Yuichi, and Gabriella R. Montinola. 2009. "Does Foreign Aid Support Autocrats, Democrats, or Both?" *Journal of Politics* 71(2): 704–18.

Krasner, Stephen D. 2004. "Sharing Sovereignty: New Institutions for Collapsed and Failing States." *International Security* 29(2): 85–120.

Kreimer, Alcira, John Eriksson, Robert Muscat, Margaret Arnold, Colin Scott. 1998. *The World Bank's Experience with Post-Conflict Reconstruction*. Washington, DC: World Bank Operations Evaluation Department.

Kreimer, Alcira, Paul Collier, Collin S. Scott, Margaret Arnold. 2000. *Uganda: Post-Conflict Reconstruction Country Case Study Series*. Washington, DC: World Bank Operations Evaluation Department.

Kreutz, Joakim. 2010. "How and When Armed Conflicts End: Introducing the UCDP Conflict Termination Dataset." *Journal of Peace Research* 47(2): 243–50.

Kron, Josh. 2011. "Uganda's Oil Could Be Gift That Becomes a Curse." *The New York Times*, November 25.

Kumar, Krishna, ed. 1997. *Rebuilding Societies after Civil War: Critical Roles for International Assistance*. Boulder, CO: Lynne Rienner Publishers.

Kuperman, Alan J. 2001. *The Limits of Humanitarian Intervention: Genocide in Rwanda*. Washington, DC: Brookings Institution Press.

Kuziemko, Ilyana, and Eric Werker. 2006. "How Much Is a Seat on the Security Council Worth? Foreign Aid and Bribery at the United Nations." *Journal of Political Economy* 114(5): 905–30.

Lacina, Bethany, and Nils Petter Gleditsch. 2005. "Monitoring Trends in Global Combat: A New Dataset of Battle Deaths." *European Journal of Population* 21(23): 145–66.

LaFraniere, Sharon. 2006. "In Oil-Rich Angola, Cholera Preys Upon Poorest." *The New York Times*, June 16.

LaFraniere, Sharon. 2007. "As Angola Rebuilds, Most Find Their Poverty Persists." *The New York Times*, October 14.

Lake, David A., and Matthew A. Baum. 2001. "The Invisible Hand of Democracy: Political Control and the Provision of Public Services." *Comparative Political Studies* 34(6): 587–621.

Lalá, Anícia, and Laudemiro Francisco. 2006. "The Difficulties of Donor Coordination: Police and Judicial Reform in Mozambique." *Civil Wars* 8(2): 163–80.

Landau, Luis. 1998. *Rebuilding the Mozambique Economy: Assessment of a Development Partnership*. Washington, DC: The World Bank.

Langseth, Peter, James Katorobo, E.A. Brett, and J.C. Munene, eds. 1995. *Uganda: Landmarks in Rebuilding a Nation*. Kampala: Fountain Publishers.

Lateef, K. Sarwarin. 1991. "Structural Adjustment in Uganda: The Initial Experience." In *Changing Uganda: The Dilemmas of Structural Adjustment & Revolutionary Change*, eds. Holger Bernt and Michael Twaddle. London: James Currey Ltd., 20–41.

Le Billon, Philippe. 2001a. "The Political Ecology of War: Natural Resources and Armed Conflict." *Political Geography* 20: 561–84.

Le Billon, Philippe. 2001b. "Angola's Political Economy of War: The Role of Oil and Diamonds, 1975–2000." *African Affairs* 100: 55–80.

Leeds, Brett Ashley, Jeffrey M. Ritter, Sara McLaughlin Mitchell, and Andrew G. Long. 2002. "Alliance Treaty Obligations and Provisions, 1815–1944." *International Interactions* 28(3): 261–84.

Leeds, Brett Ashley. 2005. "The Alliance Treaty Obligations and Provisions Project." Accessed February 2, 2010. http://atop.rice.edu/.

Legum, Colin. 1976. "The Soviet Union, China and the West in Southern Africa." *Foreign Affairs* 54(4): 745–62.

Leslie, Winsome J. 1987. *The World Bank & Structural Transformation in Developing Countries: The Case of Zaire*. Boulder, CO: Lynne Rienner Publishers.

Licht, Amanda A. 2010. "Coming into Money: The Impact of Foreign Aid on Leader Survival." *Journal of Conflict Resolution* 54(1): 58–87.

Licklider, Roy. 1995. "The Consequences of Negotiated Settlements in Civil Wars: 1945–1993." *American Political Science Review* 89(3): 681–90.

Liebenow, J. Gus. 1987. *The Quest for Democracy*. Bloomington: Indiana University Press.

Lieberman, Evan S. 2005. "Nested Analysis as a Mixed-Method Strategy for Cross-National Research." *American Political Science Review* 99(3): 435–52.

Liniger-Goumez, Max. 1989. *Small Is Not Always Beautiful: The Story of Equatorial Guinea*. Savage, MD: Rowman and Littlefield.

Londregan, John B., and Keith T. Poole. 1990. "Poverty, the Coup Trap, and the Seizure of Executive Power." *World Politics* 42(2): 151–83.

Looney, Robert. 2009. "The Omani and Bahraini Paths to Development: Rare and Contrasting Oil-based Economic Success Stories." United Nations University – World Institute for Development Economics Research. Research Paper No. 2009/38 Accessed August 3, 2014. http://www.wider.unu.edu/stc/repec/pdfs/rp2009/RP2009-38.pdf,

Lum, Thomas, Hannah Fischer, Julissa Gomez-Granger, and Anne Leland. 2009. "China's Foreign Aid Activities in Africa, Latin America, and Southeast Asia." Washington, DC: Congressional Research Service.

Luttwak, Edward. 1968. *Coup d'Etat: A Practical Handbook*. London: Allen Lane.

Macrae, Joanna, Anthony B. Zwi, and Lucy Gilson. 2006. "A Triple Burden for Health Sector Reform: 'Post'-Conflict Rehabilitation in Uganda." *Social Science and Medicine* 42(7): 1095–108.

Mallaby, Sebastian. 2004. *The World's Banker: A Story of Failed States, Financial Crises, and the Wealth and Poverty of Nations*. New York: Penguin Press.

Mamdani, Mahmood. 2001. *When Victims Become Killers: Colonialism, Nativism, and the Genocide in Rwanda*. Princeton, NJ: Princeton University Press.

Manning, Carrie. 1998. "Constructing Opposition in Mozambique: Renamo as Political Party." *Journal of Southern African Studies* 24(1): 161–89.

Manning, Carrie. 2001. "Competition and Accommodation in Post-Conflict Democracy: The Case of Mozambique." *Democratization* 8(2): 140–68.

Manning, Carrie. 2002. *The Politics of Peace in Mozambique: Post-Conflict Democratization, 1992–2000*. Westport, CT: Praeger.

Manning, Carrie. 2009. "Mozambique." In *External Democracy Promotion in Post-Conflict Zones: Evidence from Case Studies*, ed. Christoph Zürcher. Berlin: Freie Universität Berlin.

Manning, Carrie. 2010. "Mozambique's Slide into One-Party Rule." *Journal of Democracy* 21(2): 151–65.

Manning, Carrie, and Monica Marlbrough. 2010. "Bilateral Donors and Aid Conditionality in Post-Conflict Peacebuilding: The Case of Mozambique." *Journal of Modern African Studies* 48(1): 143–69.

Manthorpe, Jonathan. 1992. "Both Feast and Famine Can Be Fatal in Mozambique." *The Gazette (Montreal)*, October 29.

Marcum, John A. 1969. *The Angolan Revolution*. Cambridge, MA: M.I.T. Press.

Maren, Michael. 1997. *The Road to Hell: The Ravaging Effects of Foreign Aid and International Charity*. New York: Free Press.

Marshall, Monty G., Keith Jaggers, and Ted Robert Gurr. 2009. "Polity IV Project: Political Regime Characteristics and Transitions, 1800–2008." Vienna, VA: Center for Systemic Peace.

Marshall, Monty G., and Donna Ramsey Marshall. 2010. "Coup D'*État* Events." Vienna, VA: Center for Systemic Peace.

Martens, Bertin, Uwe Mummert, Peter Murrell, and Paul Seabright. 2002. *The Institutional Economics of Foreign Aid*. Cambridge, UK: Cambridge University Press.

Masimba, Josephine. 1994. "Mozambique-Politics: Will the Peace Hold?" *Inter Press Service*, October 20.

McEwen, Andrew. 1986a. "Chalker Advice for Uganda." *London Times*, December 5.

McEwen, Andrew. 1986b. "UK Links Africa Aid to Reforms." *London Times*, November 18.

McGillivray, Mark, Simon Feeny, Niels Hermes, and Robert Lensink. 2006. "Controversies Over the Impact of Development Aid: It Works; It Doesn't; It Can, But that Depends." *Journal of International Development* 18: 1031–50.

McSherry, Brendan. 2006. "The Political Economy of Oil in Equatorial Guinea." *African Studies Quarterly* 8(3): 23–45.

Médecins Sans Frontières. 2011. "Central African Republic: A State of Silent Crisis." Amsterdam: Médecins Sans Frontières.

Messiant, Christine. 2001. "The Eduardo Dos Santos Foundation: or, How Angola's Regime is Taking over Civil Society." *African Affairs* 100(399): 287–309.

Messiant, Christine, Brigitte Lachartre, and Michel Cahen. 2008. *L'Angola Postcolonial*. Paris: Karthala.

Milner, Helen V., Daniel L. Nielson, and Michael G. Findley. 2013. "Which Devil in Development? A Randomized Study of Citizen Actions Supporting Foreign Aid in Uganda." Princeton University.

Ministry of Planning and Economic Development. 1990. "Background to the Budget 1990–1991." Kampala.

Minter, William. 1972. *Portuguese Africa and the West*. New York: Monthly Review Press.

Minter, William. 1994. *Apartheid's Contras: An Inquiry into the Roots of War in Angola and Mozambique*. Johannesburg: Witwatersrand University Press.

Mo Ibrahim Foundation. 2007. "Joaquim Chissano Wins the Largest Prize in the World." October 22.

Moore, Mick. 2004. "Revenues, State Formation, and the Quality of Governance in Developing Countries." *International Political Science Review* 25(3): 297–319.

Moran, Mary H. 2008. *Liberia: The Violence of Democracy*. Philadelphia: University of Pennsylvania Press.

Morck, Randall, and Bernard Yeung. 2011. "Economics, History, and Causation." *Business History Review* 85(1): 39–63.

Morrison, Kevin M. 2007. "Natural Resources, Aid, and Democratization: A Best-Case Scenario." *Public Choice* 131(3/4): 365–86.

Morrison, Kevin M. 2009. "Oil, Nontax Revenue, and the Redistributional Foundations of Regime Stability." *International Organization* 63(1): 107–38.

Moser, Kath A., David A. Leon, and Davidson R. Gwatkin. 2005. "How Does Progress Towards the Child Mortality Millennium Development Goal Affect Inequalities Between the Poorest and the Least Poor? Analysis of Demographic and Health Survey Data." 331(7526): 1180–82.

Moyo, Dambisa. 2009. *Dead Aid: Why Aid Is Not Working and How There Is Another Way for Africa*. London: Allen Lane.

Mozambique News Agency. 2002. "Deputies United Over Their Pensions." *Africa News*, September 12.

Mugyenyi, Joshua B. 1991. "IMF Conditionality and Structural Adjustment under the National Resistance Movement." In *Changing Uganda*, eds. Holger Bernt Hansen and Michael Twaddle. London: James Currey Ltd.

Murdoch, James, and Todd Sandler. 2004. "Civil Wars and Economic Growth: Spatial Dispersion." *American Journal of Political Science* 48(1): 138–51.

Murshed, Syed Mansoob. 2010. *Explaining Civil War: A Rational Choice Approach*. Cheltenham, UK: Edward Elgar.

Musoke, David. 1991. "Uganda: Broad-Based Coalition Government May Soon End." *Inter Press Service*. April 10.

Mutibwa, Phares Mukasa. 1992. *Uganda since Independence: A Story of Unfulfilled Hopes*. Trenton, NJ: Africa World Press.

Mutumba, Richard. 2005. "Norway Cuts Aid Over Kisanja." *Kampala Monitor*. July 19.

Mwenda, Andrew. 2006. "Foreign Aid and the Weakening of Democratic Accountability in Uganda." Foreign Policy Briefing No. 88. Washington, D.C.: CATO Institute.

Mwenda, Andrew 2010. "Uganda's Politics of Foreign Aid and Violent Conflict: The Political Uses of the LRA Rebellion." In *The Lord's Resistance Army: Myth and Reality*, eds. Tim Allen and Koen Vlassenroot. London: Zed Books Ltd., 45–58.

Mwenda, Andrew M., and Roger Tangri. 2005. "Patronage Politics, Donor Reforms, and Regime Consolidation in Uganda." *African Affairs* 104(416): 449–67.

Najman, Boris, and Gael Raballand, eds. 2007. *The Economics and Politics of Oil in the Caspian Basin: The Redistribution of Oil Revenues in Azerbaijan and Central Asia*. New York: Routledge.

National Bank of Rwanda. 2004. "Annual Report 2003." Kigali, Rwanda.

Naudé, Wim A., Amelia Uliafnova Santos Paulino, and Mark McGillivray, eds. 2011. *Fragile States: Causes, Costs, and Responses*, UNU-Wider Studies in Development Economics. Oxford: Oxford University Press.

Navia, Patricio, and Thomas D. Zweifel. 2003. "Democracy, Dictatorship, and Infant Mortality Revisited." *Journal of Democracy* 14(3): 90–103.

Neumayer, Eric. 2003. *The Pattern of Aid Giving: The Impact of Good Governance on Development Assistance*. London: Routledge.

Newitt, Malyn. 1995. *A History of Mozambique*. London: Hurst & Company.
New Times. 2005. "Uganda: President Museveni Shows Signs of Backsliding." *Africa News*, July 8.
Ng'ethe, Njuguna. 1995. "Strongmen, State Formation, Collapse, and Reconstruction in Africa." In *Collapsed States: The Disintegration and Restoration of Legitimate Authority*, ed. I. William Zartman. Boulder, CO: Lynne Rienner Publishers.
Nielsen, Richard A., Michael G. Findley, Zachary S. Davis, Tara Candland, and Daniel L. Nielson. 2011. "Foreign Aid Shocks as a Cause of Violent Armed Conflict." *American Journal of Political Science* 55(2): 219–32.
Nobel Prize. 2013. "Ellen Johnson Sirleaf—Biographical." Accessed March 17, 2014. http://www.nobelprize.org/nobel_prizes/peace/laureates/2011/johnson_sirleaf-bio.html.
O'Callaghan, Mary-Louise. 2001. "Solomons Plotters Get Poll Handout." *The Australian*, November 8.
O'Reilly, Marc J. 1998. "Omanibalancing: Oman Confronts an Uncertain Future." *The Middle East Journal* 52(1): 70–84.
Obidegwu, Chukwuma. 2003. "The Search for Post-Conflict Socio-Economic Change, 1995–2001." Africa Region Working Paper Series No. 27678. Washington, DC: World Bank.
Odongo, Onyango. 2000. *A Political History of Uganda: The Origin of Museveni's Referendum 2000*. Kampala: Monitor Publications.
OECD. 2001. "The DAC Guidelines: Helping Prevent Violent Conflict." Paris.
OECD. 2008. "Is it ODA?" Factsheet. Organisation for Economic Co-operation and Development.
OECD. 2012. "International Development Statistics." Accessed March 29, 2012. http://www.oecd.org/dataoecd/50/17/5037721.htm.
Office of Foreign Assets Control. 2009. "Effectiveness of U.S. Economic Sanctions With Respect to Sudan." Washington, DC: Report to the U.S. Congress.
Okoth, Oketcho, and Ellen Subin. 1995. "Final Evaluation: Child Survival Project in Semuto and Butuntumula, Luwero District—Uganda." Washington, DC: AMREF Uganda Project.
Olson, Mancur. 1993. "Dictatorship, Democracy, and Development." *The American Political Science Review* 87(3): 567–76.
Organski, A. F. K., and Jacek Kugler. 1980. *The War Ledger*. Chicago: University of Chicago Press.
Ottaway, Marina. 1988. "Mozambique: From Symbolic Socialism to Symbolic Reform." *Journal of Modern African Studies* 26(2): 211–26.
Owtram, Francis. 2008. *Modern History of Oman: Formation of the State since 1920*. London: I. B. Tauris.
Pack, Howard, and Janet Pack. 1993. "Foreign Aid and the Question of Fungibility." *Review of Economics and Statistics* 75(2): 258–65.

Paige, Jeffery M. 1997. *Coffee and Power: Revolution and the Rise of Democracy in Central America*. Cambridge, MA: Harvard University Press.

Paluck, Elizabeth Levy, and Donald P. Green. 2009. "Deference, Dissent, and Dispute Resolution: An Experimental Intervention Using Mass Media to Change Norms and Behavior in Rwanda." *American Political Science Review* 103(4): 622–44.

Paris, Roland. 2004. *At War's End: Building Peace after Civil Conflict*. New York: Cambridge University Press.

Paris, Roland, and Timothy D. Sisk, eds. 2009. *The Dilemmas of Statebuilding: Confronting the Contradictions of Postwar Peace Operations*. London: Routledge.

Paus, Eva. 1996. "Exports and the Consolidation of Peace." In *Economic Policy for Building Peace: The Lessons of El Salvador*, ed. James K. Boyce. Boulder, CO: Lynne Rienner.

Pawson, Lara. 2007. "Angola Calls a Halt to IMF Talks." *British Broadcasting Corporation*, March 13.

Peterson, John E. 2007. *Oman's Insurgencies: The Sultanate's Struggle for Supremacy*. London: Saqi.

Pfeiffer, James. 2003. "International NGOs and Primary Health Care in Mozambique: The Need for a New Model of Collaboration." *Social Science & Medicine* 56: 725–38.

Pickard-Cambridge, Claire. 1998. "Mozambique's GDP put at $2 Billion." *Business Day*, June 26.

Pilster, Ulrich H., and Tobias Böhmelt. 2011. "Coup-Proofing and Military Effectiveness in Interstate Wars, 1967–99." *Conflict Management and Peace Science* 28(4): 1–20.

Pimlott, John. 1985. "Armed Forces and Modern Counter-Insurgency." In *The British Army: The Dhofar Campaign, 1970–1975*, eds. Ian Beckett and John Pimlott. New York: St. Martin's Press, 16–45.

Pitcher, M. Anne. 2002. *Transforming Mozambique: The Politics of Privatization, 1975–2000*. New York: Cambridge University Press.

Political Risk Services Group. 2007. "International Country Risk Guide." East Syracuse, NY.

Ponzio, Richard. 2011. *Democratic Peacebuilding: Aiding Afghanistan and Other Fragile States*. Oxford; New York: Oxford University Press.

Porto, João Gomes. 2003. "Cabinda: Notes on a Soon-To-Be-Forgotten War." Pretoria, South Africa: Institute for Security Studies.

Pottie, David. 2001. "Electoral Management and Democratic Governance in Southern Africa." *Politikon* 28(2): 133–55.

Powell, Jonathan. 2012. "Determinants of the Attempting and Outcome of Coups d'etat." *Journal of Conflict Resolution* 56(6): 1017–40.

Powell, Jonathan M., and Clayton L. Thyne. 2011. "Global Instances of Coups from 1950 to 2010: A New Dataset." *Journal of Peace Research* 48(2): 249–59.

Pritchett, Lant, and Michael Woolcock. 2004. "Solutions when the Solution is the Problem: Arraying the Disarray in Development." *World Development* 32(2): 191–212.

Prunier, Gérard. 1995. *The Rwanda Crisis: History of a Genocide.* New York: Columbia University Press.

Pugh, Michael. 2002. "Postwar Political Economy in Bosnia and Herzegovina: The Spoils of Peace." *Global Governance* 8(4): 467–82.

Pugh, Michael. 2004. "Rubbing Salt into War Wounds: Shadow Economies and Peacebuilding in Bosnia and Kosovo." *Problems of Post-Communism* 51(3): 53–60.

Pugh, Michael, Neil Cooper, and Jonathan Goodhand. 2004. *War Economies in a Regional Context: Challenges of Transformation.* Boulder, CO: Lynne Rienner.

Quinlivan, James T. 1999. "Coup-Proofing: Its Practice and Consequences in the Middle East." *International Security* 24(2): 131–65.

Rádio de Portugal. 1997. "Opposition Renamo Party Reportedly Has No Money for Local Elections." May 1.

Rádio Maputo. 1996. "Opposition Leader Dhlakama Returns Home after European Tour." June 3.

Rádio Mozambique. 1998. "Renamo Leader Meets Chirac, Promises No Return to War." July 1.

Ray, Bryan. 2008. *Dangerous Frontiers: Campaigning in Somaliland and Oman.* Barnsley, UK: Pen and Sword.

Reno, William. 1998. *Warlord Politics and African States.* Boulder: Lynne Rienner Publishers.

Reno, William. 2002. "Uganda's Politics of War and Debt Relief." *Review of International Political Economy* 9(3): 415–35.

Roessler, Philip. 2011. "The Enemy Within: Personal Rule, Coups, and Civil War in Africa." *World Politics* 63(2): 300–46.

Roque, Paula Cristina. 2008. "Angolan Legislative Elections: Analysing the MPLA's Triumph." Situation Report. Pretoria, South Africa: Institute for Security Studies.

Roque, Paula Cristina. 2009. "Angola's Façade Democracy." *Journal of Democracy* 20(4): 137–50.

Roque, Paula Cristina. 2011. "Angola: Parallel Governments, Oil and Neopatrimonial System Reproduction." Situation Report. Pretoria, South Africa: Institute for Security Studies.

Rose, Andrew K. 2005. "Does the WTO Make Trade More Stable?" *Open Economies Review* 16(1): 7–22.

Ross, Michael L. 2004. "How Do Natural Resources Influence Civil War? Evidence from Thirteen Cases." *International Organization* 58(1): 35–67.

Ross, Michael L. 2006a. "A Closer Look at Oil, Diamonds, and Civil War." *Annual Review of Political Science* 9: 265–300.

Ross, Michael L. 2006b. "Is Democracy Good for the Poor?" *American Journal of Political Science* 50(4): 860–74.

Ross, Michael. L. 2012. *The Oil Curse: How Petroleum Wealth Shapes the Development of Nations.* Princeton, NJ: Princeton University Press.

Rule, Sheila. 1987. "Uganda, At Peace, Is Facing Economic Battles." *The New York Times*, January 28.
Rwegayura, Anaclet. 1992. "Uganda: Ban on Political Parties Stirs Emotions." *Inter Press Service*, September 22.
Sachs, Jeffrey. 2003. "Institutions Don't Rule: Direct Effects of Geography on Per Capita Income." Cambridge, MA: National Bureau of Economic Research Working Paper 9490.
Saul, John S. 1985. *A Difficult Road: The Transition to Socialism in Mozambique*. New York: Monthly Review Press.
Saul, John S. 1991. "Mozambique: The Failure of Socialism?" *Transformation* 14: 104–10.
Savun, Burcu, and Daniel C. Tirone. 2011. "Foreign Aid, Democratization, and Civil Conflict: How Does Democracy Aid Affect Civil Conflict?" *American Journal of Political Science* 55 (2): 233–46.
Savun, Burcu, and Daniel C. Tirone. 2012. "Exogenous Shocks, Foreign Aid, and Civil Conflict." *International Organization* 66(3): 363–93.
Schirmer, Jennifer. 1998. *The Guatemalan Military Project: A Violence Called Democracy*. Philadelphia, PA: University of Pennsylvania Press.
Schmidtchen, Dieter. 1999. "To Help or Not to Help: The Samaritan's Dilemma Revisited." CSLE Discussion Paper. Saarbrücken, Germany: Universität des Saarlandes.
Scott, Catherine V. 1988. "Socialism and the 'Soft State' in Africa: An Analysis of Angola and Mozambique." *Journal of Modern African Studies* 26(1): 23–36.
Seay, Laura E. 2012. "What's Wrong with Dodd-Frank 1502? Conflict Minerals, Civilian Livelihoods, and the Unintended Consequences of Western Advocacy." Washington, DC: Center for Global Development.
Sesay, Max Ahmadu. 1996. "Politics and Society in Post-War Liberia." *Journal of Modern African Studies* 34: 395–420.
Shankleman, Jill. 2006. *Oil, Profits, and Peace: Does Business Have a Role in Peacemaking?* Washington, DC: United States Institute of Peace Press.
Sharer, Robert L., Hema R. De Zoysa, and Calvin A. McDonald. 1995. *Uganda: Adjustment with Growth, 1987–94*. Washington, DC: International Monetary Fund.
Shaw, Angus. 1992. "Famine Victims Die from Overeating." *Associated Press*, November 1.
Shaxson, Nicholas, João Neves, and Fernando Pacheco. 2008. "Drivers of Change: Angola." London: Department for International Development.
Sherman, Jake H. 2000. "Profit vs. Peace: The Clandestine Diamond Economy of Angola." *Journal of International Affairs* 53(2): 699–719.
Smith, Alistair. 2008. "The Perils of Unearned Income." *Journal of Politics* 70(3): 780–93.
Soares de Oliveira, Ricardo. 2007. "Business Success, Angola-Style: Postcolonial Politics and the Rise and Rise of Sonangol." *Journal of Modern African Studies* 45(4): 595–619.

Soares de Oliveira, Ricardo. 2011. "Illiberal Peacebuilding in Angola." *Journal of Modern African Studies* 49(2): 287–314.
Spence, Jack, David R. Dye, Paula Worby, Carmen Rosa de Leon-Escribano, Vickers George, and Mike Lanchin. 1998. "Promise and Reality: Implementation of the Guatemalan Peace Accords." Cambridge, MA: Hemisphere Initiatives.
Stanley, William. 1996. *The Protection Racket State: Elite Politics, Military Extortion, and Civil War in El Salvador*. Philadelphia, PA: Temple University Press.
Stanley, William, and Charles Call. 1997. "Building a New Civilian Police Force in El Salvador." In *Rebuilding Societies After Civil Wars: Critical Roles for International Assistance*, ed. Krishna Kumar. Boulder, CO: Lynne Rienner, 107–33.
Stanley, William, and David Holiday. 1997. "Peace Mission Strategy and Domestic Actors: United Nations Mediation, Verification, and Institution Building in El Salvador." *International Peacekeeping* 4(2): 22–49.
Stanley, William, and Robert Loosle. 1998. "Peace and Public Insecurity: The Civilian Police Component of Peace Operations in El Salvador." In *Policing the New World Disorder: Peace Operations and the Public Security Function*, ed. Robert Oakley. Washington, DC: National Defense University Press, 67–108.
Stanley, William. 1999. "Building New Police Forces in El Salvador and Guatemala: Learning and Counter-Learning." *International Peacekeeping* 6(4): 113–14.
Stewart, Frances, and Valpy Fitzgerald. 2001. *War and Underdevelopment*. Oxford: Oxford University Press.
Stockholm International Peace Research Institute. 1984. *SIPRI Yearbook*. Stockholm: Almquist & Wiksell.
Stone, Randall W. 2002. *Lending Credibility: The International Monetary Fund and the Post-Communist Transition*. Princeton, NJ: Princeton University Press.
Stone, Randall W. 2004. "The Political Economy of IMF Lending in Africa." *American Political Science Review* 98 (4): 577–91.
Stone, Randall W. 2010. "Buying Influence: Development Aid between the Cold War and the War on Terror." Unpublished Manuscript. University of Rochester, Rochester, NY.
Synge, Richard. 1997. *Mozambique: UN Peacekeeping in Action, 1992–94*. Washington, DC: United States Institute of Peace Press.
Tangri, Roger. 2006. "Politics and Presidential Term Limits in Uganda." In *Legacies of Power: Leadership Change and Former Presidents in African Politics* eds. Roger Southall and Henning Melber. Cape Town: Human Sciences Research Council Press.
Tarragó, Oscar E., and Giorgio L. Martinelli. 1996. "Integrated Health, Water and Sanitation Project: Beira and Chibabava District, Sofala Province—Final Evaluation." Prepared for: Africare Mozambique. USAID/Africare Project No. 656-0217-G-00-3022-00. Washington, DC: USAID
Tarrow, Sidney. 2010. "The Strategy of Paired Comparison: Toward a Theory of Practice." *Comparative Political Studies* 43(2): 230–59.
Televisão de Moçambique. 1995. "Dhlakama Renews Appeal for Government Funding of Renamo." February 25.

Thacker, Strom C. 1999. "The High Politics of IMF Lending." *World Politics* 52(1): 38–75.
Themnér, Lotta, and Peter Wallensteen. 2011. "Armed Conflict, 1946–2010." *Journal of Peace Research* 48(4): 525–36.
Therkildsen, Ole. 2001. "Efficiency, Accountability and Implementation Public Sector Reform in East and Southern Africa." Democracy, Governance and Human Rights Programme Paper. New York: United Nations Research Institute for Social Development.
Thwaites, Peter. 1995. *Muscat Command: The Muscat Regiment in Oman in 1967.* London: Leo Cooper.
Tindigarukayo, Jimmy K. 1988. "Uganda, 1979–85: Leadership in Transition." *Journal of Modern African Studies* 26(4): 607–22.
Titeca, Kristof. 2010. "The Spiritual Order of the LRA." In *The Lord's Resistance Army: Myth and Reality*, eds. Tim Allen and Koen Vlassenroot. London: Zed Books Ltd., 59–73.
Toft, Monica Duffy. 2010. *Securing the Peace: The Durable Settlement of Civil Wars.* Princeton, NJ: Princeton University Press.
Tomz, Michael, Gary King, and Langche Zeng. 2003. "ReLogit: Rare Events Logistic Regression." *Journal of Statistical Software* 8(2): 1–27.
Tomz, Michael, Jason Wittenberg, and Gary King. 2003. "CLARIFY: Software for Interpreting and Presenting Statistical Results." *Journal of Statistical Software* 8 (1). Accessed August 1, 2014. http://gking.harvard.edu.
Tostensen, Arne, and Beate Bull. 2002. "Are Smart Sanctions Feasible?" *World Politics* 54(3): 373–403.
Tripp, Aili Mari. 2010. *Museveni's Uganda: Paradoxes of Power in a Hybrid Regime.* Boulder, CO: Lynne Rienner.
Trouillot, Michel-Rolph. 1990. *Haiti: State Against Nation.* New York: Monthly Review Press.
Trouillot, Michel-Rolph. 1994. "Haiti's Nightmare and the Lessons of History." *North American Congress on Latin America*: 39–50.
Truth Commission for El Salvador. 1993. "From Madness to Hope: The 12-Year War in El Salvador." Report of the Commission on the Truth for El Salvador. New York and San Salvador: United Nations.
UN Integrated Regional Information Networks. 2004. "Angola: Pipeline Blockages Cut Off Food Aid to Beneficiaries." February 13.
UN News Centre. 2006. "Huge Funding Shortfall Forces UN to End Feeding Programme in Angola." October 13.
UNICEF. 2014. "Central African Republic: The Big Picture." Accessed March 5, 2014. http://www.unicef.org/infobycountry/car_2465.html.
United Nations. 1994a. "Programa Consolidado de Assistência Humanitária 1992–1994." Maputo, Mozambique.
United Nations. 1994b. "Report of the Secretary-General on the UN Operation in Mozambique." Security Council S/1994/803. July 7. New York.
United Nations. 1995. "The United Nations and El Salvador, 1990–1995." United Nations Blue Book Series. New York: United Nations Public Documents.

United Nations. 1998. "The Guatemalan Peace Agreements." New York.
United Nations. 2000. "Mozambique: United Nations System Common Country Assessment." Maputo, Mozambique.
United Nations. 2002. "Security Council is Told Peace in Democratic Republic of Congo Needs Solution of Economic Issues that Contributed to Conflict." Press Release SC/7547. Security Council 4634th Meeting (PM), New York
United Nations. 2010. "Human Development Report 2010: The Real Wealth of Nations: Pathways to Human Development." New York: United Nations Development Programme.
United Nations. 2012. "Peacekeeping Operations." Accessed November 1, 2012. http://www.un.org/en/peacekeeping/operations/.
United Nations Development Program. 2007. "Support to the Police of the Republic of Mozambique: Project Outcome Evaluation Phase I, II, and III Final Report." Outcome Evaluation Mission Report. October, New York.
United Nations Development Program. 2009. "Assessment of Development Results: Guatemala." New York: United Nations.
United Nations Development Program. 2013. "About Azerbaijan." Accessed December 3, 2013. http://www.az.undp.org/content/azerbaijan/en/home/countryinfo/.
U.S. Army/Marine Corps. 2006. "Counterinsurgency Field Manual." Washington, DC.
U.S. General Accounting Office. 1994. "El Salvador: Implementation of Post-War Programs Slower than Expected." GAO Report, Washington, DC.
U.S. State Department. 1995. "Country Reports on Human Rights Practices: Mozambique: 1994." Accessed August 7, 2007. http://www.state.gov.
USAID. 2005. "USAID/Mozambique: Strategic Objective Close Out Report." Washington, DC.
Uzoigwe, Godfrey N. 1983. "Uganda and Parliamentary Government." *Journal of Modern African Studies* 21(2): 253–71.
Van Acker, Frank. 2004. "Uganda and The Lord's Resistance Army: The New Order No One Ordered." *African Affairs* 103(412): 335–57.
van de Walle, Nicolas. 2001. *African Economies and the Politics of Permanent Crisis, 1979–1999*. New York: Cambridge University Press.
van der Veen, A. Maurits. 2011. *Ideas, Interests and Foreign Aid*. New York: Cambridge University Press.
Victora, Cesar G., Adam Wagstaff, Schellenberg Armstrong, Davidson Gwatkin, Mariam Cleason, and Jean-Pierre Habicht. 2003. "Applying an Equity Lens to Child Health and Mortality: More of the Same is Not Enough." *The Lancet* 362(9379): 233–41.
Vines, Alex. 1996. *Renamo: From Terrorism to Democracy in Mozambique*. York: Centre for Southern African Studies, University of York.
Vines, Alex. 1998. "The Business of Peace: 'Tiny' Rowland, Financial Incentives and the Mozambican Settlement." In *The Mozambican Peace Process in Perspective*, eds. Jeremy Armon, Dylan Hendrickson, and Alex Vines. London: Conciliation Resources, 66–74.

Vines, Alex, Nicholas Shaxson, and Lisa Rimli. 2005. *Angola: Drivers of Change*. London: Chatham House.

Vokes, Richard. 2012. "The Politics of Oil in Uganda." *African Affairs* 111(443): 303–14.

Vreeland, James Raymond. 2003. *The IMF and Economic Development*. Cambridge: Cambridge University Press.

Vreeland, James Raymond. 2008. "The Effect of Political Regime on Civil War: Unpacking Anocracy." *Journal of Conflict Resolution* 52(3): 401–25.

Wakabi, Wairagala. 2006. "Health Crisis Worsens in Central African Republic." Accessed May 5, 2008. http://www.thelancet.com.

Walter, Barbara F. 1997. "The Critical Barrier to Civil War Settlement." *International Organization* 51(3): 335–64.

Walter, Barbara F. 2011. "Why Bad Governance Leads to Repeat Civil War." University of California, San Diego.

Wantchekon, Leonard. 2004. "The Paradox of "Warlord" Democracy: A Theoretical Investigation." *American Political Science Review* 98(1): 17–33.

Weinstein, Jeremy M. 2002. "Mozambique: A Fading U.N. Success Story." *Journal of Democracy* 13(1): 141–56.

Weinstein, Jeremy M. 2005. "Autonomous Recovery and International Intervention in Comparative Perspective." Washington, DC: Center for Global Development.

Weinstein, Jeremy M. 2006. *Inside Rebellion: The Politics of Insurgent Violence*. New York: Cambridge University Press.

Weiss-Fagen, Patricia. 1996. "El Salvador: Lessons in Peace Consolidation." In *Beyond Sovereignty: Collectively Defending Democracy in the Americas*, ed. Tom Farer. Baltimore, MD: Johns Hopkins University Press.

Widner, Jennifer A. 1994. *Economic Change and Political Liberalization in Sub-Saharan Africa*. Baltimore, MD: Johns Hopkins University Press.

Williams, Robert G. 1994. *States and Social Evolution: Coffee and the Rise of National Governments in Central America*. Chapel Hill: University of North Carolina Press.

Wise, Michael. 1986. "Agrarian Reform in El Salvador, Process and Progress." San Salvador, El Salvador: U.S. Agency for International Development.

Wood, Elisabeth. 1996. "Economic Structure, Agrarian Elites, and Democracy: The Anomalous Case of El Salvador." New York: New York University.

Wood, Elisabeth. 1999. "Civil War Settlement: Modeling the Bases of Compromise." Paper presented at the 95th Annual Meeting of the American Political Science Association, September 2–5, Atlanta.

Wood, Elisabeth. 2000. *Forging Democracy from Below: Insurgent Transitions in South Africa and El Salvador*. New York: Cambridge University Press.

Wood, Elisabeth Jean. 2001. "An Insurgent Path to Democracy Popular Mobilization, Economic Interests, and Regime Transition in South Africa and El Salvador." *Comparative Political Studies* 34(8): 862–88.

Wood, Geoffrey. 2004. "Business and Politics in a Criminal State: The Case of Equatorial Guinea." *African Affairs* 103(413): 547–67.

World Bank. 2001. "The World Bank Operations Manual Operational Policies: Development Cooperation and Conflict." OP 2.30. Washington, DC: World Bank.

World Bank. 2002. "Democratic Republic of Congo: World Bank Supports the Country's Emergency Rehabilitation Program." Press Release No. 2003/049/AFR. Washington, DC: World Bank.

World Bank. 2003. "Azerbaijan: Building Competitiveness—An Integrated Non-Oil Trade and Investment Strategy (INOTIS) (In Two Volumes) Volume I: Summary Report." Report No. 25818-AZ. Poverty Reduction and Economic Management Unit. Washington, DC: World Bank.

World Bank. 2004. "Implementation Completion Report on a Credit in the Amount of SDR $66.3 Million to the Government of Mozambique for a Health Sector Recovery." Report No. 26963.Washington, DC: World Bank.

World Bank. 2005a. "Angola: Public Expenditure Management and Financial Accountability." Report No. 29036-AO. Washington, DC: World Bank.

World Bank. 2005b. "Mozambique: Country Economic Memorandum: Sustaining Growth and Reducing Poverty." Report No. 32615-MZ. Washington, DC: World Bank.

World Bank. 2006a. "From Curse to Blessing: Natural Resources and Institutional Quality." *Environment Matters Annual Review* (July 2005–June 2006), Washington, DC.

World Bank. 2006b. "ALCID Conditionality Database." Washington, DC: World Bank.

World Bank. 2006c. "Angola Country Economic Memorandum: Oil, Broad-based Growth, and Equity." Washington, DC: : World Bank.

World Bank. 2007a. "Angola: Country Assistance Evaluation." Report No. 39829, Washington, DC.

World Bank. 2007b. "Angola: Oil, Broad-Based Growth, and Equity." A World Bank Country Study. No. 40531. Washington, DC: World Bank.

World Bank. 2009a. "Guatemala Poverty Assessment: Good Performance at Low Levels." Central America Department. Report No. 43920-GT,. Washington, DC: World Bank.

World Bank. 2009b. "Cambodia Sustaining Rapid Growth in a Challenging Environment: Country Economic Memorandum." Report No. 49158-KH., Washington, DC: World Bank.

World Bank. 2010. "World Development Indicators." World Bank. Accessed February 10, 2011. http://databank.worldbank.org.

World Bank. 2011. "World Development Report 2011: Conflict, Security, and Development." Washington, DC.

World Bank. 2012a. "World Development Indicators." The World Bank. Accessed June 24, 2012. http://databank.worldbank.org.

World Bank. 2012b. "Projects and Operations." Accessed March 2, 2012. http://www.worldbank.org/projects.

World Health Organization. 2007. "Cholera Country Profile: Angola." Global Task Force on Cholera Control, Geneva: World Bank.

Worrall, John. 1981. "Uganda Leader's Key Problem May Be His Own Army." *The Christian Science Monitor*, November 24.

Wright, Joseph. 2008. "To Invest or Insure? How Authoritarian Time Horizons Impact Foreign Aid Effectiveness." *Comparative Political Studies* 41(7): 971–1000.

Wright, Joseph, and Matthew S. Winters. 2010. "The Politics of Effective Foreign Aid." *Annual Review of Political Science* 13: 61–80.

Young, Tom. 1988. "The Politics of Development in Angola and Mozambique." *African Affairs* 87(347): 165–84.

Zürcher, Christoph, Carrie L. Manning, Kristie D. Evenson, Rachel Hayman, Sarah Riese, and Nora Roehner. 2013. *Costly Democracy: Peacebuilding and Democratization after War*. Stanford, CA: Stanford University Press.

SUBJECT INDEX

Figures and tables are indicated by "f" and "t" following the page numbers.

Afghanistan
  aid to, 1–2, 141–144
  state-building effort in, 11–12
Africa, U.S. attitude toward, 64
African Development Bank, 107, 110
Africare, 76
Agriculture, in Mozambique, 76–77
Aid. *See* Foreign aid
Aid curse, xxi, 3–4, 119, 121, 147. *See also* Windfall curse
AidData, 151*n*12
Ali, Moses, 102
Aliyev, Heydar, 132–133
Aliyev, Ilham, 132–133
Al-Qaeda, in Afghanistan, 142
Al-Shabaab (al-Qaeda cell), 117
Amin, Idi, 101
Angola. *See also* Mozambique vs. Angola, post-conflict reconstruction in
  aid to, 64, 67, 73
  anti-transparency campaign by, 139–140
  cholera in, 75
  civil war, foreign involvement in, 61
  IMF's work with, 65–66
  OECD members as bilateral and multilateral donors to, 65–66
  power consolidation in, 78–79
  sanctions against, 135
  stonewalling aid gatekeepers in, 65–67
  UN mandate in, 62
  windfall income for, 61–62
  World Bank's work with, 65, 66, 76
  World Food Program's work in, 71
Annan, Kofi, 96
Aristide, Jean-Bertrand, 129
Armed Conflicts Database, 31, 38, 39
Armed Forces for the Defense of Mozambique, 80
Arzú Irigoyen, Alvaro, 125
Austerity measures, required by IMF and World Bank, 20–21
Australia, Solomon Islands, aid to, 18
Authoritarianism, 146
Azerbaijan, post-conflict reconstruction in, 132–133, 134

SUBJECT INDEX

Background (existing) institutions, 27
Baganda people, 102, 103
Bangui Agreements (1997), 94
Bank Information Center, 139
Baseline model, of nonstrategic-desperation hypothesis, 38–40
Baseline reconstruction, 38, 50
Bicesse Accords (1991), 90
Biden, Joe, 12
Binaisa, Godfrey, 102
Bin Laden, Osama, 142
Blood (conflict) diamonds, 137–138
Bosnia, aid effectiveness in, 4, 125–126
Britain. *See* United Kingdom
British Broadcasting Corporation, on nonstrategic donors to Uganda, 107
British Petroleum, 139
Buchanan, James, 22
Bush, George W., 138, 142, 143
Butuntumula, Uganda, health care projects in, 111
Bypassing governments, as policy counteracting windfall curse, 141–144

Cabinda, Angola
  insurgency in, 91–92
  oil from, 62
Cambodia
  aid effectiveness in, 127
  as low windfall country, 37
Canada, aid to Uganda, 110
Carter Center, 158n35
Case studies. *See* Mozambique vs. Angola; Uganda
Cashew industry, in Mozambique, 70
Cash handouts, power consolidation and, 15
Central African Republic
  democracy in, 94
  reconstruction in, 3, 95
Central Committee (Frelimo), 95
Chad
  coup in, 48–49
  oil production in, 117
  revenue management fund of, 138–139
Chaudhry, Kiren Aziz, 17
Chibabava, Mozambique
  clinics in, 76
  reconstruction of, xix–xx
Child Survival Project, in Uganda (USAID), 111
China
  Angola and, 61, 64, 73
  Sudan, funding for, 136–137
China Investment Fund (Angola), 79
Chirac, Jacques, 83
Chissano, Joaquim, 63, 69, 80–82, 89, 92, 95–96
Cholera, in Angola, 75
Citizens, direct income to, 161n14
Civil wars. *See also* Phoenix states
  in Angola, 90
  in Angola vs. Mozambique, 60, 61–63
  coup-proofing after, 13–15, 24
  definition of, 31
  foreign aid after, conclusions on, 28–29
  foreign aid after, improving effectiveness of, 122–146
  frequency of, xxi
  in Mozambique, xix, xxi, 89
  probability of resumption of, 2
  resumptions of, 152n9
  in statistical model, 38, 40
  in Uganda, 101–103
Clean Diamond Trade Act (2003), 138
Coalition building, by Museveni, 115
Cold War aid agreements, 35
Colonial rule, effects of, in Mozambique vs. Angola, 85–86
Comissão Conjunta Politico-Militar (Angola), 90
Commander's Emergency Response Program, 144
Communal villages, 87
Concern (NGO), 71
Conflict (blood) diamonds, 137–138

Consultative Group (aid donors), 72
Cooperatives, in Mozambique, 76
Correia Seabra, Veríssimo, 49
Corruption, 142. *See also* Illicit markets and money; Patronage networks
Cote d'Ivoire, diamond trade and, 138
Coups. *See also* Low-windfall coup-proofing hypothesis
    coup-proofing, 13, 14–15, 24
    definition of, 14
    risk of, 48–49, 52*t*, 53*f*, 54–55*t*, 56*t*, 154*n*31
Crime, in post-conflict countries, 2
Cristiani, Alfredo, 124
Cuba, Ugandan bartering with, 104

Darfur, war in, 136
Dawson, Jeremy F., 156*n*6
Deaths
    from Angolan civil war, 88
    in El Salvador, 124
    in Guatemala, 125
    from Mozambican civil war, 89
    in Rwanda, 126
    from war, 38, 51, 155*n*11
Déby, Idriss, 139
Defense strengthening. *See* Security infrastructure
del Castillo, Graciana, 150*n*7
Democracy
    data for, in baseline model, 39
    as explanation for post-conflict reconstruction, 27
    in low-windfall coup-proofing hypothesis formula, 51
    prewar, baseline model data for, 44
    in Uganda, 159*n*1
Democratic Party (Uganda), 115, 119–120
Democratic Republic of the Congo (formerly Zaire)
    as high windfall country, 36–37
    reconstruction in, 3
    strategic importance, 35
    Ugandan looting in, 117
    World Bank aid to, 11

Denmark, Uganda, aid to, 110–111
Department for International Development (DFID, UK), 66
Destruction
    in El Salvador, 124
    in Equatorial Guinea, 128
    in Guatemala, 125
    in Liberia, 133
    post-independence, in Mozambique vs. Angola, 88–89
Development assistance, 34, 153*n*23
Dhlakama, Afonso, 63, 80, 81, 82–83, 145
Dhofar, Oman, civil war in, 130
Diamonds, resource rent from, 16, 61, 137–138
Direct income to citizens, 161*n*14
Dodd-Frank Act (2010), 161*n*12
Dombe, Mozambique, Renamo control of, 80
Donors. *See also* OECD
    aid, threats to withdraw, 22–23
    Buchanan on, 22
    nonstrategic, 17–18, 19–20, 48, 71–72, 73, 81
    strategic, 16–17, 143
Dos Santos, José Eduardo
    donor conditions, noncompliance with, 78–79
    end of civil war and, 62
    leadership abilities, 96
    1992 election and, 90–91
    popularity, 93
    reconstruction challenges faced by, 89
    wealth of, 78–79

Education, relationship to health, 76
Education aid, in Mozambique, 74
EITI (Extractive Industries Transparency Initiative), 140–141
Elections
    Angola (1992), 90, 158*n*39
    Angola (2008), 93, 94
    authoritarianism and, 146
    Cambodia (1993), 127
    Central African Republic, 94

Elections (*Cont.*)
  Liberia (2005), 133
  Mozambique (1994), 93
  Uganda (1980), 102
Elites, in Mozambique, co-opting of, 81–84
El Salvador
  aid effectiveness in, 4, 124
  U.S. aid to, 18
EPI (Expanded Program on Immunization, Uganda), 109
Equation for baseline model, 40
Equatorial Guinea, post-conflict reconstruction in, 128–129, 130, 134
Ethiopia, U.S. aid to, 161*n*16
Ethnic cleansing, in Bosnia, 125
Ethnic fractionalization, 39–40, 51
European Commission, 83
European Economic Community, aid to Uganda, 107
European Union, aid to Bosnia, 126
Existing (background) institutions, 27
Expanded Program on Immunization (EPI, Uganda), 109
Extractive Industries Transparency Initiative (EITI), 140–141
Extragovernmental aid disbursement, 143–144

Fearon, James D., 31
Federal Democratic Movement (Uganda), 102
Federal Democratic Movement of Uganda, 160*n*28
FLEC (Front for the Liberation of the Enclave Cabinda), 91–92
Followers of rivals to political leaders, 14
Food aid, to Angola, 67
Foreign aid. *See also* Aid curse; Nonstrategic aid; Strategic aid
  amount of, 2
  controversial nature of, 11–12
  data on, source of, 33
  dependence on, 6
  extragovernmental aid disbursement, 143–144
  gatekeepers of, 65–71, 105–107
  in Mozambique vs. Angola, comparison of, 77–78
  strategic, 15–17, 34–35, 143
Foreign aid effectiveness after civil war, improving, 122–146
  exceptional cases with high windfall, 130–134
  exceptional cases with low windfall, 128–130
  future research on, 144–146
  overview, 9, 122–124
  supportive cases, 124–127
  windfall curse, policies counteracting, 134–144
Foreign investments, in Angola, 86
Former Uganda National Army, 160*n*28
France, aid to Uganda, 107, 110
Frelimo (Liberation Front of Mozambique), 62–63, 79–84, 86–88, 92–95, 146
Front for the Liberation of the Enclave Cabinda (FLEC), 91–92
Future research topics, 144–146

Gatekeepers of aid, 65–71, 105–107
GDP. *See* Gross Domestic Product
Germany, aid to Uganda, 109, 110
Gertzel, Cherry, 101
"Getting to Denmark," 6, 146
Ghost workers, 20
Gleditsch, Nils Petter, 38
Global development average, 38, 50
Global Witness (NGO), 117, 137, 138, 139
Gold, resource rents from, 16
Government income. *See* Foreign aid; Natural resources and natural resource rents; Windfall income
Greater Nile Petroleum Consortium, 136
Gross Domestic Product (GDP)
  of donors, in statistical model, 55
  in Equatorial Guinea, 128

nonstrategic donor, per capita, in statistical model, 44–45
in Rwanda, 126
in Uganda, 111
Guatemala, aid effectiveness in, 4, 125
Guinea-Bissau, coup in, 49
Gulf Oil, 62
Gulf states, oil rent income in, 17
Gurr, Ted Robert, 39

Haiti, post-conflict reconstruction in, 129–130, 134
Health care, xx, 2, 74, 76, 109, 110–111
Health Sector Recovery Program (Mozambique), 74
Heston, Alan, 38
Hidden armies, in Mozambique, 80–81
High windfalls. *See* Windfall income
Holy Spirit Movement (Uganda), 115, 159*n*28
Human Rights Watch, 96, 139
Hun Sen, 127
Hypotheses on post-conflict reconstruction, limitations of, 31–32. *See also* Low-windfall coup-proofing hypothesis; Nonstrategic-desperation hypothesis

Ialá, Kumba, 49
Ibrahim Prize for Achievement in African Leadership, 95–96
IFIs (International Financial Institutions), 105
Illicit markets and money, 36, 129, 130
IMF. *See* International Monetary Fund
Improving foreign aid effectiveness after civil war. *See* Foreign aid effectiveness after civil war, improving
Income. *See also* Windfall income
in Cambodia, 127
data for, in baseline model, 38
direct, to citizens, 161*n*14
illicit money, 129, 130
in low-windfall coup-proofing hypothesis formula, 51
prewar, data for, in baseline model, 44
role of, in leaders' decisions on reconstruction, 15–23
sources of, Mozambique vs. Angola, 60
Income, role of, in coup-proofing, 15–23. *See also* Foreign aid
nonstrategic aid, as creator of phoenix states, 20–22
nonstrategic aid, as payment for security and handouts, 17–19
nonstrategic aid, threats to withdraw, 22–23
nonstrategic donor demands, 19–20
windfall income, 15–17
Incumbent tenure variable, 51, 155*n*11
India, aid to Uganda, 110
Industrialization, in Mozambique vs. Angola, 85–86
Infant mortality, 33, 38, 75–76, 111, 118, 127
Institutions
post-conflict, as explanation for post-conflict reconstruction in Mozambique vs. Angola, 86
in post-conflict countries, quality of, 38
strength of, 3–4, 45, 50–51, 150*n*6
Instrumental variables, 155*n*15
International Country Risk Guide, on Uganda, 117
International Financial Institutions (IFIs), 105
International Monetary Fund (IMF)
Angola, work with, 65–66, 140
Bosnia, aid to, 126
Cambodia and, 127
Frelimo on, 95
Mozambique, work with, 67–68, 73
nonstrategic aid, role in, 19
program assessment of, 139
structural demands, modifications of, 20–21
Uganda, work with, 105–107
Inverted windfall variable, 36
Iraq, aid to, 1–2, 141, 143–144

Irregular entry variable, 51, 155*n*11
Islands of efficiency, 149*n*3 (ch.1)
Italy
    Mozambique, aid to, 82
    Uganda, aid to, 110

Jaggers, Keith, 39
Japan, aid to Uganda, 107, 109
Johnson Sirleaf, Ellen, 133–134

Kampala, Uganda, unrest in, 112–113
Karzai, Hamid, 142
Kayiira, Andrew, 102
Kimberley Process Certification Scheme, 137–138
Kiyonga, Crispus, 114
Kony, Joseph, 115–116
Kreutz, Joakim, 39
Kugler, Jacek, 149*n*1 (ch.1)

Lacina, Bethany, 38
Laos, as high windfall country, 36
Lawyers, as aid beneficiaries, 18
Leaders. *See also* Mozambique vs. Angola, post-conflict reconstruction in
    good, 131, 134
    Mozambican vs. Angolan, 60
    political decision-making of, 13
    popularity of, 28
    post-conflict, in Mozambique vs. Angola, 95–96
    spending by, 47–48, 56–57
    in Uganda, 119–121
Leaders' decisions on reconstruction, 11–29
    conclusions on, 28–29
    income, role of, 15–23
    overview, 7–8, 11–13
    post-conflict reconstruction, alternative explanations for, 26–28
    post-conflict reconstruction, incentive-based model for, 24–26
    power consolidation following civil wars, 13–15

Lebanon, as low windfall country, 37
Leeds, Brett Ashley, 34
Liberation Front of Mozambique (Frelimo), 62–63, 79–84, 86–88, 92–95, 146
Liberia, post-conflict reconstruction in, 133–134
Libya, civil war in, xxi
Lord's Resistance Army (LRA), 115–116, 117
Low windfall, 37, 103–105, 124–130
Low-windfall coup-proofing hypothesis, 47–57. *See also* Nonstrategic-desperation hypothesis
    conclusions on, 56–57, 147
    description of, 25–26, 29, 122
    exceptions to, 128–134
    main results of, 51–55
    overview, 47–48
    robustness of, 55–56
    testing of, 48–51
LRA (Lord's Resistance Army), 115–116, 117
Luanda, Angola, planned modernization of, 74–75
Lule, Yusuf, 102

Machel, Samora, 87
Malaria ecology variable, 155*n*13
Marshall, Monty, 39
Mauritania, civil war in, xxi
Micro-level experiments, 31
Military alliances, 34–35
Ministry of Finance, Planning, and Economic Development (MOFPED, Uganda), 110
Ministry of Health (Mozambique), 74
Ministry of Planning and Economic Development (Uganda), 109–110
Ministry of Public Works (Angola), 79
Mobutu Sese Seko, 17
Moi, Daniel arap, 102
Morais, Pedro de, 89
Mozambican National Resistance (Renamo), 82, 92, 145

Mozambique
- embracing aid gatekeepers in, 67–70
- foreign aid, dependence on, xxi, 70, 74
- on foreign aid, 68–69
- as one-party state, 146
- overview, 144
- as phoenix state, xix–xx
- possible aid curse in, xxi
- power consolidation in, 79–84
- reconstruction priorities in, 73

Mozambique vs. Angola, post-conflict reconstruction in, 58–98
- aid effectiveness, comparison of, 77–78
- aid gatekeepers, stonewalling vs. embracing of, 65–71
- Angola, power consolidation in, 78–79
- civil war in Angola vs. Mozambique, 61–63
- comparison of, 74–77
- conclusions on, 97–98
- differences in, alternative explanations for, 84–96
- Mozambique, power consolidation in, 79–84
- nonstrategic donor responses, 71–72
- overview, 8–9, 58–61
- paying for, differences in, 72–74
- windfall income comparison and, 63–64

Mozambique vs. Angola, post-conflict reconstruction in, alternative explanations for differences in, 84–96
- colonial rule, 85–86
- post-conflict democracy, 94–95
- post-conflict leadership, 95–96
- post-conflict popularity, need for, 92–94
- post-independence destruction, 88–89
- post-independence institutions, 87–88
- unresolved insurgency, 91–92
- UN security guarantees, 89–91

MPLA (People's Movement for the Liberation of Angola), 61–63, 86–88, 91–94
Mubarak, Hosni, 135
Museveni, Yoweri
- aid income, questions of use of, 101
- leadership capabilities, 100, 119–121, 122
- nonstrategic aid donors and, 105–107
- power consolidation by, 112–116, 146
- Uganda, rule of, 99
- Ugandan civil war and, 101–103
- Ugandan finances and, 103–105
- windfall income and, 118
Musharraf, Pervez, 49
Mwenda, Andrew, 116

Nagorny Karabakh, Azerbaijan, civil war in, 132
National Army for the Liberation of Uganda, 160n28
National election commission (Mozambique), 83
National Health Service (Mozambique), 74
National Resistance Army (NRA, Uganda), 102, 114, 116
National Resistance Movement system, 103
National Union for the Total Independence of Angola (UNITA), 61–63, 88, 90–91, 93, 135, 137
Natural resources and natural resource rents, 5, 15–16, 36, 117–119. *See also* Windfall income
Negotiated settlement, data for, in baseline model, 39
Netherlands, aid to Mozambique, 81, 83
New York Times
- on Afghanistan, 142
- on Angola's anti-transparency campaign, 139–140
NGOs (nongovernmental organizations), use of, by strategic donors, 143

Nguema Biyogo, Francisco Macias, 128
Nonstrategic aid. *See also* Nonstrategic donors
  as creator of phoenix states, 20–22
  donor demands, 19–20
  donors of, 48, 71–72
  effect on reconstruction, as windfall changes, 43*f*
  impact of, 6, 8
  in low-windfall coup-proofing hypothesis formula, 49
  measurement of, 35
  as payment for security and handouts, 17–19
  refusal of, in high windfall regimes, 77
  scatterplots for, 37*f*
  threats to withdraw, 22–23
  to Uganda, 105–112, 118
  as variable for nonstrategic-desperation hypothesis, 33–35
Nonstrategic-desperation hypothesis. *See also* Low-windfall coup-proofing hypothesis
  baseline model of, 38–40
  conclusions on, 147
  dependent variable for, 33
  description of, 24–25, 29, 122
  independent variables for, 33–37
  main results of model of, 40–41
  robustness of model, 41–45
  scatterplot analysis of, 37–38
  testing of, 32–37
Nonstrategic donor gross domestic product (GDP) per capita, 44–45
Nonstrategic donors, 17–18, 19–20, 48, 71–72, 73, 81
North Korea, Uganda's bartering with, 104
Norway, aid to Uganda, 118
NRA (National Resistance Army, Uganda), 102, 114, 116

Obama, Barack, 143
Obiang Nguema M'basogo, Teodoro, 128
Obote, Milton, 102–103, 106, 115, 120

OECD
  Development Assistance Committee donors, 7
  development assistance guidelines, 18
  foreign aid from, 33–34, 65–66, 72
  Mozambique, work with, 73
Off-budget expenditures, in Uganda, 110
Office of National Reconstruction (Angola), 79
Oil and oil income, 16, 61–62, 91, 117, 136, 138–139
Okello, Tito, 102
Oman, post-conflict reconstruction in, 130–132, 134
Operation Enduring Freedom, 142
Operation Production (Mozambique), 88
Opposition factions, strong, as explanation for post-conflict reconstruction, 27–28
Organization for Security and Cooperation in Europe, 126
Organski, A. F. K., 149*n*1 (ch.1)
Ovimbundu people, 61

Pakistan
  coup in, 49
  strategic importance to U.S., 35
Paradox of plenty, 150*n*9
Patassé, Ange-Félix, 94
Patronage networks, 98, 128
Peacekeeping operations, 152–153*n*19
Peer-evaluated certification schemes, 137
People's Assemblies (Mozambique and Angola), 87
People's Movement for the Liberation of Angola (MPLA), 61–63, 86–88, 91–94
Per capita income, in Cambodia, 127
Persistent opposition, as explanation for post-conflict reconstruction, 27–28
Pfeiffer, James, 158*n*28
Philippines, U.S. aid to, 161*n*16
Phoenix states, 1–10. *See also* Mozambique vs. Angola, post-conflict reconstruction in

SUBJECT INDEX

chapter overviews, 7–9
conclusions on, 10
examples of, 4
foreign aid to, 3–4
overview, 1–2
post-conflict reconstruction, importance of, 2
reconstruction, need for incentives for, 5–6
success stories of, 124–127
testable argument for, need for, 4–5
Police, 18, 80–81
Political administration under colonial rule, in Mozambique vs. Angola, 85
Political institutions, strong, as explanation for post-conflict reconstruction, 27
Political stability, 129, 130
Political will, 22
Popularity, post-conflict need for, in Mozambique vs. Angola, 92–94
Population density variable, 51, 155n13
Portugal
  colonial rule of Angola and Mozambique, 85, 86
  Mozambican civil war, involvement in, 62
Post-conflict democracy, in Mozambique vs. Angola, 94–95
Post-conflict leadership, in Mozambique vs. Angola, 95–96
Post-conflict popularity, need for, in Mozambique vs. Angola, 92–94
Post-conflict reconstruction. *See also* Nonstrategic-desperation hypothesis
  academic attention to, 4–5
  aid, relationship to, 12, 20–22
  alternative explanations for, 26–28
  conclusions on, 147
  empirical questions on, xx–xxi
  foreign aid effectiveness after civil war, improving, 122–146
  importance of, 2
  incentive-based model for, 24–26

leaders' choices and, 21–22
leaders' decisions on, 11–29
in Mozambique vs. Angola, 58–98
nonstrategic aid and, scatterplots for, 37f
phoenix states, 1–10, 124–127
as phrase, 1
regression analysis of factors affecting, 42t
statistical analysis of, 30–46
statistical analysis of coup risks, 47–57
successful, description of, 20
in Uganda, 99–121
Post-independence destruction, in Mozambique vs. Angola, 88–89
Post-independence institutions, in Mozambique vs. Angola, 87–88
Powell, Jonathan, 23, 48, 152n5
Power consolidation, 13–15, 112–116, 146
Presidential Guard (Dhlakama's hidden army), 80
Prewar democracy, baseline model data for, 44
Prewar income, baseline model data for, 44

Qaboos bin Said, Sultan of Oman, 131–132

Rapid Intervention Police (Angola), 91
Rapid Intervention Police (Mozambique), 80–81
Reconstruction. *See* Post-conflict reconstruction
Red Cross, on situation in Chibabava, xx
Refugees, 88, 89, 126, 132
Renamo (Mozambican National Resistance), 82, 92, 145
Reno, Will, 117
Resource (windfall) curse, 7, 9, 36, 117, 147
Revenue management funds, 138–139
Rhodesia, involvement in Mozambican civil war, 62

Richter, Andreas W., 156*n*6
Rivals to political leaders, 13, 14, 15, 145
Robustness, of nonstrategic-desperation hypothesis model, 41–45
Roque, Paula, 78, 93
Rose, Andrew K., 34
Rule of law, 77
Rwanda, aid to, 4, 126–127, 153*n*20

Said bin Taimur, Sultan of Oman, 131–132
Samaritan's Dilemma, 22
Sanctions, 134, 135–137
Saudi Development Bank, 107
Savimbi, Jonas Malheiro, 62, 90
Scandinavian countries, involvement in Mozambican civil war, 62
Scatterplot analysis, of nonstrategic-desperation hypothesis, 37–38
Secret police, in Mozambique, 87
Security infrastructures, 14–15, 78, 80–81, 113–114, 145
Seminario Angolense (newspaper), on the rich in Angola, 78–79
Semuto, Uganda, health care projects in, 111
Shared colonial history, strategic importance of, 34
Sharif, Nawaz, 49
Shelter Afrique, 110
Sirleaf, Ellen Johnson, 133–134
Soares de Oliveira, Ricardo, 63–64, 78
Socioeconomic reconstruction. *See* Post-conflict reconstruction
Solomon Islands, nonstrategic aid to, 18
Somalia
  post-conflict reconstruction in, 130
  U.S. aid to Uganda and, 117
Sonangol (Angolan national oil company), 63
South Africa
  Angolan civil war, involvement in, 61
  Mozambican civil war, involvement in, 62

Soviet Union
  Afghanistan, invasion of, 141
  Angolan civil war, involvement in, 61
  Mozambique and, 62, 64
Spain, aid to Mozambique, 81
Split-panel data, 156*n*6
State capacity levels, 27
Statistical analysis of coup risks, 47–57
  conclusions on, 56–57
  low-windfall coup-proofing hypothesis, 48–51
  main results of model, 51–55
  overview, 8, 47–48
  robustness of model, 56
Statistical analysis of post-conflict reconstruction, 30–46
  baseline model, 38–40
  conclusions on, 45–46
  main results of model, 40–41
  nonstrategic-desperation hypothesis, 32–37
  overview, 8, 30–32
  robustness of model, 41–45
  scatterplot analysis, 37–38
Stonewalling vs. embracing gatekeepers of aid, in Mozambique vs. Angola, 65–71
Strategic aid, 15–17, 34–35, 143
Structural adjustments and demands, 19–20, 67, 70–71, 75, 105, 112
Sudan
  Kony, support of, 116
  sanctions against, 135–137
  strategic importance to UK, 35
  U.S. War on Terror and, 117
Sudapet (Sudan oil company), 136
Sweden, aid to Mozambique, 83
Switzerland, aid to Mozambique, 83
Syria, civil war in, xxi

Tajikistan, civil war in, xxi
Taliban, 142, 143
Tanzania, invasion of Uganda, 101–102
Taylor, Charles, 133
Ten-Point Program (Museveni), 120

SUBJECT INDEX 201

Term limits, 118
Thyne, Clayton L., 48, 152n5
Tied aid, 22
Tindigarukayo, Jimmy, 101
Tombalbaye, François, 48–49
Transparency, as policy counteracting windfall curse, 139–141
Tumusiime-Mutebile, Emmanuel, 107

Uganda, 99–121
   cabinet, size of, 160n35
   civil war in, 101–103
   conclusions on, 121
   donors' reduced aid to, 22
   leadership of, 119–121
   low windfall in, 103–105
   newfound natural resources and strategic importance, 117–119
   nonstrategic aid, increase in, 107–112
   overview, 9, 99–101, 144–145
   power consolidation and, 112–116
   satisfying gatekeepers of nonstrategic aid in, 105–107
Uganda Freedom Army, 102
Uganda Freedom Movement, 160n28
Uganda National Army, Former, 160n28
Uganda National Rescue Front, 102, 106n28
Ugandan Military Commission, 102
Ugandan People's Army, 160n28
Ugandan People's Congress, 102, 115
Ugandan People's Democratic Army (formerly Ugandan National Liberation Army), 115
Unemployment, 2
UNICEF (United Nations Children's Fund), 76, 109
UNITA (National Union for the Total Independence of Angola), 61–63, 88, 90–91, 93, 135, 137
United Kingdom (UK)
   Department for International Development, 66
   EITI and, 140–141
   on Obote, 120
   Oman, aid to, 130–131
   Sudan's strategic importance to, 35
   Uganda, aid to, 104, 107
   on Ugandan reconstruction, 110
United Nations (UN)
   Afghanistan, resolution on, 142
   on Angola, 66, 67
   Angola and, 61, 62
   Bosnia, aid to, 126
   Cambodia, intervention in, 127
   Central African Republic, forces in, 94
   donor-recipient voting at, 154n6
   El Salvador, intervention in, 124
   Mozambique, quick impact disaster relief programs in, 73
   Renamo, support to, 82
   security guarantees, 39, 89–91, 155n5
   on Sudan, 136
   Uganda, aid to, 109–110
United Nations Children's Fund (UNICEF), 76, 109
United Nations Development Program, 20, 83, 132–133, 134
United Nations General Assembly (UNGA), diamond certification, resolution on, 137
United Nations Humanitarian Affairs, xix
United States
   Afghanistan, aid to, 141–144
   Agency for International Development, 64, 66, 69–70, 92–93, 111
   Azerbaijan's strategic importance to, 132
   Clean Diamond Trade Act (2003), 138
   Democratic Republic of the Congo's strategic importance to, 35
   El Salvador, aid to, 18, 124
   Iraq, aid to, 141
   Pakistan's strategic importance to, 35
   Sudan, sanctions against, 135–136
   Uganda, aid to, 100, 107, 110
   on Uganda, 104, 105
   War on Terror, Uganda and, 117
   Zaire, aid to, 17

Unresolved insurgencies, in Mozambique vs. Angola, 91–92

Vaccinations, in Mozambique, 76
Venezuela, diamond trade and, 138
Vicente, Manuel, 139
Vreeland, James, 39

Walter, Barbara F., 31
War deaths, 38, 51, 155n11
War destruction. *See* Destruction
War duration, 38, 51
War on Terror (U.S.), 117, 142–143
West Germany, aid to Uganda, 107
Windfall (resource) curse, 7, 9, 36, 117, 147
Windfall curse, policies counteracting, 134–144. *See also* Aid curse
  bypassing governments, 141–144
  Kimberley Process Certification Scheme, 137–138
  overview, 134–135
  revenue management funds, 138–139
  sanctions, 135–137
  transparency, 139–141
Windfall income. *See also* Uganda
  aid effectiveness in exceptional cases with high, 130–134
  in Angola, 79
  in Angola vs. Mozambique, 61, 63–64
  in Azerbaijan, 132
  conclusions on, 147
  countries with high, 36
  coup-proofing and, 15–17, 154n31
  coup risk and, 154n31, 156n7
  definition of, 36
  illicit money as, 129, 130
  leadership and, 96
  low, 37, 103–105, 124–130
  in low-windfall coup-proofing hypothesis formula, 49
  in Oman, 130
  regimes with high, coup-proofing of, 77
  resource rents and, 5
Women, education of, in Mozambique, 76
World Bank
  Angola, work with, 65, 66, 75
  on Angola, 64, 75, 78, 140
  on Azerbaijan, 133
  Bosnia, aid to, 126
  Cambodia and, 127
  Chad, support for, 138
  Democratic Republic of the Congo, aid to, 11
  on El Salvador, 4
  Frelimo on, 95
  Genuine Savings Project, 36
  Mozambique, work with, 67–68, 73, 76
  on Mozambique, xix, 69, 70, 72
  operational methodology, 157n14
  on pre-conditions for sustainable development, 18
  program assessment of, 139
  on Rwanda, 126–127
  structural demands by, 19, 20–21
  on threats to withdraw funding, 22–23
  Uganda, work with, 105, 107–108, 109, 110
World Food Program, 71

Years since war ended variable, 39
Yemen, foreign aid to, 17
Yugoslavia
  Uganda, aid to, 110
  Ugandan bartering with, 104

Zaire. *See* Democratic Republic of the Congo
Zimbabwe, diamond trade and, 138